SAINTS, SINNERS AND COMEDIANS
The Novels of Graham Greene

Books by Roger Sharrock

SONGS AND COMMENTS
JOHN BUNYAN
THE PILGRIM'S PROGRESS (*Arnold*)

As editor

THE PILGRIM'S PROGRESS (*Oxford University Press*)
GRACE ABOUNDING
THE HOLY WAR
SELECTED POEMS OF WORDSWORTH
SELECTED POEMS AND LETTERS OF KEATS
THE PILGRIM'S PROGRESS (*Penguin Books*)
PELICAN ENGLISH PROSE

SAINTS, SINNERS AND COMEDIANS:
The Novels of Graham Greene

by Roger Sharrock

BURNS & OATES

UNIVERSITY OF NOTRE DAME PRESS

Burns & Oates
Wellwood, North Farm Road,
Tunbridge Wells, Kent, TN2 3DR, England

University of Notre Dame Press
Notre Dame, Indiana 46556, USA

First published in Great Britain and U.S.A. 1984

ISBN (UK) 0 86012 134 8 (hardback)
          0 86012 141 0 (paperback)
ISBN (USA) 0 268 01713 1

Phototypeset by Saxon, Derby
Printed and bound in Great Britain by
Biddles Ltd, Guildford and King's Lynn

Contents

Perhaps what you mean by 'escaping' is somewhat parallel to what I feel, as though one didn't belong to this world at all, and that one is obliged to act a part in a very odd comedy, where one does it (and it is a very odd part) seriously, and yet half-laughing at it all, at the bottom of one's heart, and one feels that it has no importance except that it is God's Will. My habitual feeling is that the world is so extremely odd, and everything in it so surprising. Why *should* there be green grass and liquid water, and why *have* I got hands and feet?

The Spiritual Letters of Dom John Chapman, OSB
(second edition, 1954) p.51.

Author's preface

This is a book about the novels of Graham Greene. It is not a life of the author and biographical facts are only introduced when they seem to bear a necessary part in the explanation of his development as a novelist. Likewise reference to the plays and short stories (with the exception of the long tale *Under the Garden*) is only marginal and brought in when relevant to my account of the novels.

The treatment is chronological but not scrupulously so. That is to say, I have discussed *A Burnt-Out Case* out of sequence so as to place it with the novels in which Catholic characters and problems of Christian belief and morality play a major role. I have moved *Travels with My Aunt* out of sequence so as to take it with *Monsignor Quixote* as an example of Greene's late comic art. I have tried to treat each novel as an individual entity; however, I do come roughly to divide the whole work into three phases: a pre-war one, a phase of Catholic novels, and a later group of books in which the Christian themes, if not wholly absent, are removed to a greater distance. I use 'Catholic novel' simply as a convenient descriptive term and not as implying any doctrinal intention. Mr Greene has declared that he is a novelist who happens to be a Catholic, not a theologian. If in the end I seem to have devoted rather more pages to the middle novels than to the later ones, it is perhaps because they seem to raise more problems, not because I think them better than the later ones.

I must thank Mr Graham Greene for his kindness and encouragement, including his permission to quote extensively from his works. I have profited from conversation on the novels over a number of years with Father Leopoldo Durán; during the composition of the book I had the stimulus of frequent discussion with Peregrine Sharrock; I am in debt to Professor Raymond Chapman of the London School of Economics who read part of the book in type-script and made helpful comments.

Versions of Chapter 3 and 4 have appeared respectively in *Essays and Studies by Members of the English Association* edited by Beatrice White (1983) and *Proceedings of the 1982 ELLAK Symposium* (The English Language and Literature Association of Korea, 1983) and I am grateful to the editors for permission to use this material.

March 1984   *Roger Sharrock*

CHAPTER 1

Two Generations of a Novelist

I

Graham Greene is almost certainly the most distinguished English novelist writing today. A book on his fiction needs no excuse. One is aware, of course, that while a writer lives the tale is not complete: the next novel may change the total pattern of his whole life's work. The interim judgments of so many contemporary studies of former writers abound in misinterpretation and errors of proportion; Cervantes was nearly sixty before the publication of the first part of *Don Quixote* and an interim judgment passed before that would hardly have been *à propos*. But Greene in his late seventies, with fifty years of writing behind him, over twenty novels, four plays, and many short stories, as well as travel books and two autobiographies, has charted a course and it is fitting to describe the long voyage.

In a period when the critical interpretation of living writers has proliferated, serious criticism of Greene has been in inverse proportion to his quality and his reputation with the general reader. Many lesser writers of his own and the next generation have been far more frequently the subjects of academic articles and research theses. The reason for this is intimately related to the peculiar nature of his achievement. Learning his trade during the major phase of the modern movement and the highbrow novel he has never ceased to be a popular writer in the ordinary sense of one who communicates to a wide uncliqueish public while retaining the full force of his personal vision and technical accomplishment. He used to classify his fiction into entertainments and novels, but eventually and properly he dropped the distinction. All the books he once called entertainments are novels, though they may tend to have happy, or fairly happy, endings, and, as in *The Ministry of Fear* or *The Confidential Agent*, the major themes of alienation and pity are fully present; all his novels are entertaining. He has been translated into many languages and has become a world writer in the contemporary sense which is not that used by Goethe: he is there on the revolving bookstall in the airport or supermarket alongside the books of disaster movies and the paperbacks with soft-pornographic covers.

Greene's great technical achievement has been the elevation of the form of the thriller into a medium for serious fiction. He has of course a predecessor in Conrad (especially in *The Secret Agent*) and it is to be remembered that the first English detective story is Dickens's *Bleak House* with its Inspector Bucket; but in the mid-twentieth century he has made the form of the mystery story peculiarly his own as an instrument for the expression of contemporary betrayal and violence. J.I.M. Stewart, who has himself attempted to do the same thing, has spoken somewhat coyly of this development:

> . . . that early phase of the popular 'thriller' in which unscrupulous diplomats, ruthless revolutionaries, commissioners of police, and other picturesque persons are represented as involved in espionage, counter-espionage, and the contriving or preventing of acts of political violence . . . . a territory later brought within the bounds of serious fiction . . . . by Mr Graham Greene.[1]

But what is more important in the adaptation than the background of police detection or secret intelligence is its direction towards the moral and psychological treatment of the impact of violence and the nature of betrayal; the plots expose among both hunters and hunted the alienated man who is looking beyond betrayal for his true identity. The deception may be that of the criminal and murderer Pinkie in *Brighton Rock*; or that of the bad priest who is a drunkard and has a bastard child in *The Power and the Glory*; it may be the adultery of Bendrix involving the betrayal of his friend in *The End of the Affair*, the lies about himself of the confidence man Jones in *The Comedians*, or the double agent's role of Maurice Castle in *The Human Factor*. The criminal is detected, the confidence man exposed: human beings may be naturally treacherous but cannot ultimately deceive themselves or God.

When Greene's reputation was first established in the books published before the Second World War, and perhaps even as it stood soon after that war, there was a sense of limitation of powers, of a writer ploughing a narrow and obsessive furrow. The hunted figure in a shabby mackintosh against a shabby urban background conveyed an oppressive personal vision of a world evil and corrupt. Soon this world was to be christened Greeneland by reviewers to mark its personal obsessiveness. Yet other writers acknowledged as masters have offered their own brands of claustrophobic vision, Dostoievsky and Kafka for instance. Greene has always had a large awareness of this possible limitation of his field of view; when there was a *New Statesman* competition for a parody of a contemporary novelist he carried off the prize with a portrait from Greeneland. At that time I saw his work as that of a craftsman exploiting a single vein of his own morbid psychology, advancing between the ill-lit decaying build-ings of a cul-de-sac. He seemed in this way to belong more among certain technically dedicated French novelists — Jouhandeau, perhaps, or Céline — than to any in the more expansive, outward-directed English scene. In the same period the critics had a label to mark the restriction of his talent. He was a 'Catholic novelist', whatever that means: he was an exotic specimen in the Anglo-Saxon literary zoo. Certainly many Catholics have never been happy about the theology implied in *Brighton Rock* or *The Heart of the Matter*. They would perceive a dangerous gap in the novels between the depiction of fallen human nature and the workings of divine grace. The mysteriousness of God's grace is inexplicable, an orthodox enough view, but it seems very far away, and in fiction it is the accent not the doctrine

that matters. It was always possible to compare Greene the
convert with François Mauriac and to argue in the latter's
favour that, with the faith in his bones and a known,
convincing regional background, he was able to escape
heresy. But did Greeneland really exist or was it not the
product of a personal trauma? Here was another reason for
denying Greene major status. It is worth noticing, however,
before pursuing this question further that in retrospect, as
we look back on a period that completed the progressive
secularization of English life and letters, the two most
outstanding novelists, Greene and Evelyn Waugh, were
both Catholic converts. If we add the example of T.S. Eliot
and W.H. Auden as Christian poets, no wonder that
Kathleen Nott in *The Emperor's Clothes*, writing with secularist prejudice, was acid on the fissure between these writers
and the general culture.[2]

Greene then was too popular, too obsessed, and he was a
Catholic. Only the second objection is worth critical consideration. But in the later novels from a *A Burnt-Out Case*
(1961) onwards, and especially in *The Comedians*, *Travels
with My Aunt*, *The Honorary Consul*, and *The Human Factor*,
the perspective has altered.

First of all, quite apart from the crowning of his achievement in these books, the circumstances of the times have
altered our view of his work. The world has caught up with
Greene, for better or worse. The best artist has always been
prophetic. When Wordsworth spoke of the uniformity of
occupations producing 'a craving for extraordinary incident' and of the fierce storm 'of sorrow barricadoed
evermore Within the walls of cities',[3] he was writing before
he and most people had been directly affected by an
alienating industrialization still in its infancy. The art of the
Surrealists anticipated the deformation of ordinary reality
by air attack in 1939–45: staircases and chimney pieces
floated free in empty air; a chest of drawers with one
drawer hanging open lolled suspended at the edge of an
exposed upper floor. After 1939 civilization has suffered a
similar deformation and invasion of its human living space
through war, revolution, the impact of the world of the
concentration camps and technological depersonalization.

The result has been a turning in of the western mind upon itself in the face of experiences too terrible for the imagination to bear. Neurosis has become the rule, not the exception (Freud in the First World War had speculated whether there might possibly exist a national or general neurosis[4]) and the man in the shabby mackintosh who is running away from something is a reflection in too many mirrors.

Of course the image an age projects of itself may influence behaviour but is never an exact replica of behaviour; vices and virtues, spectacular or unspectacular, always exist side by side in any epoch, but the point is that in our own it has become harder to entertain aesthetic or sympathetic commerce with qualities like heroism or loyalty, easier to accept as prime objects for consideration evil, betrayal, and the inevitability of final failure. In a reminiscence of his boyhood Greene tells how, while he was deeply unhappy at school, his imagination was fired by Marjorie Bowen's historical romance *The Viper of Milan* and that what compelled him was its sense of evil and doom:

> As for Visconti, with his beauty, his patience and his genius for evil, I had watched him pass by many a time in his black Sunday suit smelling of mothballs. His name was Carter. He exercised terror from a distance like a snowcloud over the young fields. Goodness has only once found a perfect incarnation in a human body and never will again, but evil can always find a home there. Human nature is not black and white but black and grey. I read all that in *The Viper of Milan* and I looked round and I saw that it was so.
> . . . the sense of doom that lies over success — the feeling that the pendulum is about to swing. That too made sense; one looked around and saw the doomed everywhere — the champion runner who would one day sag over the tape; the head of the school who would atone, poor devil, during forty dreary undistinguished years. Anyway she had given me my pattern — religion later might explain it to me in other terms, but the pattern was already there — perfect evil walking in the

world where perfect good can never walk again, and only the pendulum ensures that after all in the end justice is done.[5]

As for the theme of betrayal we have seen the drama of spy and counter-spy lifted out of fiction into a world of reality stranger than any fiction. In a society which has become uncomfortable about instinctive or conventionally accepted loyalties the secret agent becomes an important and interesting figure because he, as it were, plays the game without the rules by which ordinary people have to perform. Danger may be entailed and with it a degree of separation from ordinary moral norms and a private discipline to replace them. In this discipline the meticulous observation of a code or of certain security precautions follows a pattern analogous to the compulsive behaviour of the neurotic. The association of a carefully observed code for dealing with external threats and the motivation of private psychic life is present in the forefront of most of Greene's novels. It is there in two widely different characters, the policeman Scobie in *The Heart of the Matter* and Wormold, the bogus agent, in *Our Man in Havana*.

Blackmailed by the Syrian trader Yusef, Scobie has to smuggle diamonds on to a Portuguese ship and as a result brings about the death of his loyal servant Ali, murdered by Yusef's man because he has seen one of the diamonds and may talk. The precise and secret plan for smuggling the diamonds is connected by a chain of necessity with Scobie's pity for his wife which has driven him to borrow from Yusef, and this pity which has betrayed him is a part of his deepest personality. In *Our Man in Havana* Wormold, once he has been recruited as a British agent, has to communicate with his superiors in London in an absurd book code based on an edition of Lamb's *Tales from Shakespeare*; in his case too his decision to enlist in the enterprise and obey the code is intimately linked to his personal life, his love for his daughter and desire to pamper her; all this happens at the level of fantastic comedy until Wormold, sending romanticized reports, suddenly stumbles into real political intrigue. In both cases the observance of the code obeys an inner need which leads to betrayal and the death of others. The atmosphere of underground warfare conducted by special and exclusive rules is present in many of Auden's pre-war poems:

> Though aware of our rank and alert to obey orders,
> Watching with binoculars the movement of the grass for
>   an ambush,
> The pistol cocked, the code-word committed to memory,
> . . . But careful; back to our lines; it is unsafe there,
> Passports are issued; that area is closed.[6]

In Greene the agent eventually becomes a double agent, betraying and betrayed. Greene is of the generation of Burgess, Maclean and Philby, and himself served in the intelligence services during the war. He was a friend of Philby of whom he has written an account.[7] Apart from those actual defectors, in the 1930s generation of intellectuals the inherited national and cultural loyalties were divided or suppressed by the crisis of the time: the Communist Party and the Popular Front seemed to many, however misguidedly, the only forces capable of saving Europe from Fascism and therefore the only protectors both of political freedom and of humane culture. The Chamberlain government and the 'establishment' could only be seen as collaborators with the enemy; for many who were not in a legal sense traitors a situation was created in which loyalty was directed, openly or secretly, elsewhere. In the language of its sub-culture, when using the terms Fascist and anti-Fascist, the intellectual left was drawing the distinction between *pays légal* and *pays réel* already declared by the extreme right in France. Greene was a man of the 1930s who to a large extent has continued to maintain after the war the political allegiances of that period; this is demonstrated by his sympathy for the Soviet Union and Castro's Cuba and by his anti-Americanism. From being in the 1930s and 1940s a specialist in guilt-ridden Catholic ousiders depicted in a melodramatic setting Greene becomes the prophet of a world made melodramatic by violence and of the personal alienation appropriate to that world.

The process of catching up, of the world becoming cast in
the image of the writer, is also encountered in the international settings of Greene's novels. He has always been a
tireless traveller and explorer of exotic and dangerous
places. Beginning with his journeys to Liberia and Mexico
in the 1930s his life has been a quest for the extreme
breaking points of civilization — colonial and post-colonial
Africa, the war in Indo-China or the confrontation of the
propertied classes and the miserably poor in South America. His international scope suitably reflects a world in
which, after the replacement of the steamship by the
aeroplane, and after the coming of the nuclear missile, all
wars are potentially global. His alienated man is essentially a
traveller, wandering or escaping, even if it is only escaping
from himself like Querry in *A Burnt-Out Case*. In a period of
a shrunken world and dissolving frontiers, in which even
terrorism is international, we are better able to appreciate
the *déraciné* because in this common market of the will and
its paralysis our own roots are under strain.

A number of features in the history of our sensibility and
its development over the last half-century, therefore, have
shown Greene's vision to be closer to our main concerns,
not a distorted or sectarian view of life. Another important
factor is the increasing popularity of a simplified version of
psychoanalysis as a model for the growth of the individual
personality; this model usually takes the form of focussing
on a primal trauma and the modes of its recurrence. It is so
widely diffused in fiction, and other fields like penology, as
to be almost unnoticed because it is taken for granted as the
necessary sub-structure for a large number of variations
and controversies about the details of the traumatic pattern
and the possible methods of its resolution. It has something
of the ubiquity of the theory of humours in medieval and
Renaissance physiology and psychology. Many of Greene's
heroes carry the scar of a primal wound and he has exposed
his own in his autobiographical memoir *A Sort of Life* and
elsewhere in his writings. For him as for the clinical
psychologist the child is the father of the man: 'Hell lay
about them in their infancy'. The treatment of public moral
action as having its roots in private psychic drives is a

frequent modern preconception. Psychopathology becomes a matter of degrees and the social 'norm' is just a particular type of malformation, oriented by some early secret pact with safety or success. We are prepared to meet cases, not characters. Also to be noticed is Greene's constant use of dreams to convey confusion of impulses in a person and the development towards their resolution. Finally it may be seen that the psychoanalytical method, reaching backwards into childhood and deep into the stream of consciousness of a personality, is completely suited to a view of life as a battlefield (as in the title of one of his early novels) on which isolated figures move through no-man's-land, and to the author's consequent refusal to attach any overriding importance to the values of the social world. The characters are all secret agents, professionally or on account of their private existential crises.

In Greene's novels the quotidian boredom of experience is interrupted by some extraordinary incident which breaks the routine pattern, causing characters imprisoned by habit to face their true identities and come to terms with a reality beyond routine. The daily round of the *leproserie* in *A Burnt-Out Case* is interrupted by Querry's arrival and its effect on the lives of the Ryckers; the adultery of Bendrix and Sarah in *The End of the Affair* is brought to an end by Sarah's prayer during the bomb explosion and the miracles that follow it; in *Travels with my Aunt* Henry Pulling's sedate life in the suburbs is shattered by the coming of Aunt Augusta.

The routine boredom in which authenticity is frustrated need not be that of bourgeois peace: it may be represented by life in a war or by the life of violent crime. The American, Pyle, in *The Quiet American* encounters Thomas Fowler, the war correspondent, in Indo-China, decisively affecting both the latter's personal life and his attitude to the war. In *Brighton Rock* Pinkie's sordid routine as a race-course gangster is cut across both by his committing murder and by his marriage to the girl Rose, originally a cold-blooded arrangement to serve for his protection. Greene's fiction of crisis is one in which men are driven to concentrate more and more on special moments of decision and are in-

creasingly aware of discontinuity, the interruption of a
traditional mode of life or the violent impact of one culture
upon another. In the world of vast impersonal political and
economic power the way of life of individuals is changed,
curiously enough, equally by the discovery of oil and
mineral resources or by the loss of the products of those
resources.

For change to occur so as to affect the individual at all
deeply it is necessary for some time of life to be passed so
that habits have been formed. The heroes of Greene's
novels are indeed mostly characters in their late middle age
or sometimes older. So are those of a great deal more of
contemporary fiction. The typical age of the hero of earlier
fiction was in the twenties. This is true of Tom Jones, of
Julien Sorel in Stendhal's *Le Rouge et le Noir*, and of other
figures even down to the characters of James Joyce and
D.H. Lawrence. Some kind of dramatic crisis is of course
necessary for fiction; even Tristram Shandy had in the end
to be born; but in what I have generalized as the earlier
novel the drama or incident was directed towards an
initiation into life, not a break in its established routine.
Stephen Dedalus undergoes a crisis of identity but it is in
order that he may more fully possess and order the world
under the forms of art, not escape from a life that has
wholly fallen into routine and repetition (the exception to
this in Greene is the working of the *leproserie* in *A Burnt-Out
Case*; there Christian charity has been incarnated in the
daily repetitive details of testing and treatment).

The subject of middle-aged crisis, of the breaking-point
after a long period of strain, has become familiar and
acceptable. The myth of a generation gap, fuelled largely
like other contemporary myths by the media, had a very
short run. What we have really witnessed in the last
generation is the emergence of an artificial culture of
adolescence imposed from above in Marcusian fashion and
the parallel growth of our interest in change and decay
settling on the problems of the man of experience. Meanwhile for environmental and biological reasons, adolescence becomes earlier, and maturity is prolonged, old age
postponed. *Nel mezzo del cammin di nostra vita* was thirty-five,

is now about forty-five, probably the average age of a hero in a late twentieth-century novel. Crushed between teenage and middle age, the upper and nether millstones, youth, the prime subject of the earlier novel, is eclipsed, its fresh discovery of the world through action, one of the great themes of literature, for a time neglected by the imaginative writer.

Thus Greene, who on the strength of his earlier novels had been accused of being too melodramatic, is seen to have become of central importance. One is reminded of some of the probable features noted by de Tocqueville as the literary characteristics of a democratic society:

> They [the public] prefer books which may be easily be procured, quickly read, and which require no learned researches to be understood . . . above all, they must have what is unexpected and new. Accustomed to the struggle, the crosses, and the monotony of practical life, they require strong and rapid emotions, startling passages, truths or errors brilliant enough to rouse them up and to plunge them at once, as if by violence, into the midst of the subject.
>
> Style will be . . . almost always vehement and bold. Authors will aim at rapidity of execution more than at perfection of detail. Small productions will be more common than bulky books . . . The object of authors will be to astonish rather than to please, and to stir the passions more than to charm the taste.[8]

These observations reflect the form of the contemporary thriller. Imitation, like the growth of his public, must be seen as not merely an acknowledgement of Greene's skill as a story-teller but as recognition of his contribution to contemporary myth-making: his characters bear the image of human beings who are not sure that they belong in the social lives in which they find themselves and who are not at ease. Though recognizable throughout the western world these doubts are perhaps most likely to be found among the English in an England unsure of its changed role.

If Greene has reflected his times, he has, as is the way with creative artists, provided potent images in which his coevals, and the succeeding generation, can recognize their problems. Art, as well as being imitation and illumination, is prophecy, and lures the reader or spectator along paths which, before the reception of the work, were but dimly perceived. The same is the case with his Catholicism. His acute sense of sin, and belief in the reality of damnation, were at one time inclined to alienate the non-Catholic reader who would find the sensual, common-sense Ida's search for justice a more sympathetic strand in *Brighton Rock* than the dominant warped vision of Pinkie. At the same time many orthodox Catholics were upset by the dark picture he gave of Catholic life, the sexuality of many of his themes, and the possible heresy of episodes in the novels like that at the end of *The Heart of the Matter* where the suggestion seems to be that a suicide may find salvation. But all that has changed after the Second Vatican Council. The Church has given up its 'triumphalism', acknowledged the active role of the laity in its inmost life, taken stock of its social role in a world divided between poverty and riches, and renewed its recognition of the importance of the individual conscience. Moral decisions are no longer seen as prescribed by a seminarian rule of thumb. They are influenced by the nature of the individual human being and his situation. As Greene writes in his autobiography, speaking of his dilemma when he feared he was an epileptic and must therefore have no children in marriage, and when a priest could only meet it by saying, 'The Church expects you to trust God, that's all':

How differently he would have answered my question today, telling me, I have no doubt, to follow my conscience, which even then was elastic enough for almost anything. Catholics have sometimes accused me of making my clerical characters, Father Rank in *The Heart of the Matter* and Father James in *The Living Room*, fail unnecessarily before the human problems they were made to face. 'A real priest', I had been told, 'would have had something further to say, he would have shown a deeper comprehension, he wouldn't have left the situation so unchanged.' But that is exactly what in those days, before

John Roncalli was elected Pope, the priesthood was
compelled to do . . . There was only one hard answer . . .
'the Church knows all the rules'.[9]

The duty of the Church to relieve the plight of the
individual human soul, suffering, sinful, or confused, and
the knowledge that such relief must transcend the narrow
categories of a text-book of moral theology, were re-
emphasized by Vatican II. 'I come not to the righteous but
to bring sinners to repentance.'

Characters like the gangster Pinkie or the whisky priest in
The Power and the Glory can now be seen as being at the
centre of the Christian experience and not special cases on
the fringe of it, shading off into melodrama. Or only in the
sense that we are all special cases. The spirit of a changing
Church struck an answering note in the novels. Genuine
religious experience might be found in those of other
faiths, in unbelievers, in lapsed Catholics like Querry in *A
Burnt-Out Case*. As Greene says in his preface to that book in
the Collected Edition, quoting Unamuno's *The Tragic Sense
of Life*: 'Those who believe that they believe in God, but
without passion in their heart, without anguish of mind,
without uncertainty, without doubt, without an element of
despair even in their consolation, believe only in the God
Idea, not in God Himself'.[10] Greene had set the real
struggle of the mixed human heart against the conventional piety of the Catholic ghetto; the work in which he has
described this tension is assured of a more sympathetic
audience in a community moved by the oecumenical spirit
and the idea of the priesthood of all believers. What from its
dark underside had seemed morally tainted by the heresy
of Jansenism, and dangerously fideistic in theological
terms, appeared on the other side as the light of charity
surpassing the petty limits of human reasoning. 'A man can
accept anything to do with God until scholars begin to go
into details and the implications. A man can accept the
Trinity, but the arguments that follow . . . I would never try
to determine some point in differential calculus with a
two-times-two table. You end by disbelieving the calculus
. . . ' (*A Visit to Morin*).

Pinkie and the whisky priest are joined by León in *The*

Honorary Consul, the Paraguayan priest whose love of his starved and persecuted flock has led him to renounce his duties and become a revolutionary guerilla in the jungle. Here again, though his sympathy with the revolutionaries would not meet with support from all his readers, inside or outside the Church, especially from those in authority, the novel serves to highlight one of the great problems of our time: the poverty of the masses in Latin America under repressive regimes and the question whether it is right for the Christian to support the revolutionary movement and the terrorism associated with it as a form of the just war traditionally approved by the theologians from St Thomas onwards. Is it right to go even further (if there is an 'even further' than taking a human life) and embrace the Marxist interpretation of history and the class struggle as the necessary twentieth-century development of loving thy neighbour?[11] There is more to be said of Greene's political attitude which really comes down to being, like his religious belief, an attitude to the complementary roles of power and weakness; but it should be added that León, who has given up celebrating the sacraments, resumes the priestly office, however reluctantly, to say his last mass for his trapped guerilla companions in the hut where they are surrounded.

As a newer and more appreciative climate for Greene's fiction became established the later novels have broken new ground. He has entered into his full maturity as a realistic writer drawing people and scenes in Asia, Africa, South America and Hertfordshire which make the backgrounds of his earlier thrillers seem sketchy. At the same time he has shown a compassionate understanding of a wide range of characters not always found in his pre-war and wartime novels, where compassion for the seedy and the damned is not always extended to those people, grotesque or comfortable, among whom they move. Now characters who have apparently no religious dimension in their lives, whether inclining them to salvation or damnation, characters existing in the huge contemporary zone of indifference — Brown and Jones in *The Comedians*, Henry Pulling in *Travels with my Aunt*, Charlie Fortnum in *The Honorary Consul* — are rendered fully in their comedy and pathos. The moral topography of the later novels is less schematized. We are correspondingly aware that these novels are no longer 'Catholic novels', if that expression means novels written about Catholics and their problems for those aware of the theological implications. The turning-point had been reached in *A Burnt-Out Case*: Querry, like his creator, has become tired of being a Catholic artist; he has given up religious practice but even against the grain cannot avoid recognizing and following his soul's authenticity. From then on in Greene's work his subject is secular man lost to God in this world. There are anticipations of such an acceptance of the secularization of man's life in his earlier phase and in the books written immediately before *A Burnt-Out Case*. Pinkie might appear to be utterly fallen into the secular world, but there are filaments that bind him to historical Christianity and therefore make him feel lost in that world, and in his evil and horrible end the suggestion is that he may have experienced 'the appalling strangeness of the mercy of God'. Bendrix in *The End of the Affair* is a truer example of the secularized consciousness, and it is the presiding consciousness of the narrative; but it is counterbalanced by the miracles performed for and by his mistress Sarah, the only miracles to occur in Greene's fiction. We can define the later phase by calling it not sectarianly Catholic, not dealing in the miraculous; less negatively we could see it as a body of fiction celebrating each meeting and departure of human beings in the world of nature as not casual but meaningful, therefore miraculous. The novelist of spiritual dryness and despair has never been a novelist of the absurd.

These reflections on Greene's reputation, his relation to his age, and how the relation became ever more involved and intimate as Greeneland extended its frontiers, mark out an area not only of literary achievement but of a wide general and social interest; and the earlier typecasting by critics, in which the author becomes a veritable Graham Greene character himself, is now revealed as inadequate.

II

Greene was born, in 1904, into the comfortable professional class in the settled days before the First World War. The
Greenes were a large family and there were numerous
uncles and aunts and cousins. They also had their share of
distinction. One of his uncles who bore the same name
gained a knighthood for his work at the Admiralty and the
Ministry of Munitions under the Coalition government in
the First World War; he was also one of the founders of the
Naval Intelligence Service and established therefore on the
fringe of the secret world that engaged his nephew both in
life and art. His father was the headmaster of an Anglican
public school, Berkhamsted in Hertfordshire — a good
headmaster and an inspired teacher of history. Contemporaries at the school included Peter Quennell, poet and
biographer, and Claud Cockburn, Communist journalist
and editor of *The Week*. Graham Greene's paternal grand-
father went out to St Kitts in the West Indies to manage a
sugar plantation and was reputed to have fathered many
children on the island before his early death. Among his
brothers an elder one, Raymond, became a distinguished
physician and endocrinologist, a career which he combined
with serious mountaineering. A younger brother, Hugh
Carleton Greene, had a career in broadcasting administration and became Director-General of the BBC. Another
older brother, Herbert, published a book on the Spanish
Civil War; and Hugh's son, also called Graham, became a
successful publisher, serving as managing director of
Jonathan Cape Ltd.

Against this background of achievement, largely in the
field of administration, Greene's dedication to writing
stands out sharply. To be sure, his mother was a first cousin
of R.L. Stevenson, and the Stevenson influence is an early
and important one; but Greene's ambition to write was a
lonely effort. In the early pages of his autobiography *A Sort
of Life* he describes his fostering in a bustling and cheerful
family with nannies, children's party games, teas on the
lawn, and visits to uncles with exciting gardens and hiding-
places. His father was loving though distant; his mother too

was loving, though he describes her as aloof. How in this environment of bourgeois niceness and quietly accepted success did there grow up the artist of failure and the shady? Greene has given his own account of the matter. However what he has written about his childhood, in the autobiography, in his travel book on Mexico *The Lawless Roads*, and elsewhere, must be treated as evidence on the same level as certain passages in the novels and not as necessarily the heart of the matter: an artist is still an artist when he is analysing his own behaviour and motives. *A Sort of Life* is a beautifully written book, even though it tantalizes us by taking the story no further than the publication of his second novel *Stamboul Train* in 1932, even though so much of his adolescent and undergraduate experience is recalled in disarmingly presented fragments.

Greene goes back to a period of suffering and bullying at school as the first crisis of his life and one which revealed the world of his future writing; he was just thirteen and was suddenly brought face to face with horror and evil:

> One met for the first time characters, adult and adolescent, who bore about them the genuine quality of evil. There was Collifax, who practised torments with dividers; Mr Cranden with three grinning chins, a dusty gown, a kind of demoniac sensuality; from these heights evil declined towards Parlow, whose desk was filled with minute photographs — advertisements of art photos. Hell lay about them in their infancy.[12]

This passage is from the beginning of *The Lawless Roads* (1939), his book about his journey in Mexico; the insistence on human depravity is in keeping with the portrait he paints of Mexican corruption, a corruption relieved only by a few saint-like figures and actual martyrs. The famous passage from Newman which he prefixes to the book strikes a note which is maintained throughout:

> To consider the world . . . . the greatness and littleness of man, his far-reaching aims, his short duration, the curtain hung over his futurity, the disappointments of

life, the defeat of good, the success of evil, physical pain,
mental anguish, the prevalence and intensity of sin, the
pervading idolatries, the corruptions, the dreary hopeless irreligion, that condition of the whole race, so
fearfully yet exactly described in the Apostle's words,
'having no hope, and without God in the world' — all this
is a vision to dizzy and appal . . . I can only answer, that
either there is no Creator, or this living society of men is
in a true sense discarded from His presence . . . if there
be God, since there is a God, the human race is implicated
in some terrible aboriginal calamity.

Greene choses this passionately disenchanted statement
because it is an epitome of his own view. In Newman the
statement is convincing because the catalogue of human
woes works not as mere rhetoric but as an assembly of
evidence. Then there is a point in the argument where a
stage has been suppressed: 'if there be a God, since there is a
God' — some would reason that the accumulation of evil
and pain precisely denies a living God; but to experience
the horror like this, to yearn after the completion of order,
is to confirm by demanding the existence of an order that
has withdrawn. So it is with Greene. In the agony of the
schoolroom and the dormitory, the compulsions of life,
simply because what they compel is suffering, lead one to
envisage a defining freedom beyond the bounds of fallen
necessity. Back in the garden of his home adjoining the
school the sense of possible freedom became faith:

One became aware of God with an intensity — time hung
suspended — music lay on the air; anything might
happen before it became necessary to join the crowd
across the border. There was no inevitability anywhere
. . . faith was almost great enough to move mountains . . .
the great buildings rocked in the darkness.
    And so faith came to one — shapelessly, without
dogma, a presence above a croquet lawn.

Faith and the awareness of sin move correspondingly like
the weights of a pendulum. Intense realization of one gives
a corresponding assurance of the other. The coming of the

presence of faith is so beautifully rounded in the telling that it muffles the facts of the experience. The God-inspired faith than can withstand human hostility is fitting in a book about Mexico and its church of martyrs. But the boy Greene was driven to a nervous breakdown by his persecutions at Berkhamsted and to an effort to escape from school.

A Sort of Life gives a fuller and more matter-of-fact account. He states explicitly that there was no physical torture: Collifax and his dividers seem to be a dramatic construction proper enough in their place in another book. In the autobiography he explains that his sense of isolation was due to his being a traitor and a suspect, the son of the headmaster: 'I was like the son of a quisling in a country under occupation'.[13] Loyalty was not simply divided; it was extinguished. Between the civilization of the headmaster's house and the barbarism of the coarse public life of his schoolfellows he became an exile from both; he grew to be an expert in evasion and truancy.

What is common to both accounts, but is more fully documented in *A Sort of Life*, is the physical separation of school and home, their nearness and difference, and the effect on his imagination. Home and school were parts of the same building and so the dividing line was a narrow one; he was lost because the forces of ugliness had a hold on the base of his existence — 'perfect evil walking in the world where perfect good can never walk again'. He had not known before that there existed in the same house rooms so grim as those he now had to live in. A green baize door led across the frontier to worn stairs, ink-stained desks, and rooms insufficiently warmed; the dormitory was divided by pitch-pine partitions that gave inadequate privacy, and his account dwells on the violation of quiet in the nights interrupted by coughing, snoring and farting. Others survived, like a cousin who stood up to the quisling Greene brother who was head of the house; Greene survived to write out his malaise. The recurring theme of his writing is the narrowness of the barrier separating the ordinary from the dramatically significant, and therefore, the world being what it is, the ordinary from the sinister, the skull beneath the skin.

In *The Ministry of Fear* (1943), the novel perhaps most

revealing of the traumatic dreams underlying his early fiction, the clandestine operations of the bogus nursing home are carried out beyond a green baize door. Arthur Rowe goes behind it to find out the enemy's secret and to locate poor imprisoned Major Stone who has a dim idea of the secret but fears he may be mad:

> Ahead of him was the green baize door he had never seen opened, and beyond that door lay the sick bay. He was back in his own childhood, breaking out of dormitory, daring more than he really wanted to dare, proving himself. He hoped the door would be bolted on the other side; then there would be nothing he could do but creep back to bed, honour satisfied . . .

When he returns safely he feels that he has explored a strange country and come home to find it was all a dream. And Arthur Rowe is a man who, having already suffered an appalling shock, has lost his memory in a bomb incident and is only slowly recovering it. There is therefore a tension between the two worlds on either side of the green baize door which is different from the tension implied by Newman's 'aboriginal calamity', God's perfect goodness contrasted with human imperfection. Each of the worlds is so convincing in its own way that, given any unity of mind and self, which is true? Is home true and the schoolroom a nightmare, or the latter true and home an illusion? There is a side of Greene which is inclined to turn obstinately away from happiness in a plot or in the life of a person; even when misery prevails he is ready to turn the knife in the wound, as when at the end of *Brighton Rock* the reader understands that for the desolated Rose there still remains to hear played the gramophone disc recording her husband Pinkie cursing her. By the time of the post-war novels the tension is to a great extent overcome and his stories can embrace an unidealized integrity and goodness, like that of the Smiths in *The Comedians*, while fully merging them in the fallen world. But in his work until its later phase there is a tension between two dreams, a dream of innocence fallen and the nightmare of the real world from which his characters may or may not waken. Greene's exploration of the real world begins with an inverted romanticism, part discovery, part invention. This is Greeneland, a disturbed and disturbing personal fiction shot through with fragmentary perceptions of fallen contemporary life. But the urge to come to grips with the whole of which the fragments are constituent parts is imperative: Arthur Rowe goes voluntarily through the green baize door. The transition from innocence to experience is a continuing theme throughout Greene's fiction, finally controlled and distanced in the high comedy of Henry's adventures in *Travels with my Aunt*.

There is thus another pattern cutting across the uncompromising theological dualism of the passages in *The Lawless Roads* describing his childhood trauma, the epigraph from Newman, and his impressive account of finding his prime subject in *The Viper of Milan*. He has constructed an appealing myth to explain his literary endeavour but it is not the whole story. If it were, Evelyn Waugh, writing in 1939, would have had the last word: 'Mr Greene is, I think, an Augustinian Christian, a believer of the dark age of Mediterranean decadence when the barbarians were pressing along the frontiers and the City of God seemed yearly more remote and unattainable . . . Contemplation of the horrible ways in which men exercise their right of choice leads him into something very near a hatred of free-will'.[14] But there is another effort to find by experiment and travel a way of interpreting the dream, or the nightmare. The dream and the trauma of imprisonment are examined, like the map in *Treasure Island*, for clues to the shape of reality and its possible treasures. The story *Under the Garden*, included appropriately in the collection *A Sense of Reality*, offers an alternative myth of childhood initiation.

The first-person character, Wilditch, of *Under the Garden*, a great traveller, revisits his brother in the house in which they had spent part of their childhood and of which he has idyllic memories. He has just seen a surgeon who has told him that he may not survive an operation, so he is looking back from a life which may be completed. He has a vague recollection — which becomes more precise — of a dream-fantasy of his childhood visits to the house. He had waded across the water to an island in the garden, found a cave under a great tree, and descended into the earth; there he is kept prisoner by an incredibly old man and his wife. The old man, Javitt, has only one leg and his wife Maria has a roofless mouth which makes all her attempts at speech resemble 'kwak'. He has a treasure and a golden chamber-pot. He reads fifty-year-old newspapers and speaks with a hint of mastery of the general human experience.

'Sister, wife, mother, daughter, what difference does it make? Take your choice. She's a woman, isn't she?'. He brooded there on the lavatory seat like a king on his throne. 'There are two sexes,' he said. 'Don't try to make more than two definitions.' The statement sank into my mind with the same heavy mathematical certainty with which later on at school I learned the rule of Euclid about the sides of an isosceles triangle. There was a long silence.

There is much more strange wisdom from Javitt, sitting on the po or lying upon sacks, and the seven-year-old thinks that he learned more from him than from all his schoolmasters. An obstinate survivor, he harps on the theme of chosen loneliness and betrayal:

Be disloyal. It's your duty to the human race. The human race needs to survive and it's the loyal man who dies first from anxiety or a bullet or overwork. If you have to earn a living, boy, and the price they make you pay is loyalty, be a double agent — and never let either of the two sides know your real name. The same applies to women and God. They both respect a man they don't own, and they'll go on raising the price they are willing to offer. Didn't Christ say that very thing? Was the prodigal son loyal or the lost shilling or the strayed sheep? The obedient flock didn't give the shepherd any satisfaction or the loyal son interest his father.
    . . . I thought I was learning about the world and the universe from Javitt, and still to this day I wonder how it was that a child could have invented these details, or have they accumulated year by year, like coral, in the sea of the unconscious around the original dream?

The seven-year-old boy falls in love with newspaper photographs of Miss Ramsgate, a contestant for Miss England, whom Javitt claims is his and Maria's daughter. 'I looked at the photograph, at the wise eyes and the inexplicable body, and I thought, with all the ignorance children have of age and generations, I never wanted to marry anybody but her.' He nurses an ambition to find her and Javitt tells him he will have to travel very far, in warm countries, in Africa, Asia and South America, to do that — 'she was always a warm girl'. Finally the boy escapes from the cave when Javitt is asleep, although he suspects that Javitt is watching him through half-closed eyes and letting him go. He carries with him the golden chamber-pot but somehow loses it before paddling back from the island to be welcomed home by the family dog.

Under the Garden is a story rich in parable. First of all, and most importantly, it is a parable of the child's initiation into life. It is a life of fascinating mystery (the treasure), instabilty, and sexual challenge. The long passage down through the roots of the trees, fairly obviously expressing the infantile wish to return to the womb, is also the male sexual quest defined later in the ambition to pursue Miss Ramsgate. But the parable also applies to the life of the artist; the man Wilditch looking back to his childhood fantasy remembers laughter and fear with Javitt that reminds him of the first time he had known a woman, yet the wisdom of Javitt, repeatedly noted as being more authoritative than that of any schoolmaster, is the accumulated and neutrally accepted observation of human life which forms the raw material of the novelist: the inexplicable attractiveness of Miss Ramsgate, while arousing the child's sexuality, images the sensual quest of all men and all the novelist's characters. The dream, taking form in 'the sea of the unconscious', is forecast and key to a development at once generally human and individual. The general has its due, but the forecast of a peculiar individual growth predominates: as Greene says in his autobiography he had always preferred Freud to Jung. So there is the stress on infantile sexuality and the personal preoccupation with deformity: Javitt's one leg and Maria's cleft palate are parallelled by Raven's hare-lip in *A Gun for Sale* and

Smythe's birth-mark in *The End of the Affair*. In choosing powerful images for the triumph of experience over the ideal, the ideal human body against its lived and given reality, Greene may be said to design a normality of deformity for fallen man. This reflects the same standard of necessary deformity imposed upon our normal emotional response to trust and betrayal. The scheme projected of restless movement through a life is also more personal than general. 'Home's where a man lies down,' Javitt says. Wilditch meditates, 'It was as though even at seven I was accustomed to travel. All the rough journeys of the future were already in me then, like a muscle which had only to develop . . . to the self we remain always the same age'.

Before Wilditch leaves his brother's house he meets Ernest, the old gardener, and questions him indirectly about his fantasy of a tunnel under the lake and a treasure. Ernest says, 'You was hunting for something. That's what I said to the folk round here when you were away in those savage parts — not even coming back for your uncle's funeral. "You take my word," I said to them, "he hasn't changed, he's off hunting for something, like he always did, though I doubt if he knows what he's after"'. The theme of search and initiation, the prime stuff of romance, can be found in all Greene's novels in varying degrees. His characters are at the end of journeys from innocence and desire before the aboriginal calamity claims them.

The elements of which Wilditch's dream or accretion of dream is compounded are various and they lie close to the centre of Greene's personal and imaginative experience as a child. The house and garden are those of his uncle Graham, Harston Hall in Cambridgeshire, where he was taken to stay every year; it had a Shady Walk, called the Dark Walk in the story, and a pond with an island. It was at Harston that Greene suddenly realized he had learned to read, late for his age. He read *Dixon Brett, Detective* and his mother gave him *Coral Island*. There are echoes in the story of *Treasure Island* and of *Robinson Crusoe* (in the giant footsteps seen by the tree before the descent). The frightening capture by Javitt and his wife has some resemblance to Tom Kitten's falling into the hands of the rats in Beatrix

Potter's *The Tale of Tom Kitten*. Tom Kitten, too, fell down a hole in the chimney, a sort of tunnel, into a very dirty place. The young Wilditch names the pauses in his journey like the stages in a children's adventure story — Friday's Cave, Camp Indecision, Camp Hope. The language of wayfaring turns inevitably into the language of the self and its paradigm, the Christian theology of salvation. This complex of desire and prophecy, with its roots in folk-tale (Wilditch runs away with the po like Jack with the giant's singing hen), is composed with a high degree of conscious art, however much the writer may be drawing on actual dreams of boyhood about Harston. Wilditch is described simply as a traveller and the dream-vision is a prophecy of his whole life to come; but the parallel of the writer's commitment to his art comes strongly through. The child Wilditch had written a story published in his school magazine; in it his fantasy had been transformed into conventional schoolboy romance, brave Tom saving the family fortunes by discovering Spanish gold. Now the old man, perhaps near to death, tries to write down what really happened, and this is the bulk of the story as we have it. The drive of his early writing is to eliminate cliché and periphrasis and say what really happened, or what might really have happened. In this case his object is to fix what was real in a fantasy. The real fantasy, the normal abnormality, the holy sinner: wherever we look in Greene we find these oxymorons or contradictions in terms. They are enshrined in the lines from Browning's *Bishop Blougram's Apology* which he has said he would choose as a suitable epigraph for all his novels:

Our interest's on the dangerous edge of things.
The honest thief, the tender murderer,
The superstitious atheist, demi-rep
That loves and saves her soul in new French books —
We watch while these in equilibrium keep
The giddy line midway.

But from this dangerous edge of things to what side does the way point or is this known only to God? In the title of

Browning's psychological epic *The Ring and the Book* the
metaphor is that of the base metal (the dross of depositions
and gossip at the trial of Franceschini collected in the Old
Yellow Book) used by the goldsmith to produce a perfect
gold ring when it is cast off in the refining process. But in
Greene it is as if the gold remains imprisoned in the alloy of
experience, the boy in the dormitory, Pinkie in the hell of
Brighton, Querry caught in his misunderstood career. At
the end of the story Wilditch revisits the island, now smaller
than in memory, still clutching at the reality of his dream
and looking for the golden chamber-pot he had dropped.
He stumbles on a battered tin one with a few flecks of yellow
paint.

CHAPTER 2

Romance and the Thriller Form

I

Anne Wilson has said, writing on medieval romance,

> It is apparent that the forces which impel the fantasy to
> create a story are those of our wishes. Within the created
> world of the story, these wishes have omnipotence; but
> wishes may change, and many wishes may be present at
> once, conflicting with each other . . . Thus the story takes
> form in order to allow a number of different wishes to
> achieve expression, while, at the same time, progressing
> as a struggle to achieve the final triumph of certain
> wishes over others.[1]

Greene's first book was a volume of verse, *Babbling April*.
The title is revealing. His adolescent imagination was fired
by the romantic, sensuous aspect of Browning and by the
freedom of passion detected glowing within the stilted
verse of Sir Lewis Morris's *Epic of Hades* and Stephen
Phillips's *Paolo and Francesco*, so admired in their day. He
read these last two books on his escapes back across the
border from the school, under a hawthorn hedge on
Berkhamsted Common, his place of retreat. But long
before then he had become acquainted with the writers of
historical and contemporary romance, Rider Haggard,
Stanley Weyman, Henty and Marjorie Bowen, and the
greater masters Stevenson and Conrad. It was natural
perhaps, therefore, that his own first published novel *The
Man Within* should take the form of an historical romance

although its ambitions go far beyond a mere adventure tale. But then the true romance is always concerned in Browning's phrase with action in character, with the reconciliation of conflicting wishes. The epigraph from Sir Thomas Browne (how fond Greene is of epigraphs, as if every story can at least be disguised to seem to be a sermon on a text) announces the theme of the divided self: 'There's another man within me that's angry with me'.[2]

Greene had written two novels before *The Man Within* both of which failed to find a publisher. The first, he tells us, was about a black child born of white parents and it gave him the opportunity of projecting his own persecution at school on to a boy who suffered from the colour bar; the hero also wanted to escape from his class and accomplished this at the end by joining a ship at Cardiff as a deck-hand. The second novel was set among refugees from Carlist Spain in the nineteenth century, and was, he says in the preface in the Collected Edition, strongly influenced by the later Conrad of *The Arrow of Gold*.

These two attempts had, however, helped him to acquire the roll of the dice, and to construct in *The Man Within* a careful and skilful plot.

The background is smuggling on the Sussex coast in the early nineteenth century which the author had read about in a history of the subject. Andrews the hero has betrayed his fellow-smugglers to the revenue men; at their interception one of them has been killed and the others captured. Andrews had been led into 'the trade' by his brutal and domineering father, and his reaction against his father who had ill-treated his mother is certainly the most apparent reason for his act of treachery. Andrews shelters with a pure and saintlike woman Elizabeth; her guardian has just died which affords a motive for her to be alone on the Downs in a cottage near Lewes when he comes there. He is inspired by his feelings for her to go to the assizes at Lewes to give evidence against his former friends. Thus he will at least act like a man and justify his better nature (the man within).

Once in Lewes he is inveigled by Farne, the agent of Sir Henry Merriman, the prosecuting counsel, to meet him and, incidentally, Lucy his mistress. As he hesitates Lucy offers herself as a bribe to him to give his evidence. He does so and spends a night with her but then returns to Elizabeth at the cottage and declares his love. In his mind memories are mingled of his father and of Carlyon, the leader of the smugglers, who has been a stronger influence than his father to make him adhere to the band: Carlyon's dangerous life is governed by his romanticism and his sense of poetry, and for this he is respected by Andrews. In the third and last part of the book Andrews leaves the cottage, a hunted man; the smugglers come for him and one of them attacks Elizabeth; she stabs herself before the arrival of Carlyon who would have prevented this. Andrews returns to the cottage and is reconciled with Carlyon whom he sends away to safety. The revenue officers come, and Andrews allows himself to be arrested for Elizabeth's murder. His motive is partly to guarantee the safety of Carlyon who may be suspected, partly in some obscure way to sacrifice himself to achieve peace. As he walks away under arrest he completes this sacrifice by killing himself with a knife taken from the belt of the officer in front of him.

Andrews sees himself as two persons: the sentimental, desiring child who is above all a coward, and 'another more stern critic'. His fear is that when he cannot hear the critic speak it is because he does not exist and his self is nothing after all but a composite of sentiment and cowardice. Throughout the man within strives to make himself heard and impel him towards crises of decision: 'the inner critic who had been still for so long roused himself as though at a challenge and taunted him'.

Andrews' coward's revulsion from the hardness and cruelty of life at sea is given an interest and an edge by his ambivalent relation to his father; his companions accept him at first as the son of his father, and then, except Carlyon, they reject him when they find he is not the same as that boisterous and swaggering figure. After the act of betrayal he runs away and his former friends are hunting for him. The analogy with the adolescent Greene's traumatic isolation in the school house is striking. A sensitive outsider has his loyalty to a father tested among coarse companions in a brutal environment. In the reality the boy is bullied because he is the son of his father, a spy from the enemy camp; in the dream of the book he is rejected by his mates because he is not morally 'the son of his father'; in both cases he runs away, on to Berkhamstead Common or on to the Downs. The solution to the inner struggle is found in either case by a curious mixture of psychological analysis and sexual romanticism. Greene underwent a course of treatment with the psychoanalyst Kenneth Richmond after a breakdown caused by his suffering at school and at about the same time embarked on a period of adolescent love affairs of which the most important was with a nursemaid at home. Likewise Andrews is guided by critical knowledge of his divided personality and by romantic love for the idealized Elizabeth strangely spiced by a jealous sensuality (as when he learns she had been desired by her guardian, now dead). Elizabeth's advice is that he should recover his self-respect by following his choice out to the end: he must come forward in open court and bear witness against the smugglers at Lewes where the town is in sympathy with them and it will be hard to get a verdict for the prosecution. 'Go to Lewes, go to the Assizes, bear witness and you will have shown yourself to have more courage than they.' Andrews walks to Lewes and becomes involved in Sir Henry Merriman's case against the smugglers.

His action is a kind of gamble to reach beyond the perpetual hesitation of which Elizabeth accuses him. After running away from school and his subsequent analysis Greene entered on a long period of boredom: he tried to arouse himself from it by playing Russian roulette; he would go out on the Common with his brother's revolver with one chamber loaded: he would spin the chambers, press the revolver to his head and pull the trigger. He survived these experiments and after a time knew that he would not attempt them again. But experiments with other kinds of danger were to continue. As an undergraduate there was the brief, almost standard, flirtation with the Communist Party that was the pattern for so many of his contemporaries at Oxford and Cambridge between the wars. While still an undergraduate he had a short and romantically ridiculous episode of working for the German Government as a minor courier; the Germans were spying on the separatist movement at Trier which was being encouraged by the French under their occupation of the Rhineland. There were to be other dangerous experiments, journeys to West Africa and Mexico and elsewhere. Running away and the gamble of danger became a continuous accepted process. Even the start of his career as a novelist is looked back on by him as a gamble in the preface (1976) to *The Man Within*: after the two rejected novels it was 'the last throw of the dice in a game I had practically lost'.

Gambling plays an important part in his novels, notably in *Loser Takes All* and *Our Man in Havana*, and for many of his characters belief in God is, as it was for Pascal, in the nature of a gamble. So many actions in the novels resemble the wager of faith Pascal described in the *Pensées*, a movement of the will differing from intellectual belief or disbelief. But Andrews' gamble to overcome cowardice and indecision ends in death. Like many later characters, Scobie for instance, he desires more than anything else a kind of peace; his suicide, following that of Elizabeth, is supposed to provide that. She is 'someone who seemed to carry far behind her eyes, glimpsed only obscurely and at whiles, the promise of his two selves at one, the peace which he had discovered sometimes in music'. It is Elizabeth's spirit who presides over his voluntary end: 'Slowly his hand stole out unnoticed on an errand of supreme importance, for between the two candles there was a white set face that regarded him without pity and without disapproval, with wisdom and sanity'. The moral traces of his act are completely covered: Elizabeth has not been murdered and he has not murdered. Others are misled about the real motive. The truth is private and secret and dies with Andrews. So, in *The Heart of the Matter*, does Scobie's suicide remain a deliberately concealed secret act and motive until Wilson deduces it and tells his wife, and even then it retains a measure of secrecy, taken by her to the confessional but going no further and persisting only as something understood between Scobie and God.

The division of Andrews' personality is too crudely

presented in his attitude to the harlot Lucy and the pure
heroine Elizabeth. As he meditates when the former is
trying to seduce him:

> There was a kind of mystery in Elizabeth, a kind of
> sanctity which blurred and obscured his desire with love.
> Here was no love and no reverence. The animal in him
> could ponder her beauty crudely and lustfully, as it had
> pondered the charms of common harlots, but with the
> added spice of a reciprocated desire.

The introduction of his previous sexual experience seems
incongruous until one realizes that man in Greene is always
fallen a little even before his fall, just as he retains a kind of
innocence after all his experiences. Also this aspect of
Andrews has been anticipated by his coarse overtures to
Elizabeth at their first meeting. However the duality in the
book of a siren and an angel smacks too much of subjective
allegory. Northrop Frye has said: '. . . the popular demand
in fiction is always for a mixed form, a romantic novel just
romantic enough for the reader to project his libido on the
hero and his anima on the heroine, and just novel enough
to keep these projections in a familiar world.'[3] Greene's
hero is too palpably neurotic, his heroine too palely
evocative of moral significance, to tempt our libido or our
anima; neither is the book original enough to compel us.
The court scene has its moments; and the physical pre-
sences of the two lawyers are deftly sketched in. Greene was
at the beginning of his development in drawing convincing
quick portraits of men in power and intrigue. But the
Sussex smuggling background remains a literary matter,
and Carlyon, another projection of Andrews' dreams of
self, is a shadow off-stage. What sustain the book are the
boldness of its ambition and the good writing showing even
through fine writing. The deposit remaining in the reader's
mind, and connected with the novelist's later development,
is a sense of disgust, mainly sexual:

> 'Now I have sunk so deep that surely I've reached the
> bottom' . . . he felt no fear of death, but a terror of life, of

going on soiling himself and repenting and soiling himself again. There was, he felt, no escape. He had no will left.

This almost Jacobean disgust with life is an obsession of most of Greene's early characters.

The same theme of the incomplete personality expressed through a derivative romantic sensibility is to be met in the two novels which immediately followed, *The Name of Action* (1930) and *Rumour at Nightfall* (1931); Greene has not allowed them to be reprinted. They have plots that are engineered to serve the subjective problem, and like *The Man Within* intermingle sexual love with physical risk, now of a clandestine-political nature. *Rumour at Nightfall* is contemporary-Ruritanian and set in Trier under an imaginary dictatorship which closely recalls the separatist movement which the undergraduate Greene had observed in his role as a minor secret agent. But the feature which marks off the first three novels from their successors is the style. Greene has succumbed to the lush mannerism of some of Stevenson and the Conrad who over-elaborated Doña Rita in *The Arrow of Gold*. The first paragraph of *The Man Within* shows considerable skill but it is in 'a worn-out poetic fashion':

> He came over the top of the down as the last light failed and could almost have cried with relief at the sight of the wood below . . . The absence of the cold wind from the sea that had buffeted him for the last half hour seemed like a puff of warm air on his face, as he dropped below the level of the sky. As though the wood were a door swinging on a great hinge, a shadow moved up towards him and the grass under his feet changed from gold to green, to purple and last to a dull grey. Then night came.

There is nothing meretricious about this style; it is not emptily euphonious or merely decorative. There is an effort at work to capture the actual sensations of landscape, to convey the manner in which they harmonize with the drama of the story and the mood of fearful isolation in the hero, now to be developed. But the images are too self-conscious and elaborated too far in the direction of lyric poetry. The first rhythmical sentence makes an accomplished start but its dominant point of reference is not an experience but a writer writing about an experience. Such descriptions, and there are many of them in the book, only place a barrier between the reader and the recognizable, familiar world which the novel demands.

The tradition behind this art prose is a nineteenth-century one: the careful dedication to language of Henry James, Stevenson and Conrad, and of a lesser figure like Meredith, is related to the basic romantic literary assumption that the perfect arrangement of words can perfectly image the world, not simply as a rhetoric for exposition, entertainment or persuasion, but as an expression of its essential nature. Even with a less apparent prose artistry, the dedication is still there in Hardy and Lawrence, as it is in John Cowper Powys. When early twentieth-century modernism abandoned formal realism of character, plot and chronological narration in the novel it also moved away from the literariness of this descriptive visualizing, though it remains in much fiction of the period between the wars. If we look in this way at fiction through the texture of the prose we can see that Joyce is a modernist and Lawrence is often not: the latter develops from the rendering of emotion-charged landscape in prose in a manner close to that of Hardy, to a self-indulgence comparable to that of D'Annunzio, in writing where the projection of personal fantasy saturates and distorts any observation in words of a recognizable world; in Joyce the only literariness present is in passages of deliberate parody; huge artistic ambition remains, but it is ambition, not to transcribe an already divine beauty, but to bring aesthetic order out of the chaos of the real world. James, it should be said, though belonging to the nineteenth-century epoch of art prose (an epoch which stretches into the twentieth century with Proust and Thomas Mann) was yet often at odds with it and provided a bible for modernists in his critical essays and introductions on dramatic construction and the controlling point of view.

Greene has little to do directly with the modernist movement. Some might argue that this is simply an indication of how little it affected the main current of English fiction after about 1930, if one treats as a kind of sport the gigantic rearguard action represented by *Finnegans Wake*. It is better to consider how what at first appear to be radical, decisive innovations in art or design come gradually to be absorbed by the main current of practice, while imparting to it alterations which are taken for granted. Seeing camouflaged lorries moving up to the front at the beginning of the First World War Picasso remarked to Picabia that this was what they had invented in early Cubism.[4] Later, shop fronts became cubist as modernism filtered down into mass design. Similarly a modified form of the stream of consciousness technique and multiple points of view became the common stock of popular fiction, particularly the thriller. It is this kind of indirect, diffused modernism which we find in Greene; but the mainspring of his development is simply the urge to tell a better, tauter story, to shed adjectives and adverbs and unnecessary description. He does not cultivate the ironic disconnection of dialogue, favoured by the early Evelyn Waugh and Anthony Powell and derived from Firbank, except to a limited extent in the early novels. If there is one major influence on the increasing discipline of his technique it is that of the cinema.

Again, as with with the cubism of lorries and shop fronts, the influence of the cinema is so pervasive in twentieth-century fiction that it is hard to disentangle. We do not examine a narrative technique that we take for granted. The original ballad audience did not bother to analyse incremental repetition. But in Greene the debt is palpable because he was an amateur of the cinema from the start and its best English critic before he became a script writer. His first film reviews were written at Oxford for *Oxford Outlook* and he was a passionate reader of *Close Up*, the film magazine edited by Kenneth Macpherson and Bryher to which Marc Allegret and Pudovkin contributed. In 1935 he became the film critic of *The Spectator* and continued to be so until the outbreak of war. His experience thus spanned silent films, sound and colour; he was resistant to Technicolor: 'Technicolor plays havoc with the women's faces; they all, young and old, have the same healthy, weather-beaten skins'. There is a black-and-white quality about the people and the urban landscapes of his novels of the 1930s. Hence a preference for night scenes where it is possible to set a figure in close-up against darkness. In *England Made Me* (1935) Krogh the millionaire unofficially visits his workmen who are building a railway bridge.

> The foreman limped straight towards Krogh down the sleepers. He put a cigarette in his mouth. He looked small and thin, peering this way, peering that way in the glare of the arc lights. The man in the torn grey trousers followed him and the men on the girders shouted that the bolts were here, there, beyond . . . . The foreman caught the box and struck a match; he had to shield it with his hands from the wind. The arc lamps showed up his hands against the light like close-ups on a screen; the fingers blunted, twisted with rheumatism, the stump on the left hand.

Here the effect of spot-lit close-up is deliberate and stated but there are numerous other examples, and there are many night scenes like this. Even in daylight scenes a relentless grey predominates, as in the great silent films of Greene's apprenticeship to the cinema, *Warning Shadows* and *The Student of Prague*, or the later *Quai des Brumes*, *Le Jour se Lève*, and *Hôtel du Nord* of Marcel Carné. The lighting of a match to focus the incident is another typical device of film but this in turn derived in the history of the French cinema from the literary realism of Flaubert and Zola. The novelist's exploitation of small objects was taken up lovingly by literary-minded directors (Carné had as script-writer for some of his best films of seedy contemporary reality Jacques Prévert, the poet and novelist). 'The French novelist taught the French cinema the immense importance of the careful accessory'[5]; and the French cinema taught it to Greene. Beyond the significant detail the greyness of the silver screen predominates.

A page further on from the passage just quoted from *England Made Me*, Krogh's assistant Hall takes off by plane from London to Stockholm:

'The great rubber tyre below the window bounced twice from the rough grass and then stood poised above the bright clean air station, the white roofs, near the sea the oil-containers like rows of buttons on a grey-green suit . . . . The Zuyder Zee crawled backward as slowly as a worm; there was no sense of speed; it lay the colour of mud with inky patches, one island white buttressed against the low depressing swell'.

In *England Made Me* the grey screen records the dampness and fog of Stockholm. In the previous novel *It's a Battlefield* (1934) the background is London, usually at night, presented in a series of impressionistic shots, lights against the reflecting wetness of streets and pavements: 'The great lit globe of the Coliseum balanced above the restaurants and the cafés and the public-houses in St Martin's Lane'. Grey and greyness are constantly recurring terms setting the tone of a moral climate of failure and indecision, as in the case of Conrad Drover, waking in Milly's room, feeling the unhappiness of his love for her and his hopeless outsider's position: 'He meant the hate and the pain and the sense of guilt and the sound of crying in the *greying* room and sleeplessness and the walls shaking as the early morning lorries drove out of London'. Even when a primary colour is introduced it has to surrender to this greyness or to battle doubtfully against it; in *Brighton Rock* (1938) Ida Arnold's room behind Russell Square has a red curtain but it is an old one and does not cancel out the major tones of the encroaching evening. 'The room faced east and the sun had gone. It was cold and dusk. Ida turned on the gas-fire and drew the old scarlet velvet curtains to shut out the *grey* sky and the chimney-pots.'

This dominant shading of the screen within which the writer's camera-eye settles on small significant objects is accompanied by other devices of film technique as well as the close-up. The method of moving abruptly from one

scene or shot to another, cinematically cutting, is the major
means by which Greene attains economy of narration. The
scenes are connected by a narrative and emotional thread as
in the following passage from *Stamboul Train* (1932),
Greene's fourth novel and the one in which he decisively
breaks with his earlier manner to introduce, not the
subjective juxtapositions of modernist stream of consciousness, but the *montage* of film narrative:

> 'Braised chicken! Roast veal . . . 'The waiters called their
> way along the carriage and broke the minute's silence.
> Everyone began talking at once.
> 'I find the Hungarians take to cricket quite naturally.
> We had six matches last season.'
> 'This beer's not better. I *would* just like a glass of
> Guinness' . . . . and noisily and cheerfully with the thud
> of wheels, the clatter of plates, voices talking and the
> tingle of mirrors, the express passed a long line of
> fir-trees and the flickering Danube. In the coach the
> pressure gauge rose, the driver turned the regulator
> open, and the speed of the train was increased by five
> miles an hour.

Here a shot down the corridor of the restaurant car taking
in the hurrying waiters side-tracks to show faces talking
across the tables; this is cut to a shot through the window
showing the landscape racing by; another cut shows the
pressure gauge and widens to reveal the driver in action, an
image for increasing speed and the continuity of the
journey embracing the mounting action of several personal
dramas (some film-makers would use an external shot of
the train in motion to punctuate the narrative).
Greene learned in the 1930s not only from the visual
language of the cinema but from its language of situation.
The pursuit of a criminal, justly or unjustly accused, by the
police, is reduced to certain stock elements. The chase was
to achieve its classic expression in *The Power and the Glory*
(1940) but is already a subject in *A Gun for Sale* (1936). The
victim is assisted by a girl who is sympathetic and understanding rather than a loving partner, the police close in,

there is a temporary refuge for the fugitives who sleep on sacking in a railway shed, the night also affords an opportunity for revelations and self-revelations between them, and then there is a last failed bid at escape and the shooting down of the criminal. The scenario is part of the screen mythology of the period and is parallelled by that of Carol Reed's *Odd Man Out*, based on a novel by F.L. Green but possibly influenced in its treatment by his namesake's highly cinematic novel.[6] There are the visual features already noted: the dark outlines of the shed, railway lines and locomotives, the shadows and the coils of fog and the pale light of morning. Sound is synchronized with these images, as in the scene in the restaurant car in *Stamboul Train*: 'He caught a glimpse of their moving shadows and then an engine hooted and belched a grey plume of smoke round him'. These stock situations of pursuit, temporary physical shelter providing a setting for human exchanges under pressure, and a final ruthless renewal of the hunt, helped Greene to discipline his narrative structure at the same time as the camera image exerted a beneficial effect on sentence and paragraph.

But the encounter with the cinema for Greene and others was not confined to acquiring a new technique and a command of thriller structure having the beauty and convenience of formulaic situations in traditional epic. Paradoxically, the dream world of the cinema was cultivated for the taste of genuine common life behind the images. In the England of Chamberlain and Test cricket, the 'land of lobelias and tennis flannels', even American 'B' movies could seem to belong to a genuine popular culture, the gangster myth to reflect real good and evil; seen after the effete politeness of British romantic comedy on stage and screen the satiric anarchism of the Marx Brothers seemed therapeutic; and French realist films offered a view of the harsh actualities of life in which it was less and less possible for people to play the bourgeois party charade according to which everything in the garden was lovely. Films, and that meant in terms of bulk mainly Hollywood films, nursed desires for a world outside the nursery and the tennis court. As a medium appealing to the tastes of a wide range of social groups there had been nothing like it since the Elizabethan drama. Not for a generation was the theatre to recapture its role as interpreter of the moods of society; but the mood of the filmgoers of the 1930s and 1940s was to look outwards for images of reality, to the 'unjust lands', and the vigour of a strange new society with its intriguing mixture of rawness and decadence. Greene's fascination by the American films which he frequently pilloried is only matched by his continued dislike of many aspects of that society.

What Greene says about the truth of the camera in his film criticism of the period constantly confirms its influence on his own technique; and his reviews show that for the proper use of the camera to depict the scenes of ordinary life he had to turn to French and American films to escape from the narrow and incompetent artificiality of Elstree:

> But it is astonishing how seldom in English films a director uses the camera in this way to establish a scene, a way of life, with which he and his audience are familiar ... the social snobbery which hampers the English cinema. The material of English films, unlike French or American, is nearly always drawn from the leisured class, a class of which the director and his audience know very little. Mr Hitchcock sometimes indulges in crime or 'low life', but it is with the amused collector's air of a specialist in sensation. An English film as a rule means evening gowns by Hartnell, suitcases by Asprey. An excursion steamer to Margate ... becomes a luxury liner full of blondes in model bathing-dresses. Even in the worst French films one is not conscious of this class division, the cafes and dance-halls are of the kind familiar to the majority of the audience.[7]

Greene's novels of the 1930s sustain their melodramatic plots because, in his own words, he succeeds in establishing a scene and a way of life familiar to his audience. Sometimes the debt to his film favourites is so close as to amount to pastiche. His praise of *Sous les Toits de Paris* in another *Spectator* review discloses the probable source of the railway shed episode in *A Gun For Sale* when the police surround Raven and Anne:' . . . the darkness of a railway viaduct; the smoke blew continually across, and the dialogue was drowned in the din of shunting trucks. The steamy obscurity, the whispers, the uproar overhead combined to make the scene vividly sinister'. Selective observation like this, as with the neo-realists of the Italian cinema in the 1950s, can lead to its own brand of inverted picturesque. But at his best Greene renders faithfully the relatively unexplored surface of English life in the changing city.

The inspiration of the cinema is not of course the whole story. However closely related the literary image is to the language of *montage* (as Eisenstein emphasizes in *The Film Sense*) the novel is different because made with words. Condemning his second and third novels, forgotten failures, failures to communicate a purely personal case history, the later Greene declared that they lacked the prime requisite of simplicity of language and the sense of life as it is lived (in the preface to his *Collected Stories*). Some of his short stories of the same period have much more life and economy. The need was to create a convincing scene of action; a passage in the autobiography shows him analysing and solving the problem:

Now I can see quite clearly what went wrong. Excitement is simple: excitement is a situation, a single event. It mustn't be wrapped up in thoughts, similes, metaphors. A simile is a form of reflection, but excitement is of the moment when there is not time to reflect. Action can only be expressed by a subject, a verb and an object, perhaps a rhythm — little else. Even an adjective slows the pace or tranquillizes the nerve. I should have turned to Stevenson to learn my lesson: 'It came all of a sudden when it did, with a rush of feet and a roar, and then a shout from Alan, and the sound of blows and someone crying as if hurt. I looked back over my shoulder, and saw Mr Shuan in the doorway crossing blades with Alan.' No similes or metaphors there, not even an adjective. But I was too concerned with 'the point of view' to be aware of simpler problems, to know that the sort of novel I was trying to write, unlike a poem, was not made with words but with movement, action, character.[8]

The last sentence is an implied rejection of modernism as well as of old-style fine writing. But he goes on to qualify his statement that the novel is not made with words. He admits that the writer must discriminate in his words and that is the heart of the matter. He must not love his words, for that is the road of self-indulgence. He must so discriminate in their choice and so limit their profusion that they draw no attention to themselves and provide simply an efficient mime of action. It was the Jamesian point of view of the highbrow novel, spun out in webs of words, that had led him astray, working outwards from a cerebral conception of character which prevented him from effectively present-ing character in action. In the end it is his favourite boyhood romancer Robert Louis Stevenson, a sort of uncle commemorated in the family album, and by the friendships of Greene's aunts with Sidney Colvin and other surviving friends, who gave him the answer to the problem. Greene sees it at this period as being largely a technical problem of contriving the action to move, and this is why his prolonged study of film was so fruitful, though he does not mention it in the autobiography. But once again it is not possible completely to separate the mastery of technical means from the full emotional control of certain themes. The Stevenson who could present pure action without literary fuss (and who had put much of the latter behind him) was also the writer who could fix in an episode the moment of realiza-tion of a betrayal. Climbing the external staircase at Shaws at his uncle's bidding, David Balfour sees in a flash of summer lightning that the stairs are all broken and he is within a few inches of falling into the well: he has been sent to his death. Greene develops the same theme of the initiation of innocence into danger.[9] In 1936 he wrote of *Treasure Island* as a book in which adventurous action, buried treasure, a horrifying murder, and blind Pew, had symbolic value. It conveyed a sense of good and evil so that 'even a child can recognize the greater dignity and depth of this Scottish Presbyterian's *Mansoul* written in terms of an adventure-story for a boys' magazine'. His freshly acquired control of a moving action is used in the creation of parables of good and evil.

II

Stamboul Train (1932) saved Greene's career as a profession-al novelist. It was chosen by the Book Society which then guaranteed it a sale of 10,000 copies; he was not to fare so well again commercially until after the publication of *The Power and the Glory* (1940). It is not a good book because there is no single character sufficiently interesting to hold us. Years later when he had seen a film made out of it Greene wrote: 'By what was unchanged . . . I could see clearly what was cheap and banal enough to fit the cheap banal film'. But he had learned the lesson of how to achieve movement and excitement and he never looked back.

The book belongs to the genre in which a group of heterogeneous characters are thrown together in a closed setting, a ship or a train or an hotel, a forcing-house where they establish fresh relationships and are precipitated to-wards or rescued from crises. A long train journey provides an admirable vehicle for such a plot and the international glamour of the Orient Express adds a bonus (as it was to do for Agatha Christie). The treatment of a human and social cross-section was an attraction of the whole inter-war period: Arnold Bennett's *Imperial Palace* (1930) with its hotel setting and Lettice Cooper's *National Provincial* (1940) with a background of life in a provincial town (Leeds) are further examples. The limitation of the genre is that the width of the social cross-section prevents the development of any single individual drama; for a writer who believes in the reality of mass society this does not matter: Dos Passos' closed setting in *USA* is the whole North American conti-nent. But in Europe Sartre was perhaps wiser when he chose a hero, Mathieu, for *Les chemins de la liberté* and only fails when he switches the interest in mid-stream from Mathieu to Brunet.

Greene's random sample is less ambitious and suitably tuned for the pace and length of a conventional thriller.

Most of the characters are English: they go from the country where nothing happens to the 'unjust lands' of Auden's poem where dangerous and terrible things occur. There is Carleton Myatt, the Jewish currant merchant, going to Istanbul to conclude an important deal which will give him an overriding position in his firm. On the journey he has a brief love affair with the poor chorus-girl Coral Musker on her way to a dance engagement in Istanbul. Coral is hardened to the cruelties of life and her uneasy career, but it has not robbed her of gentleness and a residual hope. Unlike the more brittle and glamorous women he is used to she arouses a kind of pity in Myatt. From any tenderness of love in Greene's novels pity is never entirely dissociated. Richard Czinner, for five years a political refugee in England, is returning to Yugoslavia to lead a socialist revolt which has already been betrayed. The lesbian journalist Mabel Warren joins the train at Cologne with her companion, the worldly and sophisticated Janet Pardoe; her object is to get a story out of Czinner whom she has recognized. There is a middle-aged English couple, one dyspeptic, the other lecherous, and a faintly comic English clergyman; these minor figures present a picture of the English abroad like that of Alfred Hitchcock in *The Lady Vanishes* but without the solidity his characters have to fall back on. Finally there is a vulgar best-selling novelist, Savory, who drops his aitches when he can remember to. At Vienna the train is joined by Josef Grunlich, a thief on the run who has committed a brutal murder.

At Subotica in Yugoslavia Czinner is arrested. Coral is implicated because he has given her papers to post. They are locked in the waiting-room with Grunlich whose gun has been found. In an attempt to escape Czinner is shot and Coral helps him to shelter in a hut: so we have the night vigil of a man and a woman unknown to each other, on the run, and thrust together by circumstances, which is repeated in the dramatic climax of *A Gun for Sale*. The situation exerted a peculiar fascination for Greene; it mixes the elements of an almost cosy hiding-place (there are grain-sacks in the shed at Subotica) and danger outside where the enemy is searching for the escapers; it may be associated with

Greene's special hiding-place on Berkhamsted Common when he was playing truant from school: 'It was one of the most solitary lanes I have ever known . . . On one side was a ploughed field: on the other a ditch with a thick hawthorn hedge which was hollow in the centre and in which I could sit concealed and read my book . . . in my sixties I seem to smell the leaves and grasses of my hiding-place more certainly than I hear the dangerous footsteps on the path or see the countryman's boots pass by at the level of my eyes.'

Arriving at Subotica Myatt inquires for Coral without success; soldiers have stopped the car, there has been shooting, and his pity and concern are gradually giving way to a feeling that all this is nothing to do with him. By a twist of irony Coral and Czinner hear his car behind them just as they reach the hut and the escaping Grunlich manages to obtain a lift in it, lying in order to convince Myatt that he has not seen Coral. Czinner is dead by the morning and Coral is saved by Mabel Warren who is attracted by her and is coming to the end of her relationship with Janet Pardoe.

All these people are condemned to be prisoners of their own weakness. Czinner, Myatt and Coral are the most interesting and sympathetic, but they are all tossed about in varying degrees by circumstances and their automatic, conditioned response to them. Czinner, the socialist who is returning at great risk to lead a revolution against the government of a police state, would appear an heroic figure in any ordinary romance. He has come from a peasant family and been a doctor in Belgrade working selflessly in the poorest quarters of the city. Five years before he has given evidence for the prosecution in the trial for rape of a highly placed general, when already in danger of his life as a revolutionary, and the resulting charge of perjury has caused him to flee to England. But only in his fifties he seems an old man at the end of a wasted life: his education separated him from his parents who looked on him with awe; his skill as a doctor has been useless: 'He could do nothing for his own people; he could not recommend rest to the worn-out or prescribe insulin to the diabetic, because they had not the money to pay for either'. He has lost his religious faith, telling himself that God is a fiction invented by the rich to keep the poor content. 'He had blown that candle out with his own breath.' Yet in memories in his consciousness of the Host swinging in procession down crowded aisles his rationalism appears as loss rather than gain. There is a faint outline in his character of those men and women in Greene's Catholic novels who are searching through hopeless surroundings for the assurance of final peace — Rose, the whisky-priest, and Scobie. He is even stumbling towards the idea of confession and in a half-comic scene approaches the subject with the Anglican clergyman Mr Opie; the first notes are heard of the theme of the mutual incomprehensibility of the secular and Christian worlds:

> 'Yes,' said Mr Opie, 'a spiritual anthology for the lay mind, something to take the place in the English church of the Roman books of contemplation.' His thin white hand stroked the black wash-leather cover of his note-book, 'But I intend to strike deeper. The Roman books are, what shall I say? too exclusively religious. I want mine to meet all the circumstances of everyday life. Are you a cricketer?
>
> The question took Dr Czinner by surprise; he had again in memory been kneeling in darkness, making his act of contrition.

The novelist Savory joins in the discussion. The parallel between confession and psychoanalysis is glibly distorted: 'in the one case sins are said to be forgiven . . . the patient leaves the psycho-analyst with the power, as well as the intention of making a fresh start'. Words like responsibility, crisis, and man's need, which Czinner understands, are bandied about in this discussion like the counters in a game.

He feels that even as a socialist he has failed. He has not been able to help the poor. The peasants on the platform at Subotica and the soldiers who arrest him are ignorant and foolish, not really understanding what is going on. The revolt in Belgrade has failed ingloriously because it was timed three days too early. At a mockery of a court-martial at the station he is sentenced to death by Colonel Hartep, the Chief of Police. He had hoped to have stood his trial in a public court in the capital and to have made a speech which would have aroused the world. Now Hartep gives him permission to say a few words if it will give him peace of mind (this first of Greene's many policemen is no grotesque, though roughly and slightly drawn, and can combine corruption with a kindly nature). Czinner can only mouth platitudes about the fair distribution of goods for all under Communism, trying desperately to address himself to one of the guards who can make nothing of it. In the end, dying in pain, he finds that he is alone with himself. He has, he thinks, been damned by his faithfulness. The speed of the express which makes the passengers cling to its motion, leaning now this way and now that, shows him where he had gone wrong. 'One has to be very alive, very flexible, very opportunist.' Falling and falling, in great pain, he listens to the seamed faces of his mother and father telling him that they are glad and grateful and he has done what he could. The implied conclusion is that he is a good man gone wrong in his inner self and not simply through the injustice of his opponents and the stupidity of his supporters.

Myatt is a complex study, perhaps too complex for this crowded gallery where surface desires jostle each other as competitive human beings cling to the motion of the train. His Jewishness is stressed, partly because his fellow characters are consciously aware of his racial distinctiveness. He is subtle in assessing the motives of other men, ambitious, skilful and ruthless in his business schemes; his feeling for Coral goes beyond what he had expected it to be: she gives herself to him because she feels it is the right way to pay him for giving his first-class compartment up to her when she is sick with tiredness after Ostend. He is the first man she has had and he is touched by pity and tenderness; his imagination rises to the occasion and he has extravagantly generous plans for what they will do when they reach Constantinople. But already he is beginning to think of Janet Pardoe who is really beautiful as Coral is not and with whom he could marry and settle down.

Coral herself is a bundle of motives. One side of her is the already hard-bitten trouper with no illusions, used to the

life of the theatrical tour. But she is a virgin and has a
certain innocence beyond that; and she has the courage to
stay with Czinner till his death. She has the reality and
unclouded common sense of so many of Greene's working
girls. There is a resemblance to Anne in *A Gun for Sale*.
Greene's art is governed by patterns of bizarre juxtaposition. It is not for nothing that his first childhood memory is
of being pushed along in his pram with a dead dog at his
feet. So it is important that a casual act of sex in the sleeping
compartment of a train should be connected with a genuine
tenderness directed to the future — Coral breaks out that
she loves Myatt. The image of Coral returns to him at the
end when he is at the Pera Palace Hotel with Janet Pardoe
and deciding whether to become engaged to her. If he does
he can become a director of the currant firm, Stein's, and
assure his future. In the moment of choice he is flexible and
opportunist, moving with the train. He knows that if he asks
Janet to marry him he will have solved far more than his
domestic future. But he remembers Coral, ' the sudden
strangeness of their meeting when he had thought that all
was as familiar as cigarette smoke'. In choosing Janet he has
denied the possibility of this strangeness beyond opportunities and, as in similar scenes in Greene, a cock is faintly
crowing.

III

It's a Battlefield (1934) is a more powerful and ambitious
book. The background is not now a chance group on a
journey but the wasteland of loneliness, anxiety and social
decay in contemporary London. 'I had not known death
had undone so many.' Greene's London is close to that of
T.S. Eliot in *The Waste Land* but the consciousness of social
injustice and class struggle is far more pronounced. *It's a
Battlefield* is Greene's nearest approach to a political novel
of the inter-war period; although its successor *England
Made Me* (1935) has a capitalist and his assistants at the
centre of the plot and an atmosphere of financial
manipulation, the personal story is more important. In *It's a
Battlefield* all the personages are victims of a system locked in
an impersonal struggle.

The people of the book are drawn together from diverse backgrounds by their connection with a single murder case. Jim Drover, a bus driver, has been sentenced to death for the murder of a policeman in a riot at a Communist meeting. He had thought he was defending his wife from a blow and the death was almost an accident. The appeal has failed and now a petition to the Home Secretary to commute the sentence to life imprisonment is the only course to save Drover. Involved in the petition are Drover's wife Milly who loves him, his brother Conrad, Milly's sister Kay, pleasure-loving and promiscuous, who works in a match factory, a dilettante littérateur and parlour communist Mr Surrogate, his dead wife's friend Caroline Bury, a fashionable literary and artistic hostess, and the journalist Conder who is out for a story. Moving through the book with a firmness of direction not granted to any other character is the Assistant Commissioner of Police in charge of the case; he is linked to the chain the others form by being himself a friend of Caroline Bury who has him to lunch to gain his influence on behalf of Jim Drover; finally he is confronted by Conrad who, while attempting to shoot him, is fatally injured by a car. It is one of the interlocking ironies of the book that the frustrated rage of the neurotic Conrad, symbolizing all the deprivation and ignorance of the under-dog pained by intellectual consciousness, should be aimed at the figure of the Assistant Commissioner; for the Assistant Commissioner is not only a man of complete probity for whom his duty is his only life: he is bitterly aware of how the dice are loaded against absolute justice in a case like this. At one level the battle being fought in a fog is between 'them' and 'us':

He knew quite well the cause of the discrepancy; the laws were made by property owners in defence of property, that was why a Fascist could talk treason without prosecution; that was why a man who defrauded the state in defence of his private wealth did not even lose the money he had gained; that was why the burglar went to gaol for five years; that was why Drover could not so easily be reprieved — he was a Communist.

The reasons given for the discrepancy are those that might be given by the *New Statesman* or the National Council for Civil Liberties in 1934, yet they are partly contradicted by the obstinate integrity of the man thinking these thoughts. He is modelled to some extent on the Police Commissioner in Conrad's *The Secret Agent* and is like him in his tense and distant relation to his subordinates. He shares with his old housekeeper a passionate and not entirely reasoned fidelity: 'he recognized a quality he shared; it might be described loosely as love, as obstinacy, as loneliness, or even as desperation. The more one was alone, the more one clung to one's job, the only thing it was certainly right to do, the only human value valid for every change of government, and for every change of heart.' As for justice, he leaves it to magistrates, to judges and juries, and, uncomfortably, to the Home Secretary in the person of his smooth private secretary Beale who comes to sound his opinion. He has the implacable loyalty of a person in Conrad; in another policeman, the lieutenant in *The Power and the Glory*, a similar resolute single-mindedness is devoted to a fanatical moral ideal of secularism. But for the Commissioner there is no motivating cause other than doing his job. When he pushes aside the reports on Drover to take up those on a plain brutal murder case, he feels that he may be fighting for what is right, and there is just a hint that in moments of weariness or depression he may dream of 'an organisation which he could serve for higher reasons than pay, an organisation which would enlist his fidelity because of its inherent justice, its fair distribution of reward, its reasonableness'. But here the character is, we feel, being pushed too far and too hard towards a liberalized Marxism of the early Auden variety.

The epigraph to *It's a Battlefield* from A.W. Kinglake's *The Invasion of the Crimea*, describes the battle of Inkerman fought in early morning fog as being made up of 'small numberless circlets' in which 'each separate gathering of English soldiery went on fighting its own little battle in happy and advantageous ignorance of the general state of the action; nay, even very often in ignorance of the fact that any great conflict was raging'. The metaphor of the night

battle serves not only to convey the separation of man from
man and group from group in the metropolis but also the
spiritual confusion in which they live; as in Arnold's use of
the image his Londoners are

> here as on a darkling plain
> Swept with confused alarms of struggle and flight,
> Where ignorant armies clash by night.

The military image is kept continuously before the reader.
The Assistant Commissioner of Police is like a general at his
command post, 'left alone at headquarters to study the
reports from every unit; they littered his desk. But he was
not sheltered in a chateau behind miles of torn country; the
front line was only a hundred yards away, where the trams
screamed down the Embankment and the buses circled
Trafalgar Square. It was hard, he thought, to get any clear
idea of a war carried on in this piecemeal way throughout a
city'. However in addition to the battlefield metaphor there
is also the sense of the city having an independent life so
that human beings are simply components in a vast
automated puppet-play. There are several passages of
urban poetry, sad yet glittering, in which the very mechanical repetitiveness of metropolitan life exerts a fascination.
The neon-lit modern street scene was, in the 1930s, a new
enough creation to claim the special attention of poets and
writers. Louis MacNeice wrote in the same decade 'And yet
there is beauty narcotic and deciduous in this vast organism
grown out of us'[11]; somewhat earlier Walther Ruttmann's
documentary film *Berlin* had depicted the city as an organic
whole, stretching like an animal as people go to work at
dawn, relaxing like one as the montage shows us humans
and animals eating at the same time in the middle of the
day. Greene's vision comprises both the deciduous beauty
and the terror of an organism that swallows up the
individual:

> The man who tears paper patterns and the male soprano
> were performing before the pit queues, the shutters of
> the shops had all gone up, the prostitutes were moving

west. The feature pictures had come on the second time at the super-cinemas, and the taxi ranks were melting and re-forming. In the Café Français in Little Compton Street the man at the counter served two coffees and sold a packet of 'Weights'. The match factory in Battersea pounded out the last ten thousand boxes, working overtime. The cars in the Oxford Street fun-fair rattled and bounced, and the evening papers went to press for the last edition — 'The Streatham Rape and Murder. Latest Developments', 'Mr MacDonald Flies to Lossiemouth', 'Disarmament Conference Adjourns', 'Special Service for Footballers', 'Family of Insured Couple Draw £10,000. Insure Today.' At each station on the Outer Circle a train stopped every two minutes.

The processing of the city makes its own mythology through films and newspapers. To use the language of the intelligentsia of the period, the proletariat is subjected to the myth of finance-capitalism, which anticipates what Marcuse was to say about the absorbing structures of late capitalism. Greene's recording of the urban myth in action is like the findings of Charles Madge and Tom Harrisson's 'Mass Observation' published a few years later. For Mass Observation was really a documentary poetry of the kind revealed in this passage but based on a rather shaky scientific foundation; like all reportage it was imaginatively selective. It was the age of artistic obsession with the collective. There was even an Oxford Collective Poem (published in *New Verse* in 1938) cobbled together somewhat in the manner of Consequences and having as its best line 'Stone kings irresolute on a marble stair'. That generation at Oxford was in fact less to be seen in terms of a collective mind and attitude than post-war generations, but the imagination of an epoch tends to meet historical reality at a tangent, and at no time was this more true than of the imagination of the left-wing writers of the 1930s and their public. The stark image of class exploitation is presented while a fairer distribution of national income is actually being achieved and prosperity outside the distressed areas increasing. Auden writes of the poets bursting like bombs in a socialist society while the poets in Soviet Russia were being shot or sent to the camps. Yet apart from fashionable attitudes Greene's images of the collective life of the city have a visual and poetic truth that remains valid. Also *It's a Battlefield* is fired by the 'real driving force of the 1930s political mythology, a passion for social justice, to comment on the discrepancy between moral needs and social machinery. The observation of English class consciousness is, too, deft and sharp.

The Assistant Commissioner has come to his post, somewhat improbably, from service in the East, perhaps as a District Commissioner. He is yellowed by fever and remembers 'the murderer who had set fire to his own hut and died in the flames to escape capture' and how when patrolling in the jungle he had armed himself only with a walking-stick. It is interesting to notice here the beginning of Greene's fascination with the jungle before ever he had visited Africa or the east; a life of tropical hardship and exposure far from the centres of civilization is made to stand for an ultimate testing of human character and civilized moral assumptions. Joseph Conrad had set man against the background of the sea and the jungle in the same way; his *Heart of Darkness* begins with Marlow's suggestion to friends as they ride at anchor in the mouth of the Thames that to some young Roman London too was once one of the dark places of the earth, threatening corruption and chaos: 'He has to live in the midst of the incomprehensible, which is also detestable.' Greene has written an original novel but he has been aided to do so by moving away from one Conrad to another: from the gilded self-conscious prose mystification of *The Arrow of Gold* to the serious exploration of a central moral terror in *Heart of Darkness* and *The Secret Agent*. Only the metaphor has been changed, from the terrible unknown of the jungle to the sheer confusion of the battlefield. But the moral effect is the same, a stripping down of the comfortable protective idealisms designed to make a reasonable pattern out of human conduct in order to reveal the bare fact. As the Commissioner thinks, pondering the contradiction of the passion for physical cleanliness in some murderers, 'A life

spent with criminals would never fail to strip the maxims of
priests and teachers from the underlying chaos'. There is
even a link gratuitously established between the historical
Conrad and the principal among the separated contenders
on the battlefield, the most desperately separated, Conrad
Drover. Conrad seems to its owner a pretentious name
marking him off unduly from the herd. It was given him
because his parents took in lodgers and the most reliable
among the lodgers was a certain Polish seaman with that
name.

Conrad is the most alienated among the group of
characters who all find themselves more or less alone. He
admires his stronger and more active brother Jim and
enviously loves Jim's wife. He is the clever boy at school who
has got on and become a head clerk but he feels that in the
process he has somehow lost manhood. In his position he is
gnawed by anxiety; he is separated from the other clerks
who laugh at him behind his back, and socially and
economically cut off from the manager who promoted him.
He is the one most cruelly aware of the gulf fixed between
'them' and 'us' because his intelligence and his sensitiveness
separate him from those on his side of the barrier who
should be his fellows. He lives his life in an agony of
frustrated embarrassment. Early in the story when the
Assistant Commissioner is meeting the private secretary
Beale in the Savoy the latter overhears two women sitting
near them who are laughing over some story involving 'a
pram on a taxi'; he mentions it in the street and is overheard
by Conrad who is passing by. What was a subject for idle
curiosity to Beale becomes for Conrad an insulting upper-
class password; he is being deliberately mystified and
reminded of his lack of power or acknowledgment in the
world. The phrase haunts him as his despair becomes more
and more hysterical.

While the book moves from one human fragment to
another the most steadily developing theme is the progressive disintegration of Conrad. The last fifty pages, which
Greene looks back on as writing which he has never
bettered, describe the last stage of this disintegration which
leads to Conrad's death. Anxious to do something for his

brother he pits himself against the Assistant Commissioner
and buys a revolver in order to kill him. There is no justice
in a world where his brother must be condemned to die in
spite of his innocence on account of the preconceptions of
bewigged judges, preconceptions shared with the two men
in Piccadilly enjoying an arcane joke in upper-class accents.
It is ironically suitable to this chaos of values that he picks on
the one man in the situation who is completely disinterested; the Assistant Commissioner knows he is being
followed by Conrad and, although he does not know why,
he is not afraid. In the end as Conrad stands in the street,
trying to shoot at the Assistant Commissioner who is
emerging from Caroline Bury's house, Conrad is knocked
down by a car and dies in hospital. The revolver has been
loaded with blanks by the dealer who did not trust him and
the whole attempt has been futile. He has tried to achieve a
personal resolution and ended up by confirming his
alienation. He had been a man who thought other people
were looking at him and who worried that there was
something wrong with his clothes; at the end he is just the
same, wondering whether they can detect the shape of the
revolver through his pocket. His death simply sets the seal
on the dissolution of his personality.

> He was separated from everyone he loved by his hatred
> . . . It was as if I had driven my own nightmare into his
> body through the hole the bullet made (but there is no
> bullet and no hole) . . . Then he was struck in the body
> and thrown a dozen yards and could not think: what has
> done this? nor wonder: why am I here?'

A policeman asks the Assistant Commissioner 'Do you
know him, sir?' and his reply is, 'I haven't any idea who he
is'. He is a nameless casualty on the battlefield over which
his quarry had tried to preserve a certain order.

Conrad's disaster grows out of his love for Milly and its
inevitable failure when it is sexually realised. This is the first
major statement of a prevading theme of Greene's novels,
love, pity, and their betrayal by sexual closeness. She lets
him into her bed and allows him 'the pitiful pleasure of

their union'. Physical love only serves to separate him from her:

> Before their bodies had known each other, they had been
> closely acquainted; they had even shared something,
> their nerves and their suspicion, in which Jim had no part
> at all . . . He could believe that she loved him in a way, and
> that way, though it promised no satisfaction, was better
> than this shared lust, this shared ignorance of anything
> beyond a touch, a sense of physical closeness, a heat and a
> movement.

Another narrative irony is established by the parallel love affair of Milly's sister Kay, who is directly sensual and promiscuous, with the Soho French waiter Jules. Kay also sleeps with Mr Surrogate, enjoying the luxury of his beautiful pink bed. She comes home sleek and satisfied to recount her exploit to her sister, thin, bony, and miserable, as she sits brushing her hair before the bedroom mirror. The two women carry the treatment of sex far beyond the simple dichotomy of love and lust rendered in the previous novels. Kay is naturally and amorally happy; Conrad and Milly who love each other as persons are wretched. Milly is not angelic but wise, not beautiful but sexually disturbing: 'he wanted to describe her to herself, the fair fine hair, the high cheek-bones, the large mouth and the large hands and the small body; the courage of her malice and the fidelity of her despair'. If her husband's death sentence is reprieved it will be eighteen years before he is released from prison. And this is what happens. Faithfulness for so long is not to be expected. Jim tries unsuccessfully to kill himself. Conrad's futile action deprives Milly of the only person who could comfort her, a last ironic twist of the knife.

Love moves quickly through the act of sex from an animal sensuality to the separation of a pitiful unease. It is as if, reworking the crudely polarized theme of *The Man Within*, Elizabeth if loved must in the end become Lucy, the slight, all too human figure of pity has to enact the impersonal role of a whore. Love sets the final seal on the alienation of the principal characters, and this now becomes a developing theme of Greene's work. The casual physical affair of Kay and Jules, the Soho French boy who has come into a small legacy from his father's death, may seem a brilliantly touched in but extraneous episode; but it serves to point up the fatal isolation of Conrad and Milly who have chosen a union that dissolves all union. Jules, driving Kay madly and conceitedly into the country, wants a wife who is young and pretty and practised; she is more in love with him than with any of her other men. But both draw back from the brink of commitment: after sleeping together in a village inn, Gallic prudence and a bursting of the bubble of conceit on one side, a materialist eye to the future and sexual dissatisfaction with him on the other, lead them apart and away from marriage. But not into unhappiness: pity will never trap them and unlike Greene's protagonists they may lead happy lives.

The technique of *It's a Battlefield* makes it his most accomplished novel before *Brighton Rock* (1938) and ranks it among the best novels of its period. (Incidentally, the last fifty pages of the novel, in which the passage quoted on page 65 occurs were revised by Greene for the new edition of 1970.) Poetic prose has now finally given place to a truly poetic interweaving of themes, the recurrence of *leitmotiven*, which may owe something to the major novels of Virginia Woolf and particularly *Mrs Dalloway*, another finely achieved London setting. For example, the prison where Jim Drover is held is divided into blocks for various classes of offender; so is the match factory in which Kay works. The Minister's secretary has asked the prison governor what happens to the prisoners in Block C and learns that they have more butter on their bread and can read for an hour after lights out. A few pages later the manager is taking a visitor round the factory:

'That's Block A. The new employees go there for the simplest processes. Then if they work well they move to Block B, and so to Block C. Everyone in Block C is a skilled employee. Any serious mistake and they are moved back to Block B.'

Similarly the pram-on-a-taxi motif keeps echoing in Conrad's tormented mind until he has lost all sense of reality.
Kay speaks with hard common sense of class division as
lying between those who go to work early and have long
hours and those who do not; but there is a bizarre surrealist
quality about the prison/factory metaphor and Conrad's
pram-on-a-taxi image which lifts Greene's social vision
towards a perception of fundamental psychic warping very
different from the theory of class war propagated by the
official party pundits and their fellow-travellers in the
pages of *Left Review*. The yellow flag indicating fever that he
remembers from his jungle days likewise haunts the Assistant Commissioner as he walks along through the Sunday
streets, up to the National Gallery and along Pall Mall,
refusing to stop and confront the man who is following him,
just as, tired and thirsty, he had once refused to stop at a
small station in the bush displaying the flag. The more
intricately the images are intermeshed, the more they
separate the characters and reduce them to tiny units on the
misty battlefield of the city, bright for a deceptive moment
in the manner of Virginia Woolf when the West End is seen
for a while through Clarissa Dalloway's exaltation of mood:
'All the buildings in sight had dignity and proportion; the
boots was shaking a carpet outside Garland's Hotel'. The
skilful inter-locking process extends to items in the plot and
its ironies. Conrad's resolve to buy a revolver is linked with
his knowledge of a sale from 'Premises Damaged by Fire'
which he has acquired during his work at the office and
which has been previously mentioned.

Then there are the similes which are to become a
distinctive feature of Greene's work and are now applied to
the new integrated poetry of narrative. Conrad misses a
chance of aiming at the Assistant Commissioner and 'he
recalled the opportunity for murder with the same poignant sadness as a city-bred child might remember a field of
grass or corn'. Or the cars drawn against the pavement of
the street at night are seen 'like black cats crouched on a
narrow leaden roof'. One is first struck by the startling
surface incongruity of these images, their sheer strangeness, bringing together murderous desire and innocent

nostalgia, the living and the inanimate; then it is realized that the metaphorical dislocation expresses the dislocation of Conrad's mind and of the dissolving complexity of the city.

Greene does not seem to have repeated such a close poetic integration of a novel. Character and observation were to be allowed more of a say than this overall imaginative vision. We get a different, dryer, vernacular strength and comic bite when Davis, Mr Surrogate's man-servant, on the morning after tactfully pushes the hair-slide Kay has left under the bed with his foot and thinks: 'You dirty old bastard, you've been at it again'.

It's a Battlefield is about individuals involved in new mass society, and broken by it or hardened to survive in it. Even the comparatively sheltered Caroline Bury, brought on to the edge of the Drover case by Mr Surrogate and her own liberal feelings, waiting for an operation from which she does not expect to recover, has had to develop a protective shell; she with her harsh voice, her haggard, brightly painted face, 'her absurd, her expensive, her timeless clothes', seems to have been modelled on Lady Ottoline Morrell, as Mr Surrogate is an unkind portrait of John Middleton Murry, continually unfaithful to the memory of a wife who was in his case a painter. But it is misleading to talk about models, since what the novelist finds in a real life figure, as Maurice Bardèche has elegantly said of Stendhal, is not a model but 'a term of comparison'.[12] Caroline Bury utters some of the most socialist sentiments in the book:

Do you believe in the way the country is organized? Do you believe that wages should run from thirty shillings a week to fifteen thousand a year, that a manual labourer should be paid less than a man who works with his brains? They are both indispensable, they are both dog-tired at the end of their day. Do you think I've the right to leave two hundred thousand pounds to anyone I like?'

Greene was certainly some sort of socialist when he wrote this. Penal taxation has somewhat blunted the force of the third question; the problem of the second question is still with us in the shape of differentials among workers as well as managers. But long before the post-Second World War neo-Marxists and the publication in English of the earliest writings of Marx, Greene is primarily concerned with the alienation of individuals and not directly with attempts to change society. The account of a Communist Party meeting, which Greene says was based on the only one he had ever attended, in Paris, is unconvincing and seems to lack authorial interest. So George Orwell was only superficially right, only correct on the matter of general sympathy, when he wrote of Greene during the war:

> I have even thought that he might become our first Catholic fellow-traveller . . . If you look at books like *A Gun for Sale*, *England Made Me*, *The Confidential Agent* and others, you will see that there is the usual left-wing scenery. The bad men are millionaires, armaments manufacturers, etc, and the good man is sometimes a communist'.[13]

The truth is that 'the usual left-wing scenery' has more individual touches than the stock 1930s décor commonly allowed; not only Edward Upward's *Journey to the Border* (1938) but even William Plomer's sometimes observant *The Case is Altered* (1932), an attempt to show something new, youthful, and vaguely homosexual taking over from 'the old gang', seem astonishingly dated in comparison. As for good and bad men, what are really present are shades of grey, pressed upon by a man-made environment that more and more closes in, and torn by impossible decisions.

IV

In the 1930s Greene was indeed a man who, in Caroline Bury's phrase, worked with his brain and was dog-tired at the end of the day. He had to write to live. He had given up a safe job on *The Times* and thrown his stake on to the gambler's wheel of fiction; he had the responsibility of marriage and children, even though he and his wife tried to live simply for a time in a country cottage in the Home

Counties. There was the journalism, the film reviewing, and later the film scripts and treatments; and there was a book every year with the exception of 1937. In that year he was working a good deal on the brilliant and short-lived periodical *Night and Day,* edited jointly with John Marks, and brought to an untimely end by bankruptcy. This was caused by the libel action brought by Shirley Temple's lawyers: Greene had suggested in a review that in her late period as a child actor her nymphet qualities were being exploited. Greene had little luck with the law in these years. J.B. Priestley quite wrongly took himself to be caricatured in Savory, the popular novelist of *Stamboul Train.* There had been mention of a pipe, a love of Dickens, and blunt fingers. Thousands of copies of the book had already been distributed but Heinemann did not want to defend a libel action: pages had to be substituted and the author had to share the cost.

After the novel *England Made Me* (1935), there followed the so-called 'entertainments' *A Gun for Sale* (1936), *The Confidential Agent* (1939), and, to enter the war years, *The Ministry of Fear* (1943) set against the background of the London blitz. These four books with their thriller themes of hunter and hunted, men of power and little men, are closely related; while *Brighton Rock* (1938) and *The Power and the Glory* (1940), are essentially two Catholic novels in which grace and damnation hang over the hunter and the hunted, so that the pursuit is a double hunt, since the hound of heaven is in pursuit of both.

This prolific pre-war period also saw the publication of two travel books which contain material vital to some of the novels: *Journey Without Maps* (1936), Greene's account of his visit to Liberia, a first visit to West Africa which was to be followed by his official posting to Sierra Leone as an intelligence officer during the war; and *The Lawless Roads,* a description vivid as any novel of an arduous journey undertaken to see at first hand the conditions in those southern provinces of Mexico where the Catholic Church was still legally suppressed and persecuted. Stories of martyred priests that Greene heard fed his imagination while *The Power and the Glory* was forming in his mind, as did the heat and the flies, the squalor, perpetual danger and contempt for life in Mexico.

Apart from the novel *England Made Me* the other three fictions of this period were classed as 'entertainments' in the early editions. In the perspective of time the distinction between the novels and the entertainments has become blurred, and Greene dropped it himself from the lists of his books prefacing the novels in the later 1960s; it was revived on the jacket of his novella *Dr Fischer of Geneva or the Bomb Party* (1980) which is described as 'a black entertainment', but this smacks more of the publisher's blurb than of the writer's considered opinion, unless an increasing withdrawal from human seriousness is at issue. The distinguishing feature of the early entertainments is that they have happy endings, however sombre, involving the final union of a man (not in *A Gun for Sale* the chief character) and a woman, and that in the narrative they move rapidly through a series of melodramatic and violent incidents (often ironic in the Hitchcock mode) with clipped, spare dialogue and accounts of action. In short, we are again in the world of the cinema thriller where declassé intellectual and classless 'general reader' provide a common audience. What merges them with the novels is that the deceptions and betrayals of the mystery story, the isolation of the doomed or hunted hero, work at a deeper level than that of plot: the characters are separated not merely by the circumstances and withholding of information necessary to the thriller form but by incommunicable pasts and childhoods and by the incomprehensibility of a world without any recognizable total moral pattern. The abolition of the distinction between 'novels' and 'entertainments' is justified because the camera eye and the sound-recording ear work with the same integrity in all the books to express this nightmare of separation.

England Made Me contains some passages illustrating Greene's flirtation with stylistic modernism. After the conversational montage of *Stamboul Train* and the echoes of Virginia Woolf in *It's a Battlefield* there are passages of stream of consciousness monologue which recall Joyce in their headlong grammatical fusion of recalled incident and psychic response. Kate Farrant's thoughts in bed with Krogh are an example; she thinks of her twin-brother Anthony with whom she feels a near-incestuous bond:

> Never seen so tired now asleep so cold his hand. Anthony asleep now, the scar below the eye, the knife slipping upwards suddenly through the rabbit's fur, the scream, he went on screaming, the rabbit's fur, no control, the matron said. I woke in the middle of the night hearing him fifty miles away. Knew he was in pain. Father ill. They wouldn't let me go. The French exam all that day long, the irregular verbs and twice the supervisor went out with me to the lavatory . . . Awake sleeping hand cold all settled . . . Tiger burning bright in Tivoli, immortal eye, the hand against my side, feet touching mine; even there the women watched him . . . what shoulder, and what art, to see the rockets throwing down their spears.

The broken sentences blend pity of the pain of Anthony whom she had helped to endure the misery of school, who had cut himself leaving a scar, with her feeling for Krogh, the industrial tycoon whose power and its precariousness is suggested by the reminiscence of Blake's 'Tyger' ('When the stars threw down their spears') connecting phallic bond with the fireworks they have lately seen in the Tivoli Gardens, which rose in their trajectory sharply to the sky and then as suddenly fell. There is also a poetry of place less present in the pure thrillers (or more pure thrillers); but it is always directed and consciously applied to the revelation of a subjective predicament and this is to become increasingly the rule in the novels. Stockholm, the setting of *England Made Me,* is brilliantly sketched, but never as a tourist background. Krogh walking at Tivoli recalls his career of building up a financial empire from extreme poverty, but what he sees around him can only be rendered as loss. The present in its severing from memory can only appear meaningless to him:

> The gentle creaking of the wooden boards under the dancers' feet; the orderly crowd moving in two lines up

the shooting-booths, down past the fortune-tellers, the switchback, the scenic railways; the sudden cool courts at either end with the coloured fountains rustling between the black sky and the white concrete; the seats by the lake side; the light of a ferryboat moving away like a bicycle lamp over the dark polished lake: these were Sweden as much as the silver birch woods round Vätten, the brightly painted wooden hut, the duck staggering in mid-air, his mother waiting on the tiny quay; but the images had no longer any meaning for him, he was like a man without a passport, without a nationality; like a man who could only speak Esperanto.

England Made Me assembles a collection of exiles. Krogh himself is exiled by his riches from the life in which he grew up as a workman and craftsman designing the machine cutter that started his business; even though the lights all over his vast office building flash out the letters 'G.K.' they are 'the lights of a semaphore conveying over the vast distances which separated him from other men'. Minty, the journalist, remarks: 'He's only one of us. He has no more roots than we have'. Kate has brought her brother, Anthony, to Stockholm to find him a job with Krogh. Krogh likes him and eventually takes him on as his bodyguard. Anthony, weak and feckless, has drifted from job to job and country to country, and at thirty-three is living on his charm with the assistance of an unearned Old Harrovian tie. His sister, mistress to Krogh without loving him, has character and hardness as well as good looks, but both are exiled from their shared past and from England, though she has made her firm compromise with the nihilistic materialism of the future:

> Deliberately she turned away from the thought that there had been a straightness about the poor national past which the international present did without. It hadn't been very grand, but in their class at any rate there had been gentleness and kindness once.

One does not escape a hint of the large comfortable family

life at Berkhamsted. Yet it is Anthony, the corrupted faker of a dozen careers, who retains an element of 'conscience' sufficient to precipitate the drama and bring about his own death. As with all Greene's early characters of significance, and some later ones, Anthony's weakness and falsity go back to a lost childhood, to the trauma of school and, in Kate's view, to the impossibly high standard set by a too-demanding parent:

> Anthony learning (the beating in the nursery, the tears before the boarding school) to keep a stiff upper lip, Anthony learning (the beating in the study when he brought home the smutty book with the pretty pictures) that you must honour other men's sisters. Anthony learning to love with moderation. Anthony in Aden, Anthony in Shanghai, Anthony farther away from me than he had ever been, Anthony making good; yes, he loved Anthony and he ruined Anthony and he was tormented by Anthony until the end.

But beyond the habitual lying, the drifting and the easy womanizing, something absorbed almost against his will in this childhood has rubbed off upon Anthony which makes him more a citizen of the moral world than the other exile with his very different but equally betrayed background, Krogh. Kate acknowledges that 'He was all the moral consciousness . . . that they could summon up between them' and sees that somehow his sheer lack of resolution has a side, not of weakness, but of a possible spiritual disengagement from the terrible world chosen by the other characters: ' . . . somewhere on that straight steel track down which his brain now so quickly drove there burned a permanent red light; somewhere he would stop, waver, make a hash of things. He wasn't unscrupulous enough to be successful. He was in a different class from Krogh.' So there is exile and exile in this waste land: a shared rootlessness but unshared and distinct relations to the roots, severed or clutching.

Among the other exiles is Minty, the failed journalist who
lives on a small allowance from home, the habit of dogging
Krogh for a story, and the inevitable connection with the
British Embassy which brings him once a year to the Old
Harrovian Dinner. In his filthy room and with his physical
unattractiveness ('Crooked and yellow and pigeon-
chested') he may seem to have excelled in the abandonment
of genuine human contact practised by all the other
characters. He, too, has 'been slowly broken in by parents,
by schoolmasters, by strangers in the street'. He has come
without hope to the shabby room, the editor's criticisms, the
stump of cigarette in the soap-tray, and an only too
symbolic spider which he has kept for five days under a
tooth-glass: ' . . . like the spider withered, blown out no
longer to meet contempt; his body stretched doggo in the
attitude of death, he lay there humbly tempting God to lift
the glass'. What distinguishes Minty is that underneath a
flourish of camp Anglo-Catholic affectation he believes in
God and can therefore tempt him. He feels the sheer
spiritual horror behind the frustrations of life as they are
registered by the others; under his moral tooth-glass he has
imprisoned a warped recognition of sainthood. He is not
even as positive as the 'crippled saint' to whom G. S. Fraser
has likened him:

> . . . almost wholly devoted, in spite of his weakness and
> insignificance, to a genuine vision of goodness, and at the
> same time a man with a terribly acute and painful
> intuition of evil. He is a kind of crippled saint — a man
> whose real goodness can never find adequate outward
> expression, because of the terrible sense of inferiority
> which crushes his spirit and makes him miserable.[14]

But Minty's 'genuine vision of goodness' only amounts to a
journalist's needling of Hall, Krogh's assistant, after
Anthony's funeral because he suspects him of the latter's
death ('You didn't send a wreath . . . didn't you and he get
on together?') and a dim sense in talking to Kate later that
Anthony was his friend though he cannot bring himself to
use the word. Minty finally remains under his tooth-glass

and it is to the heroes of the later 'Catholic' novels that we have to look to recognize a 'flawed sainthood'.

V

After *England Made Me,* two more entertainments followed in the pre-war period: *A Gun for Sale* (1936) and *The Confidential Agent* (1939).

A Gun For Sale is an accomplished thriller. Raven, the hired killer, murders a European social democratic minister on the orders of an armaments manufacturer, Sir Marcus Stein; he is pursued to Nottwich in the English Midlands and the girl Anne and her detective fiancé are involved. Raven is shot down after killing Stein and his accomplice. The book is imbued by a sense of the immorality of international capitalism and the plight of the exploited; it is also overshadowed by the fear of approaching war. Raven, with his twisted bitterness, his hare-lip and disturbed childhood, is a rough sketch for Pinkie in *Brighton Rock,* and the skilful quickening of pace of the pursuit also provides a model for the later book. Nottwich is Nottingham where Greene began his career as a journalist. The north begins at Nottingham, and for a young man from the home counties it must have seemed a foreign country. So, if we discount the somewhat Ruritanian *Stamboul Train,* Nottwich is the first of many faithfully observed exotic settings. The camera eye takes in 'two rows of small-tiled neo-Gothic houses lined up as carefully as a company on parade' and picks out how 'the dusk came up from the dark wounded ground and the glow of furnaces became visible beyond the long black ridge of slag-heaps'.

The Confidential Agent is a strangely phantasmagoric thriller, and it is not difficult to believe Greene's confession that he wrote it in six weeks under the stimulus of benzedrine and in the intervals of composing *The Power and the Glory.* The secret agent D., seeking coal for his beleaguered government, is clearly an emissary of the dying Spanish Republic, but this is a book of initials and vague terrors, not of political or social realities. D., an Old French scholar with a sense of failure who has found an unheroic earlier version of the Roland and Oliver story, is out of his depth in an England seething with treachery and contradiction, and his malaise affects the general atmosphere. The most effective element in the narrative is the sharp reversal of interest when, in the second part, D., the pursued, becomes in his turn the revenging pursuer. Greene was to use this device again in *The Ministry of Fear* and *Our Man in Havana*.

Greene's novels and entertainments of the 1930s adapted cinematic techniques to fiction; some of them indeed, and many of those that followed, have been turned into films. So it is appropriate to consider amongst them one of Greene's most celebrated short novels *The Third Man* (1950) since it marks the last stage of his involvement with the cinema. But *The Third Man* was written at Alexander Korda's suggestion to be the basis of a film directed by Carol Reed, although it was written as a complete story, not as a 'treatment' or shooting script.

Rollo Martins goes to Vienna immediately after the war at the invitation of Harry Lime, the friend whom he had admired from school onwards. He is in time to attend his friend's funeral. In trying to track down Harry Lime's murderer he comes to realize that he is in pursuit of Harry himself who had been prominent in black-market dealing in adulterated penicillin, which can kill or maim. In a classic chase through the sewers of the city Rollo shoots Harry. Greene has said that the story 'was never intended to be more than the raw material for a picture'. But many themes to be developed elsewhere are present: the total corruption of an intelligent and humorous man by power and money; the betrayal of the betrayer by the decent ordinary friend who is driven to make a stand (this is played over more effectively and with psychological complication in *The Quiet American*).

Whether or not it was because his period of film reviewing and script-writing was over, the novels written after 1950 are less cinematic in scene and montage. The influence of film has been absorbed and contained.

CHAPTER 3

The Pursued and the Pursuer

I

Brighton Rock (1938) was the first of Graham Greene's
novels to have a clear, popular success. It was begun as an
'entertainment' and, indeed, published as such in the
United States; however, it grew naturally into its religious
dimension and marks the beginning of that phase of
Greene's work in which he clearly presents himself as a
Roman Catholic novelist.

Against the deceptively brilliant atmosphere of a seaside
Bank Holiday, Greene focusses on The Boy, Pinkie,
brought up as a Catholic, but now involved in the seedy
gangsterism of 1930s Brighton. Cyril Connolly has described two Brightons, the coffee-table Brighton of Geor-
gian terraces, the piers and the best hotels, and then the
Brighton of *Brighton Rock,* 'one of the ugliest seaside towns
in the world climbing upwards in row after row of jerry-
built brick and slate . . . of dreary department stores and
stained steel windows, of neon-lit trinket shops along the
front, of pebble beaches littered with layabouts, of race-
gangs, receivers, graft and gloomy industrial suburbs'.[1]
Greene manipulates his lyricism in order to reveal the other
ugly and dangerous Brighton under the coffee-table surface, the skull beneath the skin.

Against this background Greene constructs the tautest
thriller plot of his career so far. It is only the overwhelming
power of the obsession with evil and the dramatic involvement of the three central characters that surpass in intensity

the sheer skill in contrivance, both in the relating together
of incidents and in narrative speed and economy. The first
words seize and compel by immediate terror and at the
same time allow entrance to an action already in progress:
'Hale knew, before he had been in Brighton three hours,
that they mean to murder him'. Hale, the low-life outsider,
is marked out for punishment by the gang. He is the 'Mr
Kolly Kibber' of a popular newspaper, a man hired to leave
cards at various points in the town for tourists to pick up; if
one holds a card and can identify him from his picture in
the paper a prize can be claimed (it was a seaside diversion
of the 1930s). Pinkie recognizes Hale who tries to shelter
from the gang by picking up the cheerful, sensual barmaid
Ida Arnold; but while he is waiting on the front for her to
come out of the lavatory he is taken away and murdered by
them. Spicer, one of the gang, plants the cards that Kolly
Kibber should have planted at fixed times so as to create an
alibi. One of these is placed underneath a table-cloth in
Snow's restaurant. Pinkie goes to retrieve the card himself
in case a waitress has seen Spicer and noticed that he is not
the man in the newspaper photograph. The waitress is
Rose, a new girl in the restaurant, and she has indeed seen
the man who left it; Pinkie knows that he cannot let her go
and he murmurs 'I'll be seeing you . . . You and me have
things in common': one of the two fatal involvements of the
novel is under way.

The second is soon under way also: Ida is shocked by the
death of Hale; after attending his funeral she begins to
make inquiries and then her relentless sense of fair play sets
her on the trail that leads to Snow's and Rose and then to
Pinkie who is attempting to maintain his alibi while struggling to dominate the gang he has taken over and to
compete with the rich gangster Mr Colleoni who has a suite
at the Cosmopolitan. A recalcitrant bookmaker, Brewer, is
'carved up' by Pinkie; then he himself is slashed at the
racecourse by Colleoni's thugs and sheltered in a cellar
behind Snow's by Rose. Their relationship develops, but in
his conscious mind at any rate he decides to marry her
simply in order that she will not be able to give evidence
against him. Since they are both under age the marriage is

arranged by a crooked lawyer, Prewett. Pinkie has been warned by the police to leave Brighton but stays because he has nowhere else to go. He marries Rose in a registry office having obtained, for a down payment, the consent of her parents. The gang begins to break up; Spicer's nerve is cracking and Pinkie pushes him through rotting banisters to his death at the foot of the staircase; Cubitt is now afraid and tries to desert to Colleoni; while in the Hotel Cosmopolitan he is pumped for information by Ida who almost succeeds in extracting from him the secret of Hale's death. Ida has two confrontations with Rose, before and after the marriage, endeavouring to make her give up Pinkie and denounce him, but Rose is unswervingly loyal. Pinkie, however, is suspicious of everyone: he persuades Prewett to go to France to get him out of the way because of his knowledge of Spicer's murder; ironically enough, he distrusts his one loyal subordinate Dallow; and after Ida has spoken to her he fears the devoted Rose who is intelligent enough to have deduced that he has committed murder. The hunters are closing in, Ida and her lover Phil Corkery. Pinkie persuades Rose to undertake a suicide pact but his intention is to kill her and remain alive himself, free forever from incriminating witnesses. They drive out to Peacehaven and she meditates her resolve:

> It was said to be the worst act of all, the act of despair, the sin without forgiveness; sitting there in the smell of petrol she tried to realize despair, the mortal sin, but she couldn't; it didn't feel like despair. He was going to damn himself, but she was going to show them that they couldn't damn him without damning her too: there was nothing he could do, she wouldn't do: she felt capable of sharing any murder.

Meanwhile Ida pretends that Prewett has been brought back by the police and confessed his knowledge of Spicer's death; she threatens Dallow with her knowledge of both murders and goes with him and a policeman in pursuit of Pinkie: they catch up with him on the cliffs just after he has put a gun into Rose's hands. She throws the gun away and, in a paroxysm of hatred, ironically misled into thinking that both she and Dallow have betrayed him, he throws acid at her face. It blows back on to his. He throws himself over the cliff in agony. The conclusion comes, as it does later in *The Heart of the Matter,* in the confessional. The priest comforts Rose, telling her that her love may have redeemed her, that in the strange mercy of God even Pinkie may be saved, and that if there is a child she should pray for him to be a saint. She leaves the confessional to play the recorded message which Pinkie had given her as a wedding present. The message was: 'God damn you, you little bitch, why can't you go back home for ever and let me be?' 'She walked rapidly in the thin June sunlight towards the worst horror of all'.

Greene does not write from within the Catholic faith, however, like François Mauriac or Léon Bloy; nor does he review even his secularised or unbelieving characters from its perspective. In his principal Catholic novels — *Brighton Rock, The Power and the Glory, The Heart of the Matter, The End of the Affair* — there is always a tension, a peculiarly English tension, not simply between the world and the spirit, but between two equally balanced and desperately antagonistic points of view. Pinkie can make nothing of the common sense of fair play in Ida, the big-breasted barmaid who hunts him; nor can his girl Rose. Rose says, 'I'd rather burn like you than be like her . . . She's ignorant'. Ida in her turn regards the sense of sin and the belief in repentance which Rose and Pinkie share as simply monstrous: '"That's just religion", the woman said. "Believe me. It's the world we got to deal with."' Ida marches under the standard of plain human right and wrong and because Pinkie is wicked, her secularized, anti-religious view throws possibly a more glaring light on the action than the Catholic one, when that is supported by such miserable sinners, and when Ida is supported by all fleshly, indulgent Brighton, out for a good time but careful not to break certain of the commandments if only for the sake of prudence. If we are led at the end to leave her garish spotlight and accept the view implied by the less favourably lit Rose and Pinkie it is by a paradoxical reversal of ordinary (English) values. In the alienated world where, for most, God has died, the sinner who is conscious of his sin becomes a holy sinner, a stranger and a scandal to others but feeling, however dimly, his own isolated importance:

> From behind he looked younger than he was in his dark thin ready-made suit a little too big for him at the hips, but when you met him face to face he looked older, the slatey eyes were touched with the annihilating eternity from which he had come and to which he went.

Pinkie's isolation in the horror of moral reality is like that of T. S. Eliot's Sweeney, another murderer, though Sweeney's demon has a coarser moral fabric and lacks the precise orthodox framework of sin, repentance and damnation which Pinkie in desperation still retains:

> When you're alone like he was alone
> You're either or neither
> I tell you again it don't apply
> Death or life or life or death
> Death is life and life is death.

For Ida death and life do apply and are distinct categories because there is no eternity in which they may become continuous, only the clear limited sense of a present world in which human beings enjoy that life, pursue happiness, and postpone that death.

The characteristic pattern of a Greene novel begins to emerge here. There is continuous attention to the psychological-moral history of an individual who stands on the brink of decisive action: the attention focuses on the long road of personal motivation stretching from some early traumatic insult — Czinner's failed idealism in *Stamboul Train* or Conrad Drover's sense of inferiority in relation to his brother in *It's a Battlefield*; even comparatively minor characters like Jules, in *It's a Battlefield,* are exposed to the same moral chronology, every man is a history. But in the novels before *Brighton Rock* evil and violence wear a social face; the theme of social injustice had grown stronger in *It's a Battlefield, England Made Me* and *A Gun for Sale* which expose a corrupt establishment and an impersonal social system. The formalized analogy between the grades of convict in the prison and the grades of worker in the factory in *It's a Battlefield,* redolent of German expressionism,[2] is characteristic. In that novel the condemnation of the system is partially relieved by the figure of the Assistant Commissioner, the honest public servant who makes the system work while having little faith in it. Such a character is absent from the following novels, and by *A Gun for Sale* Raven, the pathetic assassin, and the heroine are for a time united in Manichean isolation, opposed by a wholly evil world, before the stock happy ending. In fact, though Greene might seem to be moving towards a more and more explicit political analysis of the tensions of bourgeois industrial society, what he finds peculiarly fascinating are the alienated characters produced by such tensions, the sterile charm of an Anthony Farrant or the strange mutual trust of Anne and Raven. Now in *Brighton Rock,* with its almost melodramatic contrast of Catholic and secular values, there is the first major change in his work since his development from romance; there is less room for implied social criticism of the staple 1930s left-wing type when salvation and damnation divide the stage between them. But the change is not total. The Boy, Pinkie, bears the scars of a deprived childhood in the wretched slums of Kemp Town; he is divided not only from decent people but from the big-time gangster Colleoni by the line which separates poverty from riches: other people are better dressed and better washed than he is. As in the earlier novels the force of social determinism merges with the primal horror of the individual, in Pinkie's case the horror of sex experienced by him as he listened to his parents in bed in the room he had to share. He revisits the area after slum clearance:

> The streets narrowed uphill above the Steyne: the shabby secret behind the bright corsage, the deformed breast. Every step was a retreat. He thought he had escaped for ever by the whole length of the parade, and now extreme poverty took him back: a shop where a shingle could be had for two shillings in the same

building as a coffin-maker's who worked in oak, elm or lead: no window-dressing but one child's coffin dusty with disuse and the list of hairdressing prices ... His home was gone: a flat place among the rubble may have marked its hearth; the room at the bend of the stairs where the Saturday night exercise had taken place was now just air. He wondered with horror whether it all had to be built again for him; it looked better as air.

Likewise Pinkie's spiritual drama is played out, not on a bare stage, but against the tawdry pleasure-seeking crowds of Brighton on the bank holiday, crowds that uncoil endlessly as they move on to the Palace Pier, 'like a twisted piece of wire, two by two, each with an air of sober and determined gaiety'. The highly special flavour of Brighton, its blowsy elegance, is a better subject for Greene's observer's eye than the London West End of *It's a Battlefield* or the industrial Nottwich (Nottingham) of *A Gun for Sale* because of its particularity and because his interest in the sinister underside of appearances finds a better vehicle in the holiday dream. The dreamers are trying to escape from themselves, just as the stalls and ice-cream parlours and the bright colours of the racecourse disguise the greed and crime which flourish underneath the surface. Thus the faithful recording of the details of the bright surface world ends by emphasizing the brittleness and deceptiveness of appearances; the sensuous glitter of the place is far the best foil for Rose's sad integrity and Pinkie's sour bitterness. Pinkie is a monster of perverse energy and aggrandizement who makes his accomplices and the unfortunate bookmaker Brewer fear him. Only Rose loves him. 'His young-ancient poker face told nothing'. ' . . . he jerked his narrow shoulders back at the memory that he'd killed his man, and these bogies who thought they were clever weren't clever enough to discover that. He trailed the clouds of his own glory after him: hell lay about him in his infancy. He was ready for more deaths.' Writing a few years before the publication of the early books of Jean Genet and his canonization by Sartre, and a generation before the near-canonization of Myra Hindley by certain journalists,

Greene might be thought to anticipate the sympathetic interest of a whole period in the workings of the criminal mind. But he plays fair with the reader in one way and less fair in another. Pinkie bears the scars of his stunted upbringing in Nelson Place but that is never used as a simple excuse for his conduct. He becomes human to us because, as well as being frightening, he can be pathetic. The police inspector treats him like a child: 'You're too young to run a racket if you ask me'. Dallow and Cubitt as older men patronize and tease him over his attempt on Spicer's girl and his marriage to Rose; the attendant at the shooting-gallery insults him when he asks for the time and tells him he is not providing any phoney alibis.

Typically, Greene's hero is a small-time failure, and pitifully aware into the bargain of his psychological and sexual immaturity. On the other hand, the pitifulness of Pinkie, the creatureliness which offsets even his hideous cruelty to Rose, takes on a different shape in the religious dimension of the novel. As a Catholic, however lapsed and ignorant, he shares with Rose a consciousness of 'the ravaged and disputed territory between the two eternities'; he is not merely an understandable human being, in fact in this light he can be totally condemned on the human level and this would not matter: he is the powerful protagonist in a struggle beside which the Brighton world of law, order and the pursuit of happiness is a puppet play. Ida, who points up the struggle by denying it, belongs to a light world in contrast to Pinkie's darkness, a world in which she can declare, 'It's a good life', and think that there is no place in the world in which she feels a stranger: 'the word meant nothing to her'. Pinkie is always a stranger and with everyone apart from the God who is hidden from him. For him, as for Pascal, it is the astonishing and unjust idea of the transmission of sin to all men which makes sense of life as it is.

The intimations of the presence of the hidden God are necessarily few and outweighed by acknowledgment of the horror of life, often by literary parody, as in the educated Prewett's observation, 'Why this is Hell, nor are we out of it'. The Boy can be moved by music, jazz songs or the Mass:

'Why I was in a choir once,' the Boy confided and suddenly he began to sing softly in his spoilt boy's voice: 'Agnus dei qui tollis peccata mundi, dona nobis pacem.' In his voice a whole lost world — the lighted corner below the organ, the smell of incense and laundered surplices, and the music . . . it didn't matter what music — 'Agnus dei,' 'lovely to look at, beautiful to hold,' 'the starling on our walks,' 'credo in unum Dominum' — any music moved him, speaking of things he didn't understand.

With Rose on their first visit to Peacehaven he is firm in his belief in hell and shares her scorn of Ida who 'doesn't believe in a thing', but he has to be prompted by Rose about the possibility of mercy. A memory floats up into his mind: 'You know what they say — "Between the stirrup and the ground, he something sought and something found" "Mercy". "That's right: Mercy".' Later, escaping wounded from the razor gang, he remembers the verse, and thinks that he cannot be saved without repentance and that he has no time. Here Greene the theological novelist is still playing fair with the reader: the intimations of mercy intrude only slightly into a world inexorably oriented towards hell; Rose hints at a forgiveness always open to the sinner but Pinkie's end in hatred and pain leaves no possibility of a death-bed repentance, rather an appalling prospect of annihilation: 'It was as if he'd been withdrawn suddenly out of any existence — past or present, whipped away into zero — nothing.' When leaving Rose's parents after bribing them to consent to the marriage Pinkie experiences the sense of complete negation that corresponds to a totally evil will: 'A dim desire for annihilation stretched in him: the vast superiority of vacancy.' He is prepared for his own death in its finality and if some other force is trying to break in upon him he resists it:

An enormous emotion beat on him; it was like something trying to get in; the pressure of gigantic wings against the glass. *Dona nobis pacem.* He withstood it, with all the bitter force of the school bench, the cement playground, the St. Pancras waiting-room, Dallow's and Judy's secret lust, and the cold unhappy moment on the pier. If the glass broke, if the beast — whatever it was — got in, God knows what it would do. He had a sense of huge havoc — the confession, the penance and the sacrament — an awful distraction, and he drove blind into the rain. He could see nothing through the cracked stained windscreen.

The image of a divine animal in pursuit is unmistakeable but it is to have no easy prey. Pinkie sees nothing through the windscreen, nothing outside the enclosed world of the self. If salvation is to come it is in a different way, as suggested by the old priest with his cold and his smell of eucalyptus, through the prayers of Rose, if she survives 'the worst horror of all', and perhaps through the minute working of tenderness against the grain of his contempt for her: 'Somewhere, like a beggar outside a shuttered house, tenderness stirred, but he was bound in habit of hate.'

So what has been called Greene's fairness to the reader precludes miraculous intervention or a sensational repentance. Pinkie might even be said to have embraced a technical suicide. It is Rose's ordinary love and the stirring animal tenderness it has drawn that offer the only escape from the nightmare limits drawn by Mr Prewett. Where the novelist departs from this human dimension is in his insistence that any Catholic is superior to any Protestant or agnostic, not in virtue, but in his knowledge of the nature of life; good and evil are seen as supernatural categories reaching far beyond humanist right and wrong, and it is with a stroke of melodrama that the abandoned Pinkie is set up to teach a proper theological view of reality, not only to honest, cheerful Ida, but to all of us in fallen England.

What Greene is doing is to press to an extreme that exploration of the holy sinner and his role which we first encounter in Dostoievsky. The character was further studied and developed in France by Léon Bloy and Georges Bernanos. The sinner who may have special access to divine grace is not of course a nineteenth-century discovery but implicit in the whole drive of the Gospel: 'I come not to bring the righteous but sinners to repentance'. However it was in the nineteenth century that the alliance of middle-

class respectable Catholicism, *les bien-pensants,* and the social
and political establishment, invited a response based on an
appeal to the unworldliness and uncomfortableness of
Christian values. Kierkegaard's attack on Christendom and
Bloy's rather ungodly rejoicing over the fact that the stalls
of a fashionable exhibition in the Bois de Boulogne had
been burnt down are both symptoms. After T.E. Hulme's
belated rediscovery of original sin the movement reaches
England with Eliot's effective presentation of his Sweeney
figure, eloquent in his incoherence. Charles Péguy, the
French radical Catholic thinker and poet, who must have
been in Greene's mind when he wrote the book, lays out the
assumption behind the character of the holy sinner:

> Sin and the sinner are an intrinsic part of Christianity . . .
> it is a relationship of communion . . . The sinner and the
> saint are two parts, two pieces both equally integral to the
> mechanics of Christendom.
>
>   A man who is not a Christian is a man who does not sin,
> who cannot commit a sin . . . and literally, a man who is a
> sinner, a man who has sinned, is a Christian; even in his
> sin he is a Christian . . . The sinner holds out his hand to
> the saint . . . The saint holds out his hand to the sinner . . .
> and together they make a chain and ascend towards
> Christ.[3]

The passage is crucial to understanding Greene and his
characters, their profession of a sinful humility which clings
to the roles of sanctity and will not leave go; a sentence from
it is used as epigraph to *The Heart of the Matter.* It is easy to
see here how the essentially paradoxical expression of the
sinner's relation to Christianity can lead to a dramatic
polarization of the issue as between the informed sinner
and the blind and confident world. If it is stated that such an
opposition is endemic to the Christian life the exponents of
the holy sinner need to be reminded that if that sinner is
informed by grace he will repent and cease to be a sinner.
They cannot have their cake and eat it too, but the lurid
appeal of that Baudelairean figure with his burden of bitter
knowledge was too effective to discard as a prime munition

in the war against the entrenched philistinism of the
bourgeoisie. Greene has brought the character to its
furthest stage of development by depicting a human being
who is thoroughly depraved and only capable of flickers of
remorse or tenderness, significant though they may be for
his final end. Yet he is still enlisted in the struggle against
bourgeois values. Bourgeois values may seem a misnomer,
for Pinkie does not face the hypocritical respectability
found in the settings of Mauriac or Bernanos; Ida Arnold
sleeps uninhibitedly with her admirers and Mr Colleoni is a
gangster who no longer has to dirty his hands with violence.
Pinkie when cast in his theological role has no very virtuous
opponents. But Greene has shown tact in letting Rose be the
chief vehicle of grace against the world, and Rose is not a
holy sinner but a holy fool, or one on the way to becoming
that by a life of extreme and abject service, like the poor
women in Bloy; Greene returns to the type in Clara in *The
Honorary Consul,* and she, as well as offering sacrificial
devotion, is to some extent a sinner too because she is a
prostitute.

A flaw in the character may be detected where the
parobolic role works against the human creation, the
thin-shouldered boy having his one good suit pressed to go
to Colleoni. The flaw marks also a frontier of credibility and
it may be thought that this is passed when Pinkie is made to
say to Rose in one of their tentative theological discussions,
'*Credo in unum Sathanas*'. Remembering his days in the choir
may skirt sentimentality but this feat of language is beyond
the Boy because his polarizing role is forcing him beyond
his inherent capabilities: this language of parody and
allusion is that of Greene himself in his comments on the
action or in his legitimate manipulation of Mr Prewett as a
mouthpiece (a *conscious* character in the Jamesian sense).
Pinkie's function as the worst of sinners who is therefore the
most interesting to God is echoed in similar attempts to
manipulate the plot in the direction of parable. When Ida is
interrogating him Cubitt denies Pinkie thrice as Peter does
Christ: '"I've seen you with him", she lied: a courtyard, a
serving wench beside the fire, the cock-crowing.' This
biblical cock-crowing is to be heard again.

This flaw or division in Pinkie between the delinquent and the holy sinner is less conspicuous, then, because the faint stirrings towards recognition of another person in the latter, his suspension of hatred, are shown convincingly in human terms in the former; the beating wings of the divine pursuer are not posed stagily over the lay-figure of a master-sinner but evoked exactly to convey a genuine trembling of spirit, a moment of physical possession merging into tenderness ('he hadn't hated her — he hadn't even hated the act'):

> He was beside her, watching her: she faced him back with a worried candour, and he found that he believed her as much as he believed anyone; his restless cocky pride subsided: he felt an odd sense of peace, as if — for a while — he hadn't got to plan.

Greene has in fact reworked the original paradox of the holy sinner into a new and brilliant pattern but he has done this at the expense of creating a strange emotional inconsistency in the novel. While apparently uncompromising in his depiction of a wholly fallen world and an infinite gulf between corruption and divine grace he shows Pinkie, through Rose, learning the beginnings of physical gentleness as a mode of release from his self-absorbed hatred. The Jansenist horror of the body present not only in Pinkie's consciousness but throughout the imagery of the narrative is offset by the daring and contradictory suggestion of redemption through the mystery of flesh.[4]

If on the other side of the contradiction Pinkie still has too great a weight of moral symbolism to carry for a Brighton delinquent teenager, the reader is less conscious of this on account of the energetic commitment of the writer to his creation. Greene has a habit of assigning colour names like his own to some of his more important characters; the Boy introduces himself to Colleoni as 'Mr P. Brown', and another redeemable failure, a comic, not a tragic one, is called Brown in *The Comedians*. This teasing with proper names may not be of high significance but it does achieve two purposes: it declares the author's personal involvement with the character, and by the act of naming with the names of primary colours it stresses at once the unique individuality of the person in his place in the spectrum and his ultimate union with other persons in the white light of eternity. So the inconsistencies in Pinkie, the clash between his 'realistic' function and his mythic role as great sinner, are reconciled by the creator's share in the intensity of his alienation. In fact, everywhere Greene escapes the limits of his contradictions. He does not *know* a Brighton gangster, but he does know the disputed borderland behind the green baize door, and Brighton is itself a borderland where racegoers, tourists, gangsters and local slum dwellers mix: his city is a junction where all aliens meet, not a root of the indigenous like Mauriac's Bordeaux. If realistic description is violently converted into the metaphysical ('his young-ancient poker face') this interpretation of the representative image distorts it in order to present post-industrial man in the throes of an inner vision horribly spontaneous because free from certainty.

Greene's characterization matches the intentions of early expressionist art in its deliberate distortion of the faces of subjects from common life in order to express their inner agony. Expressionist technique contributed to the necessary exaggeration of features and gestures in the early silent cinema; Fritz Lang and other directors carried it forward into the talking pictures which Greene was reviewing in the 1930s. A remark of Kokoschka about his paintings of the war period in a letter to the art historian Hans Tietze could describe the rendering of the struggle of hatred and embryo love in Pinkie:

What I'm trying to do now is to construct compositions from human faces (models like the people who happen to have been sticking it out with me here . . . with the result that they virtually haunt me, like nightmares), and in these compositions entities conflict, oppose each other rigidly, like hate and love, and in each picture I'm looking for the dramatic 'accident' which will weld the individual spirits into a higher order.[5]

The opposing entities in *Brighton Rock* are salvation and damnation and they are violently presented in the distorted face of an old woman seen by Pinkie immediately after his marriage when he walks the streets alone in the early morning:

> He could just see the rotting discoloured face: it was like the sight of damnation. Then he heard the whisper: 'Blessed art thou among women,' saw the grey fingers fumbling at the beads. This was not one of the damned: he watched with horrified fascination: this was one of the saved.

This is a rare indication, like the cracks in his armour in regard to Rose, that Pinkie may escape damnation; by a certain sleight of hand the woman's physical degradation may stand for his moral degradation: salvation is the other side of the horror of Nelson Place and does not belong with the scrubbed and healthy.

In terms of the novel Kokoschka's dramatic accident is provided by Pinkie's chance encounter with Rose in the restaurant. He is led towards his worst action, the cold-blooded deception, the cruelty of the gramophone record-ing, the suicide pact from which he is to be the survivor. But by the accident the war between the two eternities is engaged and the means of grace problematically offered. The other dramatic accident is Ida's meeting with Hale which leads to her pursuit of the Boy; this is the convention-al chase of the thriller while the simple, passive Rose's involvement sets in train a divine hunting. In thriller terms we are meant to ask who gets there first. But Ida as a sort of vigilante private eye has another function. Her zeal for fair play and her sheer human curiosity counterpoint the Catholic values of the boy and girl, open in Rose, scornfully suppressed in Pinkie, and throw the novel open to being a debate on human standards, on account of the richness and uncompromising solidity of Ida's personality. The odds may be finally weighted in favour of the Catholic view, but this openness of the novel is a fact which separates it from the universe of resolute and confirmed faith which is encountered in Bloy and Bernanos. Greene's effect is achieved partly by the successful vitality of Ida but also by his agonized penetration into Pinkie's nihilism.

The two encounters of Rose and Ida have much of parable about them but the sharp differences of character and situation endow them with human substance. Ida's hearty sensual confidence goes with a common humanist assumption that she knows what is best for other people ('I'm going to make you listen') but she is up against something she does not understand and can only interpret as 'acting morbid'. 'He's wicked. I'm not a Puritan, mind. But I've always been on the side of Right. You're young. You'll have plenty of boys before you're finished. You'll have plenty of fun — if you don't let them get a grip on you. It's natural. Like breathing. Don't take away the notion I'm against love. I should say not. Me. Ida Arnold. They'd laugh.' Only she talks in abstractions with capital letters; Pinkie and Rose never do. Likewise only she is really superstitious, consulting the ouija board about the future; for Rose and Pinkie heaven and hell are bare facts, not speculations. Simple, uneducated and immature, Rose can only resist Ida by sticking obstinately by her absolute devotion to Pinkie and by a dimly felt contempt of all the older woman calls experience:

> 'You'll grow out of it. All you need is a bit of experience.'
> The Nelson Place eyes stared back at her without understanding: driven to her hole the small animal peered out at the bright and breezy world: in the hole were murder, copulation, extreme poverty, fidelity and the love and fear of God.

Even as a terrified, crouching animal Rose is not diminished because she is sustained by a larger force, and it is she who looks out at Ida with 'her innocent and experienced eyes'. The second interview is even more shot through with misunderstanding and consequent irony. Ida is appalled that Rose knows Pinkie is a murderer and is apparently unmoved. 'You've got to be saved', she says, unaware of the *frisson* that word sets up. When she says 'Your life's in

danger', Rose replies, 'If that's all . . . ' and Ida is deeply
shocked at this dismissal of the only value she recognizes.
Tortured by the shock of mutual non-recognition and the
testing of their most intimate beliefs the faces of both
women are transformed into expressionist contortions
lifting them out of the realistic mode. Ida's plump, good-
natured, ageing face stares out at Rose 'like an idiot's from
the ruins of a bombed home'. Rose's child's face becomes
bony and determined so that 'all the fight there was in the
world lay there — warships cleared for action and bombing
fleets took flight between the set eyes and the stubborn
mouth.' When Ida, beaten to her last guard, declares
defiantly that she knows the difference between Right and
Wrong, Rose effectively withholds any reply: ' . . . the
woman was quite right: the two words meant nothing to
her. Their taste was extinguished by stronger foods —
Good and Evil. The woman could tell her nothing she
didn't know about these — she knew by tests as clear as
mathematics that Pinkie was evil — what did it matter in
that case whether he was right or wrong?'

Ida functions as a symbol of secularized middle-class
society yet her own generous warmth can sustain this
function convincingly without its seeming to be special
pleading. She appears as the avenging angel of abstract
human justice, and it is to be wondered whether any
novelist could draw her in the present age when the
secularized society has through its legislative organs abolished the death penalty. Ida's standards exhibit easy-going
vagueness at some points but are definite on the question of
justice.[6] By surrendering the belief that some behaviour
warrants punishment as wholly wrong her successors have
abandoned Protestant-middle-class self-righteousness and
sawn off the slender branch on which they maintained
themselves. In treating the criminal as a case they have
come half-way to meeting the Christian who believes all
men are sick with mortality and original sin. The principle
of fairness or justice is necessary because otherwise there
would be warfare between competing egos: what is basically
a degradation of the morality of the enlightenment would
be exposed to the remorseless critique of Sade who saw that,

if a law of nature prevailed, there was no limit other than satiety to the kind or degree of personal pleasures a natural being might seek. What, however, is most characteristic of Ida's attitude is that, in spite of her warmth and cheeriness, her committments are never total but always prudentially limited. She can feel concern for people (she likes Rose at first, seeing her as a nice little thing), but never love. Love would require the innate idea of love planted in the heart of man, and like all the English middle class Ida is an unconscious follower of Locke, who did not believe in innate ideas:

> Her friends —they were everywhere under the bright glittering Brighton air. They followed their wives obediently into fishmongers, they carried the children's buckets to the beach, they lingered round the bars waiting for opening time, they took a penny peep on the pier at 'A night of Love'. She had only to appeal to any of them, for Ida Arnold was on the right side. She was cheery, she was healthy, she could get a bit lit with the best of them. She liked a good time, her big breasts bore their carnality frankly down the Old Steyne, but you could rely on her. She wouldn't tell tales to your wife, she wouldn't remind you next morning of what you wanted to forget, she was honest, she was kindly, she belonged to the great middle law-abiding class, her amusements were their amusements, her superstitions their superstitions.

Ida differs most extremely from Rose, not in the incompatibility of their distinct belief-systems, inherited or acquired, but in her incapacity for total commitment to another person such as Rose has assumed quite naturally on her marriage. Ida's comfortable sensuality which mothers men makes her into something of an earth-goddess: so she is to the weak and frightened Hale, though he tries unsuccessfully to reject her compulsion; as with Rose, she always has an ability to know what is best for other people:

> His eyes turned to the big breast; she was like darkness to him, shelter, knowledge, common-sense; his heart ached

at the sight; but, in his little inky cynical framework of bone, pride bobbed up again, taunting him 'back to the womb . . . be a mother to you . . . no more standing on your own feet.'

Ida's mindless healthy sexuality is poles apart from the horror of sex, the blend of guilt, fascination and disgust in Pinkie. Her acceptance throws into relief his anguished deprivation and his craving. Pinkie's murders are inadequate attempts to prove his manhood in the eyes of his companions. He is rough with Rose because he is afraid of her. Always in his mind is 'the frightening weekly exercise of his parents which he watched from his single bed'. Woman is seen as a devourer, interested only in getting him into bed. He tries in bravado to seduce Spicer's girl at the road-house, but when they go out to a car he realises that he cannot comply, not on account of impotence, but because she asks him, 'Have you got the doings?', and he knows that his inexperience lacks even the technology of the adult world. The incident nicely combines two aspects of his isolation, that created by a Catholic upbringing and that imposed by the fearful immaturity which makes him a looker-on at an uncomprehended adult world. The treatment of contraception, curiously rare in contemporary fiction, in the episode at the roadhouse, is contrasted with the natural assumption of Rose that she will have a child by Pinkie. When Ida throws out the possibility as a terrible warning ('You better take precautions'), Rose feels ' . . . a sense of glory. A child . . . and that child would have a child . . . it was like raising an army of friends for Pinkie . . . Here was no end to what the two of them had done last night upon the bed; it was an eternal act'. The secular world is condemned to sterility and moral neutrality. The sinner and the faithful poor unite to enjoy the privilege of procreation. The forces on their side are in step with the continuity of the race and the march of the church militant. His eternal future is left in hint and mystery but the clear development in his story is one towards physical initiation. Rose, unattractive, hurt and uncomplaining, does make a man of him. However much the atmosphere of disgust is established on their wedding night, by the sordid room, her 'dumb, frightened and acquiescent eyes', and the unseemly jangling of the front-door bell, an echo of *Macbeth* to the reader if not to the murderer and his accomplice, he has accomplished something and will never be the same again:

> He had an odd sense of triumph: he had graduated in the last human shame — it wasn't so difficult after all. He had exposed himself and nobody had laughed. He didn't need Mr. Prewett or Spicer, only — a faint feeling of tenderness woke for his partner in the act.

Rarely can an intimation of the love that draws upwards have been so bleakly expressed, so undistinguished from animality, so blackly Jansenist in its frame of reference, but it is there. At least Greene makes no concessions to religious or romantic sentiment and is unfalteringly loyal to his imagination of what life is like for those born in Nelson Place. Where the treatment is unnecessarily harsh is in the suggestion that Pinkie and Rose make love in a state of mortal sin, not merely because of their complicity in murder, but because their civil marriage in a registry office is not a valid one; 'she knew that this evening meant nothing at all, that there hadn't been a wedding'. Rose may well believe this, but theology and Catholic tradition would argue that the promises given constitute a true marriage, and the author does not make his position clear. More in the spirit of the growth into responsibility of the girl is the moving scene on the following morning when she tries to assume adult duties, to clean up the filthy house and kitchen and make friends shyly with Pinkie's friends.

The shocking juxtaposition of hopelessness and problematic hope reaches a climax in the last pages when Rose goes to confession. The wheezing priest tells her of a man who never took the sacraments because he could not bear the idea that any man could suffer damnation. He was technically in mortal sin but some think he was a saint. No soul is cut off from mercy: 'You can't conceive, my child, nor can I or anyone — the . . . appalling . . . strangeness of the mercy of God'. The man who is not named is Charles

Péguy.[7] She walks back home to play the record. Greene avoids the error of the Catholic novelist of which Sartre accused Mauriac, of playing God to his characters.[8] If the priest is allowed to sum up it is because his is the only voice that speaks above the spiritual phantasmagoria of Bright-on: 'Why this is hell nor am I out of it,' as Prewett had put it.

Greene's increasing technical skill is shown in his hand-ling of the subsidiary characters. Personages like Mr Surrogate (*It's a Battlefield*) and Minty (*England Made Me*) generate an interest out of proportion in terms of the story. The bland Mr Colleoni and the seedy Prewett fulfil their limited functions admirably. The scene between Pinkie and the former, set against the vulgar splendour of the Cosmo-politan, is admirably economical in advancing the gang warfare side of the plot while exposing Pinkie's smarting humiliation.

The language of the novel deploys an expressionist poetry of corruption and decay. K.W. Gransden has written of the nightmarish imagery and the frequent employment of animal similes; he has also noticed Pinkie's facial distortions.[9] 'The rotten wood lay across Spicer's body, a walnut-stained eagle crouched over the kidneys.' (Pinkie's) '. . . face crinkled with the effort of amiability like an old man's'. Sex is described as a sickness, for this is a work in which the normal standards of health and vitality are torn to pieces. Pinkie and Rose rise above the comfortable humanist level of good times and experiments with plan-chette in their undeceived acceptance of the wretchedness of mortality. 'His virginity straightened in him like sex: a prick of sexual desire disturbed him like a sickness.' The imagery of sickness and poison rising in the body convey the corroding evil of Pinkie's nature; his awareness of the evil, even without repentance, marks him off from the complacent, 'partly living' majority who know neither evil nor goodness. So the imagery plays a leading part in developing the main themes.

Greene is a poetic novelist, bringing to fiction an effort comparable to that of Eliot to find linguistic means adequ-ate to the communication of 'the boredom, the horror and the glory' of modern life. In the same article K.W. Grans-

den has called Greene the most poetic of living English
prose writers. Gransden analyses his characteristic use of
similes and also his employment of the catalogue of,
usually, three descriptive phrases in apposition. Greene's
poetry is derived from that of 1920s and 1930s cinema and
though it can be nightmarish — as the cinema, an inescap-
ably sensationalist medium, often is — it can also be purely
narrative or descriptive in its isolation of a visual detail:

> The sea stretched like a piece of gay common washing in
> a tenement square across the end of the street.
>   . . . The Boy didn't answer, walking rigidly away past
> the other booths, with the smell of gun-powder on his
> fingers, holding the mother of God by the hair.
>   The spot of damp, where Frank's iron had failed to
> pass, above the Boy's breast-pocket, was slowly fading out
> in the hot Cosmopolitan air.

The first simile is purely visual and shares with the more
shocking similes only the surrealist effect of surprise, of the
unusual comparison. The cinema of the great age thrived
on pointing to the unusual, comic, pathetic or terrible, in
moving pictures of ordinary life. The other two examples
are not of similes at all: they throw into a highlight
significant details as in cinematic close-ups. The first
concentrates on the doll Pinkie has chosen as a prize at the
shooting-gallery and which he associates in his mind with
images of the Blessed Virgin seen at a church fair; dragging
it away by the hair with the smell of gunpowder on his
fingers he is desecrating the divine by the murder he has
just committed (the second image, not a visual one, works at
one remove since Hale was strangled, not shot). The last
passage, not surrealist like the first, or complex in the
manner of metaphysical poetry like the second, is the most
successful of the three. This is because a completely
ordinary visual impression is used at the primary naturalis-
tic level of narration through what-can-be-seen-to-have-
happened, then at the level of social comment on Pinkie's
relation to Colleoni in their interview, and finally at the
thematic level where Pinkie's moral and spiritual isolation is

poignantly emphasized. In the manner of film the image is repeated a few moments later — 'The spot where the iron hadn't passed was still a little damp over the Boy's breast' — but the faint detail is not clear enough for a photographic image: Greene is using the method of cinema montage to help him achieve an entirely fictional effect in which each sense is permeated by intense feeling. It is Pinkie who feels the damp spot and communicates to the reader his consciousness of poverty, his impotent rage at being out of place in the luxury hotel, and ultimately his raging sadness at being out of place in the world. There are other instances of similar narrative montage, like the soap-dish in the bedroom where Pinkie and the members of the gang keep loose change. The nightmare challenges arise not merely against a background of the ephemeral and the repetitive but spring straight out of that very daily round of bored common life; Brewer is slashed in his suburban home with a bronchitic wife coughing overhead, and Rose after the most momentous decision in her life tries to do some housework. Pinkie, who lives apart in his evil will and hardly registers the existence of other people, can yet say, 'I'm real Brighton'.

This association of the mundane with the moment of terrible truth is to be explored again and again in later novels.

II

The Power and the Glory (1940) is the first novel of Greene to be set against a studiously evoked exotic background described from personal knowledge. He had gone to Mexico in 1938 to investigate the condition of the Church after the religious persecution initiated by the socialist government. Travel to far places was to provide the material for almost all his later fiction; only *The End of the Affair* (1951) and *The Human Factor* (1978) among his subsequent novels have a London background. Mexico is followed by West Africa (Liberia having already been visited and described in *Journey Without Maps,* 1936), Indo-China, the Congo, Haiti and South America. It is as though a writer concerned with the crises of moral decision and the preceding strains deliberately sought evidence of them at the flashpoints of wars and political disturbance.

The book produced by the Mexican journey, *The Lawless Roads* (1939), is remarkable in providing not only a background for the novel but the drama of his chief character. In the desperately poor and savage province of Tabasco in the south-east the churches are burned down and for a priest to say Mass is punishable by death; a woman tells him of a single priest who had held on:

> We spoke of the Church in Tabasco (she was a Catholic) ... There was no priest, she said, left in Tabasco, no church standing, except one eight leagues away over the border in Chiapas, but the people had told him to go — they couldn't protect him any longer.[10]

Later he inquires about this man and is told, '"Oh, he was just what we call a whisky priest"'. Greene's comment is 'But who can judge what terror and hardship and isolation may have excused him in the eyes of God?' A surviving letter from the priest inspires 'an awful sense of impotence — to live in constant danger and yet be able to do so little, it hardly seemed worth the horror'. There was a story that, when drunk, the priest had baptized a boy and given him a girl's name by accident: this, too, Greene incorporates into the novel. The English dentist Mr Tench, lonely and sick of the country, is modelled on an American dentist Greene had met on his journey who had not left the little town of Frontera for five years.[11] Perhaps the closest transcription from the travel book to the novel is in the account the author gives of his appalling mule journey from Salto to Palenque; this corresponds to his whisky priest's escape journey from the province to a brief interlude of peace with the Lehr family. Greene has been charged by Francis Wyndham with occasional journalistic glibness on the grounds of style — 'tricks of observation . . . . little crudities and sensationalisms, an occasional overpithiness':[12] however, his journalist's training and continuing appreciation for the craft show much more in his instinct for being in the right place at the right time and his ability to select those morsels of information which will prove useful as copy.

In *The Lawless Roads* he declares that he loathed Mexico. He certainly endured danger, boredom and disgust there, but it seems a strange statement to make for one who has often cultivated the seedy and the decayed. The human misery and physical squalor of the country did not need a subjective stylistic emphasis to be converted into Greeneland: Greeneland was there already, even down to the irony of squalor:

> Down a slope churned up with the hoofs of mules and ragged with tree-roots there was the river — not more than two feet deep, littered with empty cans and broken bottles. Under a notice which hung on a tree reading, 'It is forbidden to deposit rubbish . . . ' all the refuse of the village was collected and slid gradually down into the river. When the rains came it would be washed away.

Greene's interest in the sordid is never perverse. He does not have a taste for squalor; his reactions to dirt and disease are normal ones; but he does perceive the artistically apt relation of sordid details to the rendering of his main theme, what he calls 'the huge universal abandonment'. Moreover, in *Brighton Rock* he had described a symbolic underground warfare between secular and religious values, just as in an earlier novel he had seen London life as a battlefield. Now he experienced a country where the conflict was open with guns and firing squads, and martyrs of the latter like the Jesuit Fr Miguel Pro — '. . . there is no peace anywhere where there is life, but there are . . . quiet and active sectors of the line'. Mexico was one of the active sectors, bringing to the surface of politics the struggle Greene saw everywhere in the heart of modern man. In Mexico faith and extreme suffering went together, thus embodying in a real situation the critique of humanist materialism which in *Brighton Rock* had only been developed by an intellectual, even contrived montage moving from the self-assurance of Ida Arnold to the old woman with a decayed face mumbling over her beads. In Mexico,

Old men came plodding in their dungarees on bare feet,
tired out with work, and again I thought: how could one
grudge them the gaudy splendour of giltwork, the
incense, the distant immaculate figure upon the cloud?
The candles were lit, and suddenly little electric lights
sprayed out all round the Virgin's head. Even if it were all
untrue and there were no God, surely life was happier
with the supernatural promise than with the petty social
fulfilment, the tiny pension and machine-made furni-
ture.

Here and elsewhere in this phase of his work Greene tends
to use the piety of the poor too much as a stick with which to
beat the Americanised *petit-bourgeois*; however there is no
doubt that he found in Mexico a ready-made arena for the
contest between Christian folly and humanist prudence,
the death that leads to eternal life and the life-enhancement
that becomes a living death.

After the teeming thriller plot of *Brighton Rock*, with its
three principals and numerous minor characters, *The Power
and the Glory* is an impressively simple drama in which two
human beings, with wholly different aims, confront each
other, the whisky priest and the police lieutenant. The story
is one of pursuit, escape, and finally capture and death. The
priest, though conscious that he is in mortal sin, continues
as best he can as the only surviving minister of the Church
in the churchless state of Tabasco to hear confessions, to
baptize, and even to say Mass; the lieutenant is dedicated to
wiping out what he regards as ignorance, superstition and
exploitation. These dominant personages are not however
placed on an empty stage: the priest in his flight meets
peons, policemen, children, the English dentist, the little
girl of the English owner of a banana plantation, a
good-hearted German-American Lutheran couple, the
Lehrs, people in prison. These encounters do not affect his
life, like Pinkie's growing relationship to Rose in *Brighton
Rock*; they demonstrate the fixed basis of his conduct, a
mingled guilt, humility and resolve to carry on with his
duty, even when terrified.

All that might be described as a development in his

nature is a heightened perception, magnified by exhaustion and fever, of where he had stood all along. This deeper view into motive, compelled by a person's dramatic crisis and often accentuated by physical strain, is a frequent prelude to the climactic decisions of modern fiction: Mathieu, reviewing his past as he fires at the Germans from the church-tower in Sartre's *La mort dans l'âme*; the last phantasmagoric hours of the Consul in Malcolm Lowry's *Under the Volcano*; his whole life flashing past the protagonist of William Golding's *Pincher Martin* as he dies, feverish and half-conscious. These characters do not gain knowledge from experience and improve themselves in the old nineteenth-century manner: they realize more acutely the identities that have been theirs all along. They may be said to come into possession of those identities only in their final moments.

The whisky priest's final state of self-possession causes him to recross the border to certain betrayal and execution; he rejects the temptation to remain in a province where there is some toleration of the Church and where he could live comfortably in its capital. But this does not make him a changed man, only a resolved one. His freedom of choice is narrowly limited; his experience is a prison for him, as is that of Mathieu, Pincher Martin and the Consul. The question posed is whether, in his loyalty to his mission, he is a slave of circumstances just as much as in his succumbing to drunkenness and lust, or whether his sense of mortal sin declares the humility of the saint. Is he a martyr manufactured by habit and circumstances or the instrument of heroic sanctity? It is important to formulate the question like this, manufactured martyr against divine instrument, not to build up a choice for the reader between a conditioned being and some impossible ideal of a hero-saint. Greene's realistic spiritual psychology, echoed in the thought-process of the priest, fully accepts the limitations of a conditioned being. In a religion of failure sainthood consists in a further submission of being to the will of God and his paradoxical purposes.

The priest is introduced waiting to go aboard the steamer which leaves for Vera Cruz every few weeks. He is in a shabby suit and has discarded his altarstone. He is sheltered in a banana shed by Coral Fellows, the twelve-year old daughter of the plantation manager. Meanwhile the lieutenant of police plans to hunt him down and obtains permission from his chief to take a hostage from each village and shoot them if his whereabouts are not disclosed. The priest revisits the village where the woman lives who has borne his daughter. He sees the daughter, a sniggering creature, too old for her years and in danger of early corruption. The lieutenant and soldiers arrive after he has said Mass but the villagers do not betray him. He makes off for his birthplace and on the way is joined by a mestizo (half-caste) who, he suspects, intends to sell him to the police. He escapes and goes to the capital of the state, Las Casas. There he must surreptitiously obtain wine for communion; this is a dry as well as a godless state. A man professing to be a cousin of the governor sells him wine and brandy for his last pesos. He has to offer a drink to the chief of police and his friends in the hotel room where the alcohol has been provided; in a ludicrous and pathetic scene they drink the wine away. Drunk on brandy he is picked up by the Red Shirts (the atheistic vigilantes) and spends a hideous night in prison but is released in the morning, undetected by the lieutenant.

After a dreadful journey he escapes over the mountains into the neighbouring state. On the way he finds the dead body of a child who has been shot by an American gangster on the run. With the child's mother he buries the body in an Indian cemetery. Across the border of the state he is nursed and sheltered by the American Lutheran brother and sister, the Lehrs. He is able to celebrate Mass openly and to baptize and hear confessions. He prepares to leave for Las Casas, but at his departure the mestizo reappears with the story that the *gringo*, the American gangster, is mortally wounded and, since he is a Catholic, the priest must go back across the border to hear his confession. Not deceived by his betrayer but unwilling to neglect the possibility of a duty to the dying man he goes with the mestizo. He reaches the American who dies without confessing and soon afterwards the lieutenant and his men close in and arrest the priest.

That night he has some talk with the lieutenant who feels for him a grudging respect. He is shot in the morning. The following night a new priest arrives in the town.

This stark summary is faithful to the main outlines of what is in effect a morality play. What a summary cannot render is the sense of proliferating life, often wretched and poverty-stricken, often vicious, but fertile and assertive, which the priest meets at every stage of his journey. This is not contradicted by the atmosphere of violence and the proximity of death. The dentist in the first chapter sees an attractive nubile girl on the deck of the steamer *General Obregón* and thinks that in a few years she will be shapeless and worn out like the other women. Children swarm in the plazas; in a village only a few years since the last priest's visit there are scores to be baptized. A couple make love all night with urgent cries, crowded together with others in the common gaol. The incessant mosquitos are 'louder than human breath'. The buzzards flap over the tin roofs looking for carrion, and in the cemetery the crosses are 'stuck up like dry and ugly cacti'.

In this environment man seems wholly absorbed in the natural cycle of birth, copulation and death; he shares the bitter land with mules, buzzards and insects. Man feels absorption but he resists it and regards his plight as an abandonment. 'The huge universal abandonment': the theme and the word recur. The climax of the woman in gaol produces 'the finished cry of protest and abandonment and pleasure'. After his night in the cell the priest feels that he has passed into 'a region of abandonment'. Mr Tench, the dentist, hopes to return to England and his wife but knows inwardly that he never will; he has talked about his family to the priest on the run and when he sees him shot he feels 'an appalling sense of loneliness'. Mr Fellows, the plantation manager, goes through the motions of being a cheerful man in order to protect himself against an inner emptiness. His wife feels abandoned in a hostile land. In the end their daughter, who had sheltered the priest, has died, the only active will in the family, and when the wife says, 'We've got each other, dear', we know that they are wholly lost. The husband of the good Catholic mother in the port who continues in secret to teach her children the faith says to her: 'We have been abandoned here. We must get along as best we can'.

Because the action of the novel is a heightened drama it is full of ironies. One of them is that the supporting characters who see the priest pass by, and aid him, feed him, or give him drink — the people Kenneth Allott and Miriam Farris call the Bystanders[13] — are lost by their fear of abandonment, while the priest achieves moments of happiness by his total surrender to circumstances and dies with a hope of salvation only he himself fails to acknowledge. There is abandonment to the world and abandonment to the will of God, analogous to the self-surrender of the mystic, and for the human mind it is difficult to distinguish between the two. So that, waiting for his execution, the priest experiences 'only an immense disappointment because he had to go to God empty-handed, with nothing done at all'.

Those who resist the sense of abandonment tend to cling to scraps of paper. Mr Tench has the yellowing snapshot of his children; the mother of Luis and his two sisters has the pious books for children which tell over-simplified and impossibly heroic stories of boys with clear-cut vocations to the priesthood who become martyrs. Coral Fellows, perhaps the only successful resister, has her exercise books used on the correspondence course which are found pathetically abandoned in a waste-paper basket when the priest revisits the hacienda: 'If five men took three days to mow a meadow of four acres five roods, how much would two men mow in one day?' The priest has the papers relating to his happy parish days when he organized the Altar Guild and the Children of Mary. He keeps them until they have become a crumpled-up ball in his hand and then throws them away. The moment of truth is reached when these facile paper comforters are abandoned. The lieutenant has on the wall of the police station the photographs of two wanted men: the American gunman and the priest. When the hunt is over, with one dead and the other under lock and key, he tears them up: ' . . . they would never be wanted again'. He too has attained a moment of truth of a

kind but it is to perceive that his victory over the priest is a
barren one. His warfare to free his countrymen from
superstition, his interpretation of their abandonment, ends
in his own isolation. 'He felt without a purpose, as if life had
drained out of the world ... He couldn't remember
afterwards anything of his dreams except laughter, laughter all the time, and a long passage in which he could find no
door'. He had wanted to give children a bright material
future and his lonely failure is endorsed when the boy Luis
who had hero-worshipped him spits on his polished boot.

The priest is an unheroic figure who in his own eyes and
those of others has failed in his vocation. At the same time
he seems to participate in the prolific life of the country
around him while the lieutenant, cold and impersonal,
stands apart from it. He is introduced as 'a small man
dressed in a shabby dark city suit, carrying a small attaché
case'. He is unassuming and meek, the helpless little man of
modern society, almost a Charlie Chaplin figure. As he
looks at his own face under the stubble: 'It was a buffoon's
face, good enough for mild jokes to women, but unsuitable
at the altar rail'. He is a whisky priest but is never seen
helpless with drink. The occasions when he drinks most are
when he has to placate the friends of the man from whom
he has bought wine for communion and on the night before
his execution to stifle his fear. He has begotten a bastard
child and feels lovingly responsible for her though helpless
to save her:

> The child stood there, watching him with acuteness and
> contempt. They had spent no love in her conception: just
> fear and despair and half a bottle of brandy and the sense
> of loneliness had driven him to an act which horrified
> him — and this scared shame-faced overpowering love
> was the result.

By engendering another human being he has betrayed his
vows but extended his hold on the common life. Revisiting
the village where the child and her mother live, he is 'a small
gaunt man in torn peasant's clothes going for the first time
in many years, like any ordinary man, to his home'. He is

presented as supremely ordinary: he regards himself as supremely sinful: the pattern of events almost accidentally imposed on him, and wearily accepted, can be read as a demonstration of the Christian life, an obedience which of definition may not be selfishly proclaimed as Christian virtue. The pattern starts at the port where a child's plea for him to attend a sick mother causes him to miss the steamer, and ends with a death which another child, Luis, and his family will interpret as a martyrdom.

The lieutenant, his embattled opposite, is not a participator, and remains aloof from the people he is dedicated to save: he does not need sex and despises those who do. Always the priest is seen as a human animal, immersed in natural life and involved however painfully or protestingly with other men and women and other animals. He is depicted as like a typical travelling peasant, leaning forward on the pommel and beating his recalcitrant mule. Little green snakes dart away from him on the jungle path. When he returns to the Fellows' house he is desperately hungry and snatches a piece of meat away from a starving dog; only his awareness of his animality distinguishes him:

> For a moment he became furious — that a mongrel bitch with a broken back should steal the only food. He swore at it — popular expressions picked up beside band-stands: he would have been surprised in other circumstances that they came so readily to his tongue. Then suddenly he laughed: this was human dignity disputing with a bitch over a bone.

By virtue of physical reduction to a near-animal level the priest can speak with an authority rarely granted to the better fed of that narrow but all-important margin of self-consciousness which defines man.

The reader is made constantly aware of the priest's bodily functions, his pain and his sweat; in the cramped cell he has to squat with his feet under him and they gradually become numb; and when, exhausted by the mountain journey across the border, he realizes that he has come at last to a church that is not desecrated or burned down, the emotion of relief and peace is as much a physical experience to him as was his early suffering: 'leaning his head against the white wall, he fell asleep, with home between his shoulder blades'. Also he can entertain a sense of the tenuous beauty of natural things: 'A horse cried in the early morning, tethered to a tree, and all the freshness of the morning came in through the open door'.

The lieutenant, on the contrary, has attempted to abolish the animal. The priest has a sense of humour grounded on the absurdity of life, the paradox of man as the great amphibian straddling the worlds of animal and spirit, just as he has a shrewd peasant common sense which sees through the whining lies of the half-caste immediately. The lieutenant is not a realist but a fanatical believer in a theory which he has embraced with all the intensity of mystical vision:

> It infuriated him to think that there were still people in the state who believed in a loving and merciful God. There are mystics who are said to have experienced God directly. He was a mystic, too, and what he had experienced was vacancy — a complete certainty in the existence of a dying, cooling world, of human beings who had evolved from animals for no purpose at all. He knew.
> . . . . Heat stood in the room like an enemy. But he believed against the evidence of his senses in the cold empty ether spaces . . . this was his own land, and he would have walled it in if he could with steel until he had eradicated from it everything which reminded him of how it had once appeared to a miserable child. He wanted to destroy everything: to be alone without any memories at all.

This urge to universal destruction motivated by memories of an unhappy childhood is in complete contrast to the priest's aspiration, however faltering, towards universal love, prompted by the pain he feels on leaving his daughter: 'One mustn't have human affections — or rather one must love every soul as if it were one's own child. The passion to protect must extend itself over a world — but he felt it

tethered and aching like a hobbled animal to the tree
trunk.' Again he slips naturally into animal imagery to
communicate the frustration against which he struggles.
The lieutenant is a man of artifice whose smile is 'an
awkward movement of the lips', and whose would-be
gesture of affection when he pinches a street boy's ear is so
overdone that the boy winces. It is significant that we never
see him naked: the nearest he comes to that is to take off his
boots.

The opposition between the priest and the lieutenant
may seem total but Greene, in his most theologically
Christian book, eschews an absolute Manichean division
between the divine and the human. Both are men, and love
obscurely penetrates into every corner. The lieutenant is 'a
little dapper figure of hate concealing his secret love'; but
when he dismisses the priest after his night in the cell, not
yet recognizing him, he gives him five pesos (the price of a
Mass) and the priest replies, 'You are a good man'. Greene
in an interview has said that this was his only novel written
to a thesis: at first this seems unlikely when one compares its
charity with the harsh dualism imposed on *Brighton Rock*
(though the thesis in that book was apparently an afterthought) but if Christianity in our secular world means not
a way out of, but a way of looking in with understanding,
with the possibility of openness, mystery rather than killing
certainty, one can see what he meant.

What, too, makes it difficult to accept the idea of a book
written to a thesis is the human fullness of the ironies and
cross-indications by which the meaning (but of course it is
not a *meaning* but a perpetually haunting question) is
conveyed. Mr Tench with his acid stomach; Coral with her
precise, precocious intonation; the one yellow toe peeping
out of the half-caste's sandal and his habit of scratching
under the armpit: this realized particularity prevents any
symbolism from becoming an abstract schema. But the
symbolism is there. There are Biblical echoes. The priest
misses the steamer because he responds to a call to a sick
man, and he is described as 'the slave of his people' like
certain West African kings; the analogy is not far from that
of the sacrificial victim, the suffering servant of Isaiah,[14]

and when on the run from the police he stops at a village
and is persuaded to hear confessions he says angrily, 'I am
your servant'. As a figure of Christ, the suffering servant,
the priest has a Judas in the half-caste who intends to betray
him for money and whom he forgives in a precise,
charitable comparison of their degrees of sin: 'Christ had
died for this man too: how could he pretend with his pride
and lust and cowardice to be any more worthy of that death
than this half-caste? This man intended to betray him for
money, which he needed, and he had betrayed God not
even for real lust'. But the half-caste's sin lies not so much in
the fact of treachery which the priest is prepared to accept
but in his moral obtuseness, his arrogant assumption that
he has a right to the blood-money: 'It's fate. I was once told
by a fortune-teller ... a reward ... ' He is continually
irritated with the priest, who tends him when he has a fever,
and complains of not being trusted. Not for the first time
Greene here uses sheer comedy in the service of serious
moral discrimination.

Another parallel to the life and sacrifice of Christ is to be
found in the relationship of the priest to the American
gangster, Calver. Though verbal suggestions no doubt
perform their subliminal work it is not necessary, with
R.W.B. Lewis, to dwell on the fact that his name Calver is
rather like the name Calvary. His photograph is exposed on
the wall of the police station next to that of the priest. Both
are wanted men like Christ and Barabbas, and the lieutenant, who develops a hatred for the sleek young priest as he
is in his picture, has a preference for the criminal whose
normal passions can do no real harm to the state. As
Kenneth Allott and Miriam Farris note in *The Art of Graham
Greene*, there is a faint echo of Pilate's 'whom will ye that I
release unto you? Barabbas or Jesus which is called Christ?'
The priest's decision, prompted by the half-caste, to re-
enter Tabasco in order to hear the dying American's
confession is the occasion of his recapture and death. He is
only before the reader in his last moments, when the priest
has caught up with him, and then he is a shadowy
Bogart-like figure, working powerfully however in the
dramatic setting. There are more faint but unmistakeable

parallels to the account in St Luke's Gospel of the two thieves crucified with Christ. The gangster will not confess. He says 'You beat it out of here quick', and 'You take my gun, father,' but someone has removed it from the holster. Finally he says, 'You look after yourself. You take my knife . . . ', trying to draw it out. As the priest murmurs a conditional absolution for him he thinks that he is only one criminal trying to aid the escape of another. The 'save thyself' echo comes through clearly:

> And one of the malefactors which were hanged railed on him, saying, If thou be Christ, save thyself and us.
> But the other answering rebuked him, saying, Dost thou not fear God, seeing thou art in the same condemnation?
> And we indeed justly; for we receive the due reward of our deeds: but this man hath done nothing amiss.

The priest like Christ is asked to save himself; the violent man exercises a last act of charity in the only way he knows. In the priest's estimation they are both malefactors, but the dramatic implication, drawn from the priest's self-sacrifice, his prayer, and this last act of the gangster, is that both are saved, like Christ and the just thief. The echo leads us forward to the later verse, 'Verily I say unto thee, today shalt thou be with me in paradise'.

The significant pairing of characters and episodes is not always related to Christian symbolism. Greene now perfects his already considerable talent for endowing his people with representative force and at the same time grouping them in suggestive patterns. Of the two families the priest is sheltered by, the Lehrs are prim Lutherans, grounded in honesty and principle. They dislike Catholicism for what they regard as its ostentation and materialism; the priest, at the end of his tether, has little to show of either, and they charitably take him in. The miniature suggestiveness of this short episode is masterly. There is gentle humour in the description of the regular evening baths in the stream of Mr Lehr and his sister, the Gideon Bible in the guest-room, 'Winning Commercial Men for Christ', even the physical appearance of Mr Lehr, 'there was something upright and idealistic even in the thin elderly legs with their scrawny muscles'. The dramatic pressure is removed after the rising action of the priest's time in the capital, his night in the cell and the journey over the mountains. This is an interlude in his hunted existence. The Lehrs are good people but they are not in the front line. That their goodness is acknowledged mitigates the sense of the complete loneliness of the priest and is a development from the humble arrogance of Rose in *Brighton Rock* who can say of those outside her religion that they simply do not understand. But we are given to understand that there is something unreal about the idealism of the Lehrs: '. . . (they) had combined to drive out savagery by simply ignoring anything that conflicted with an ordinary German-American homestead. It was, in its way, an admirable way of life.' If this is the whisky priest's House Beautiful he is a Christian who is not really comprehended by his helpers. The Lehrs anticipate a fairer, less patronizing treatment of Protestant idealism in the portrait of the Smiths in *The Comedians*. Greene had to lean for long on the text 'He who is not with me is against me' before he could turn to 'In my house are many mansions'. The other family of helpers, the Fellows, are people without God in the world, Mr Fellows subsisting on a hollow cheerfulness, his wife withdrawn from reality into headaches and the past. Only their daughter Coral has a sense of responsibility and an openness to the reality behind appearances. As she shelters the priest in the banana shed:

She stood in the doorway watching them with a look of immense responsibility. Before her serious gaze they became a boy you couldn't trust and a ghost you could almost puff away: a piece of frightened air. She was very young — about thirteen — and at that age you are not afraid of many things, age and death all the things which may turn up, snake-bite and fever and rats and a bad smell.

Coral's name invokes *Coral Island* and the heroic adolescents of Ballantyne and Stevenson. Greene always takes children seriously, not because they are innocent but because they give a true account of experience; they have not yet learned to ignore or conveniently to forget. She and the priest talk together as two adults in a world of children: 'she had a keen desire to learn . . . He had answers as plain and understandable as her questions'. She begins to think about what he tells her and in between-the-lines fashion there is a premonitory hint of her conversion before a violent death which is never fully recounted in the novel:

> 'Mother,' the child said, 'do you believe there's a God?'
> The question scared Mrs Fellows, she rocked up and down and said:
> 'Of course.'
> 'I mean the Virgin Birth and — everything.'
> 'My dear, what a thing to ask. Who have you been talking to?'

Coral points away from the different receptions at the Lehr and Fellows households to another pairing of like and unlike, her contrasted relation with the priest's daughter Brigitta. Coral feels her first menstrual pains and is in agony while supervising the counting and packing of bananas. Characteristically, the child is interesting because she is on the verge of maturity, on the dangerous line between one life and another. Brigitta too is mature beyond her years, frighteningly so, and without Coral's intelligence and directness of heart; without also, it may be added, the correspondence course of Henry Beckley, B.A., Director of Private Tutorials, she is in danger of being corrupted:

> The child's snigger and the first mortal sin lay together more closely than two blinks of the eye. He put out his hand as if he could drag her back by force from — something; but he was powerless; the man or the woman waiting to complete her corruption might not yet have been born: how, could he guard her against the non-existent?

The child with her 'impudent and malicious gestures',

destined to be lost, is set beside the precise and calm Coral
who is in full possession of her individuality though
destined for a violent death. Death like a fine sealing
varnish offers a finish to existence which life denies.

Other children, as well as Coral and Brigitta, exist, and
bring into definition the flickering half-truths and un-
reasoning violence of the adult world. An Indian child is
shot by the gangster but the priest knows that even this
murder can be forgiven. A boy with a message begins the
story by preventing the priest from taking the steamer;
another boy, Luis, who had been bored before by his
mother's pious reading and had admired the lieutenant,
ends the story when he admits into his house another priest.
Both the last two episodes are crucial to the story. The
innocent body of the Indian boy with three bullet-holes in it
seems to symbolize the violence that pervades the book,
since it is a death even more pointless than those of the
hostages who are taken out of the villages to be shot. But,
given the suffering passivity of the Indians, it is also a
supreme instance of sacrifice in a work concerned with the
mysterious nature of Christian sacrifice and the effectiveness concealed under its apparent ineffectuality. The priest
accompanies the child's mother with the body to the Indian
cemetery; he is reduced by fever and exhaustion to a state
of acute sensitivity, and as she prays and he contemplates
the crosses black against the sky, he has a heightened
experience of the quality of faith which is made all the
stronger by the dark and superstitious nature of the
woman's religion:

No priest could have been concerned in the strange
rough group; it was the work of Indians and had nothing
in common with the tidy vestments of the Mass and the
elaborately worked out symbols of the liturgy. It was like
a short cut to the dark and magical heart of the faith — to
the night when the graves opened and the dead walked.
When she reached the tallest cross she unhooked the
child and held the face against the wood and then the
loins: then she crossed herself, not as ordinary Catholics
do, but in a curious and complicated pattern which

included the nose and the ears. Did she expect a miracle? and if she did, why should it not be granted her? the priest wondered. Faith, one was told, could move mountains, and here was faith — faith in the spittle that healed the blind man and the voice that raised the dead.

There is no miracle and to the priest it is 'as if God had missed an opportunity'; but the episode does indicate the other non-miraculous way in which grace is working, through the sacrifices of the priest who has paused to try to dress the child's wounds and then to assist the woman, regardless of his pursuers. It is an extraordinary passage: as often in Greene the extraordinary seems to be preferred to the normal. He talks of 'the faith' as Belloc or Waugh might, as sole repository of truth, then recognizes 'faith' in a bare desperate reduction deprived of the regular life of liturgy. We remember too that the priest is equally reduced, having had to cast away altar-stone and breviary. The only minister of the faith left in the state, a drunken sinner, is left with a congregation of one, a superstitious, half-pagan woman, and the innocent dead. The role of the child Luis is equally crucial though very different. The real witness of the priest causes him to see the pious tale of the martyr Juan read to him by his mother in a new light: he is a convert from the lieutenant's party to the Church, and what clinches it is sacrifice, the relic of the handerkerchief dipped in the victim's blood that his mother promises to obtain. With the arrival of the new priest we are returned from the potential isolation of the solitary victim for whom no miracle falls to the fruitful sacrifice of the orthodox martyr which will be repeated so as to ensure the continuous and triumphal life of the Church. In the symbolic roles of the two boys Greene leans two ways, first in a direction contrary to all those who would ignore what did not suit them, whether agnostics, Lutherans, or pious women, then through Luis to the interpretation of the priest's complete dereliction as martyrdom which will reunite him forever with his fellow Christians and with the saints, the last thing they would have expected.

The symbolic representative level of *The Power and the*

Glory is, after these examples, most effectively but quite simply demonstrated by the fact that neither the priest nor the lieutenant are given names. We know them merely by their professional labels: behind the labels worlds of life and death are conveyed. The representative level of the novel has not become barrenly argumentative on account of the realistic fullness in the portrayal of people and the description of scenes. However, when the symbolic argument between the Church and the world is pushed hard, there are some scenes that are less convincing than others. It does seem that the night in the prison cell is a much more effective and less strident piece of narration than the dialogue between the priest and lieutenant before the former's execution. Pushed into the dark, overcrowded, stinking cell, where there is only one bucket for the ordure of all the prisoners, the priest finds himself in a microcosm of the sinful world. There are thieves and murderers, an old man who, like the priest, has been separated from his daughter, a couple who make love like animals to forget their suffering, and an irritatingly self-righteous woman who has been shut up for one night for the crime of possessing holy pictures and who will be bailed out by her sister in the morning:

> This place was very like the world: overcrowded with lust and crime and unhappy love: it stank to heaven; but he realized that after all it was possible to find peace there, when you knew for certain that the time was short.

The parable effect is not forced because the episode fits naturally into the dramatic structure of the story. The priest has been arrested merely for having illicit liquor and the question is whether he will be identified by the police in the morning; even his admission to the others that he is a priest comes naturally in the strange intimacy of shared degradation. The woman asks him to hear her confession but bitterness has hardened her heart:

> 'What's the good of your saying an Act of Contrition now in this state of mind?'

'But the ugliness . . .'

'Don't believe that. It's dangerous. Because suddenly we discover that our sins have so much beauty.'

'Beauty,' she said with disgust. 'Here. In this cell. With strangers all round.'

'Such a lot of beauty. Saints talk about the beauty of suffering. Well, we are not saints, you and I. Suffering to us is just ugly. Stench and crowding and pain. *That* is beautiful in that corner — to them. It needs a lot of learning to see things with a saint's eye: a saint gets a subtle taste for beauty and can look down on poor ignorant palates like theirs. But we can't afford to.

. . . We're all fellow prisoners. I want drink at this moment more than anything, more than God. That's a sin too.' . . . It was more difficult to feel pity for her than for the half-caste, who a week ago had tagged him through the forest; but her case might be worse. He had so much excuse — poverty and fever and innumerable humiliations. He said: 'Try not to be angry. Pray for me instead.'

The priest is living out the Christian paradox without self-consciousness; he has no defensive dignity and no excuses: he giggles nervously when admitting that he will die afraid because he is in mortal sin. We are prepared for his acceptability as a saint when he disclaims sainthood. His sin has not affected his consistently steady moral judgment; and his moral discriminations here as elsewhere are those suitable to a priest, directed to the utility of souls. In the person of the woman the formal show of false Catholic propriety takes another beating: her unshakeable conviction is an instance of that ability to ignore the disturbing workings of human nature while professing to know all about it which is gently satirized in the Lehrs, magnificently put on stage in Ida Arnold. But as a Catholic the woman should know better, and the priest is harder on her, reluctantly, than he is on his betrayer or his executioner. She abides by forms because she lacks love. Even the fornicating couple have a version of this and in the desperate circumstances Greene has imagined (or reported), where the Church has become one wretched ordinary man responding to those circumstances, the priest can preach for himself and others a charity above forms, a faith beyond forms approaching that of the Indian woman who thinks her son may be brought back from the dead: only in hope for himself does he seem deficient. If a curtain falls between the world and the truth, even between the priest's God and the church of the world, there is no division between his image of God and the needs of common people. Since his whole dangerous drama depends on his resolve to bring the sacrament to his people, when he can obtain wine, he treads the sharp edge of orthodoxy and is not a holy sinner but a sinful saint. For this reason the Jansenist streak in Greene is necessarily less pronounced in this book than in the earlier ones. This does not prevent the startling declaration of extremes or contradictions, the priest's thought, for example, that venial sin is worse than mortal sin because it is more productive of pride, or his reflection when hearing the villagers' confessions that unhappy love can be more unhappy than anything but the loss of God, and that lust only becomes dangerous when it turns into love. Here under the form of advice to penitents Greene is able to introduce a favourite preoccupation, which is to provide the theme for later novels especially *The Heart of the Matter* and *The Honorary Consul*: the destructive consequences of the devouring sense of responsibility inspired by love or pity.

The prison scene convincingly develops the underlying theme of the priest who is a separated sinner only to himself, but united to God and his suffering people in love. The conversations with the lieutenant at the close smack more of the morality play. The two figures are posed against each other in debate and the scene becomes a vehicle for a critique of secularist philosophy. It is in the nature of such a debate that the loving person of the priest tends now to be treated as the expositor of a rival philosophy; the characters are too much on stage:

'No more money for saying prayers, no more money for building places to say prayers in. We'll give people food instead, teach them to read, give them books. We'll see they don't suffer.' . . . It's no good your working for your end unless you're a good man yourself. And there won't always be good men in your party. Then you'll have all the old starvation, beating, getting-rich-anyhow. But it doesn't matter so much my being a coward — and all the rest. I can put God into a man's mouth just the same — and I can give him God's pardon. It wouldn't make any difference to that if every priest in the Church was like me.'

Debating points on either side are assembled and in the play of argument the case for the Church is presented by the priest as a magical sacramentalism according to which men are saved, irrespective of their actions, by divine instruments whose efficacy is equally divorced from their moral obedience. There is no compromise in this dialectical struggle between the good works of humanism and the absolutely free grace of Catholic Christianity offered to the unworthy through the sacraments. This does not do justice to the state of mind of the priest, the main interest of the novel, or indeed to the obscure motions towards love made by those around him. Greene's great double insight is into the darkness of the human heart and the mysterious freedom of God's love to enlighten it. As the priest says: 'God *is* love. I don't say the heart doesn't feel a taste of it, but what a taste. The smallest glass of love mixed with a pint pot of ditch-water'. So much for the dimension of limited knowledge afforded by human loving; then for the dimension of bewildered ignorance when man comes to the contemplation of the idea of loving God: 'I don't know a thing about the mercy of God: I don't know how awful the human heart looks to him'. Greene's novels exist in this gap between fallen knowledge and the hidden God shrouded in our ignorance.[15] The tradition of the Church closes the gap by means of the sacraments; Greene gives prominence to the sacraments in *The Power and the Glory*, both the Eucharist and Confession, and also in his next novel *The Heart of the Matter*, but in these and other works we are shown, as it were, the void within the gap rather than an effectual bridging of it. Dramatic interest is directed to moments of participation in the sacraments where the gap seems to yawn again, a bad communion or an unsatisfactory confession, the withholding of absolution from Rose. But in *The Power and the Glory* a balance is struck between the dark heart of man and the Catholic sacramental life; the sinner becomes a martyr and his blood fertilizes the Church so that another frightened man with a suit-case is ready to smuggle himself into the persecuted province, and no doubt others after him.

This novel, the chief of Greene's Catholic novels, effects a remarkable balance between the author's personal obsessions and a theological vision of the priesthood as a medium of grace.[16] There is also in the work a perfect reconciliation of symbolic function and realistic narrative; the expressionistic heightening that Greene favours is in keeping with the extremity of the situation; and however desperate the setting seems, the reader is reminded that Christianity began in the catacombs and may be preparing to re-enter them: in 1940 the persecution of the Church was fully under way both in the Soviet Union and in Nazi Germany.

The hero of the novel, the eternal little man, slightly pudgy and complacent in the fading photograph showing him as a young priest, is turned into a saint by what appears as a complex amalgam of personal decisions and accidents. Something is accomplished in the void between the two worlds which is the author's special territory. The priest always retains the sense of his own unworthiness. He is a drunkard and has broken his vow of chastity; more seriously, he has not achieved anything: 'What an impossible fellow I am, he thought, and how useless'. The villagers are too terrified to shelter him; he cannot help his child; the American will not make his confession to him; he is caught in the end like a rat in a trap; and since the lieutenant cannot prevail on the coward Padre José to hear the priest's confession, he fears that he dies in mortal sin.

On the other side, in addition to his profound humility, there are many instances of his charity. He carries on throughout in his mortally dangerous duty: his temporary sojourn in the next state is only a brief period of rehabilita-

tion and he returns to his spiritual front line in Tabasco
when he could retire comfortably to the state capital. He
ignores the grace and comfort he brings when he can say
Mass or administer the Sacrament of Penance. He tries at
great personal risk to obtain communion wine. He forgives
the half-caste, his betrayer, not as a formal gesture but with
an impressively inward and sympathetic attempt to understand the man's needs. Most marked, and like to the
recorded signs of sainthood, is his effect on all the people he
meets: the effect ranges from the first stirring of religious
consciousness in Coral to a touch of pity in the dry soul of
Mr Tench the dentist. He calls out humanity in the
lieutenant who breaks his rules and the law to find another
priest for him; and this generous action works artistically
too, for it interrupts the rigid schematization of their debate
and returns us from the novel written to a thesis to the novel
that is more than that, the novel not of the opposition of
creeds, but of the inter-involvement of persons in contact
with divine grace. Above all, he is simply terrified of
physical pain, so that his task in meeting death is harder
than that of many.

Sainthood is the last thing he contemplates as he waits for
death, drugging himself with brandy, and it is only in a
dream that there is a premonition of what is happening
(ever since his uncompleted psycho-analysis Greene has
shown a fondness for dreams as a medium for communicating the true direction of the psyche):

> He had a curious dream. He dreamed he was sitting at a
> café table in front of the high altar of the cathedral.
> About six dishes were spread before him and he was
> eating hungrily. There was a smell of incense and an odd
> sense of elation. The dishes — like all food in dreams —
> did not taste of much, but he had a sense that when he
> had finished them, he would have had the best dish of all.
> A priest passed to and fro before the altar saying Mass,
> but he took no notice: the service no longer seemed to
> concern him. At last the six plates were empty; someone
> out of sight rang the sanctus bell, and the serving priest
> knelt before he raised the Host. But *he* sat on, just
> waiting, paying no attention to the God over the altar, as

if that was a God for other people and not for him. Then the glass by his plate began to fill with wine and looking up he saw that the child from the banana station was serving him. She said: 'I got it from my father's room.'

The child refers to the signal of Morse taps they had; an invisible congregation begins to tap along the aisles and when he asks what it means she says, 'News'. As the dream ends she is watching him 'with a stern, responsible and interested gaze'. As with all Greene's children and child-women the hero sees her looking at him in the expectation of his death; just as Andrews in *The Man Within* sees Elizabeth looking at him before he stabs himself. These women who concur in a man's sacrifice include Helen, the indirect cause of Scobie's death in *The Heart of the Matter*.

This dream, so brilliantly achieved as the recognizable formal matter of a dream, combines Christian symbolism with Greene's personal style of theological thinking: there is the suggestion of a hidden God apart from the public working of the life of the church, 'as if that was a God for other people and not for him'. The heterodoxy of isolation is relieved by the echoes of the Gospels. The glass filling with wine is the sacrifice of Christ's blood signified at the Last Supper: 'This is my blood of the new testament, which is shed for many for the remission of sins' (St Matthew 26.28). Likewise 'my father's room', recalling how Coral brought mineral water for the priest from her father's stock, also alludes to 'In my house are many mansions': there is a place for the alienated priest, and it is the child who is the most spiritually mature of all the people he meets who tells him so; it is significant that the gap between truth and alienation is bridged by a secret code, a special communication for the alienated, and that yet the message received is 'News' — the good news of the Gospel broadcast to all men. Finally the last thought of the priest, suddenly without fear and only immensely disappointed at having to go to God empty-handed, is 'there was only one thing that counted — to be a saint'. The sentence is taken from Léon Bloy's novel *La désespérée*.[17]

Greene's novels are about the degrees and kinds of

failure, the unimportant worldly kind, and the supreme failure to grasp at the possibility of sanctity which is spoken of by Bloy. But it is only in *The Power and the Glory* that he shows failure transformed into sainthood. After this book he returns to the subject of ordinary failure and frustration; courage and goodness are not excluded but divine grace, always mysterious, becomes both more mysterious and more distant. 'In my house are many mansions': the saint does not abjure his human individuality and there is no reason why a writer might not create a series of wholly different heroes of the faith. But not a writer like Greene. His once-sinning, self-despising priest is the only saint his imagination could bear, with the special exception of Sarah in *The End of the Affair*, and the possible exception of the hero of *Monsignor Quixote*. There are no more apart from these, only a continuing exploration of the sinful contemporary world. From a technical point of view this means that the morality play structure of the first two Catholic novels is abandoned. Their pairs of uncompromisingly opposed characters had brought the struggle of flesh and spirit into the centre of the stage. Now the realism of the narrative is more sober and less melodramatic; there is more variety of character, psychological interplay of persons in the two African novels, *The Heart of the Matter* and *A Burnt-Out Case*, and an experiment in construction in *The End of the Affair* (a first person narrative interrupted by Sarah's journal). These are his last explicitly Catholic novels, and *A Burnt-Out Case*, about an architect who does not believe, not even in his work, is already in a kind of limbo, religious only in the analogy it implies between the sick of the leper colony and the nature of Querry, the architect's spiritual dryness. As for *The End of the Affair*, it clings to Catholicism, literally, by a miracle.

Increasingly in this period (1948–61) Greene speaks through his fictions as a moralist rather than a religious writer. Increasing worldly wisdom, and the developing skill of a great comic novelist in deploying it, aid this change of role. One might speculate as to whether another direction might have been followed in his mature work. He might have carried his expressionist realism further towards the display of extreme tension and breakdown: this is the atmosphere of the two 'entertainments' published one before and one after *The Power and the Glory*, *The Confidential Agent* (1939) and *The Ministry of Fear* (1943).

The heroes of these books move in a nightmare world where all appearances are deceptive and their precarious grip on their identities consequently weakened. Dreams abound, and the half-conscious recall of past traumatic moments. 'D' in *The Confidential Agent* keeps remembering the dead cat that was by him when he came round after being blown up in a cellar; Arthur Rowe in *The Ministry of Fear* is also blown up and the shock expunges the guilty memory of his mercy-killing of his wife.

The heightened atmosphere of wartime may have something to do with the merging of reality and fantasy in these novels; in any case the direction was not pursued; the chief persons of the later books enjoy the normal life with which he was already endowing a succession of vigorously conceived minor characters; the descriptive style becomes correspondingly less lurid and exaggerated. The horror behind the green baize door, or its equivalent, and the mark it leaves on people may still be his theme, but the treatment alters. There may be personal factors at work in the change affecting the manner in which the sexual theme, previously a background irritant, now occupies the centre of the stage, the next two novels dealing with adultery and the later *A Burnt-Out Case*, with a wrong suspicion of adultery. A novelist with so provable a sense of place now also conveys a sense of persons known, however transmogrified by his imagination. But about the change it is easier to observe that as Greene's art matured he was becoming middle-aged; perhaps also to add that when his camera-eye was focussing on scripts for Carol Reed (*The Third Man* and *The Fallen Idol*, 1950), and when he had ceased to write film criticism, his technique in fiction became decidedly less cinematic and therefore less melodramatic.

One further change in his work may be anticipated here. And yet it is less of a change than a new solution to a problem already stated in *The Power and the Glory*. The priest suffers physically in a country of suffering. Suffering, like the priest's humility and the poverty of his people, is seen as an offering to God: the poor in goods and in spirit will enter heaven when the rich and the pious may not. As in his treatment of the old woman with the decayed face saying her rosary in *Brighton Rock*, Greene is completely traditional and evangelical in his attitude: poverty may be a vehicle of grace and not an evil demanding a social transformation. And yet, when the priest preaches in this vein to the villagers, it leads him on to a sheer semantic difficulty in speaking of God's love:

> 'That is why I tell you that heaven is here: this is a part of heaven as pain is a part of pleasure . . . Pray that you will suffer more and more and more. Never get tired of suffering. The police watching you, the soldiers gathering taxes, the beating you always get from the jefe because you are too poor to pay, smallpox and fever, hunger . . . that is all part of heaven, the preparation. Perhaps without them, who can tell, you wouldn't enjoy heaven so much. Heaven would not be complete. And heaven. What is heaven?' Literary phrases from what seemed now to be another life altogether — the strict quiet life of the seminary — became confused on his tongue: the names of precious stones: Jerusalem the Golden. But these people had never seen gold.
>   . . . 'Heaven is where there is no jefe, no unjust laws, no taxes, no soldiers and no hunger. Your children do not die in heaven. Oh, it is easy to say all the things that there will *not* be in heaven: what is there is God. That is more difficult. Our words are made to describe what we know with our senses. We say 'light' but we are thinking only of the sun, 'love' . . . That perhaps means a child . . . '

The traditional theological principle that God as pure spirit cannot be known as he is in himself and must be grasped by analogy with the created things that are known, is firmly maintained; and yet the definition of heaven by negatives which precedes it carries the ulterior suggestion that it might be a Christian duty to abolish unjust laws and restrain the rage of unjust men. The suggestion is not pursued since this is a novel about love, not justice. Poverty brings a community of suffering; since the reforms of Vatican II the conception of the whole Church as the body of Christ has brought into focus the problem of social justice: does not love demand the effort to abolish hunger in the community of men in South America or South Africa as well as the effort to achieve personal salvation? If men should be freed from sin should they not also be freed from the prison of an evil social system? The priest's words lead up to these questions: they do not attempt to solve them, and when the priest tries to describe the joy of heavenly love he comes back, rightly, to his own painful love for his wretched daughter. Everyone is the prisoner of his own consciousness though he may share common elements with other men. Would a liberation of his communal conditions help, in Marxist fashion, to liberate him from this aliena-tion? This is a question the priest certainly does not ask and his stumbling attempt to explain heaven is brought to an abrupt end by the warning that his pursuers are approaching the village. In the dialogue with the lieutenant he declares emphatically that it is better to let a man 'die in dirt and wake in heaven — so long as we don't push his face in the dirt'. It is impossible to imagine such a statement in the later books. Here its exaggeration, its omission to define the boundary when leaving in the dirt begins to constitute a push, contributes to the black and white contrast of religion and the secular world. In *The Comedians*, and particularly in *The Honorary Consul*, the Church of the poor is transformed into a revolutionary movement against oppression. It is as if Greene had come to say, not like Thomas Mann that Karl Marx must read Friedrich Hölderlin, but that Léon Bloy must read Karl Marx.

CHAPTER 4

Doubt and Miracle

I

To talk of change of direction in Greene's work is of course to oversimplify; literary history tends to prefer a varied development. Greene's obsessional, almost neurotic drive constantly reasserts itself so that it is nearer to the truth to express change as a reshuffling of the cards, not the introduction of a new pack.

So, if we take the card of the holy sinner *The Heart of the Matter* belongs with the two previous books. First the depraved criminal of *Brighton Rock* who at least experiences the passage of holiness, then the ordinary sinner of *The Power and the Glory* whom God and circumstances (which means God through his circumstances) compel into a saint: now an exceptionally good and honest man Scobie, the chief character of *The Heart of the Matter*, whom God's circumstances and his own needs compel into sin and crime and leave a question mark over his final end. The police chase which is an analogue of the divine hunting has now gone; but in its place is a police drama (for Scobie is a policeman) where the trap is slowly shutting, and, not so much a divine hunt, as a human escape from the responsibilities imposed by the divine.

Then if we take the card of place, Sierra Leone on the West African coast may, after Mexico, hardly seem to be a reshuffling at all. There is no temperate zone and moral issues steam and peel in the heat; if there is a distinction it is that Mexico was an indigenous suffering and dereliction, Africa is a place for expatriates to lose their roots and go to pieces. Their books have to be wiped daily against the damp, and discussions of modern poetry seem painfully trivial and irrelevant. Even voices change: 'Here intonations changed in the course of a few months: became high-pitched and insincere, or flat and guarded'. The country changes them and separates them one from another; in *The Heart of the Matter*, in the first scene between Scobie and his wife she is separated from him by the mosquito netting under which she lies ill, with matted hair and closed eyes, resembling a dog or a cat in her complete prostration. Heat and sweat are everywhere a barrier: in bed Scobie tries to keep his body away from Louise: 'wherever they touched — if it were only a finger lying against a finger — sweat started'.

Above all else the Coast tires its white people. The picture of a native porter bowing under his load enters into the imagery of the story. The image comes to be applied to Scobie himself who lives by shouldering other people's burdens:

He was surprised how quickly she went to sleep: she was like a tired carrier who has slipped his load. She was asleep before he had finished his sentence, clutching one of his fingers like a child, breathing as easily. The load lay beside him now, and he prepared to lift it.

The metaphor broods over the whole story which may be read as an account of the increasing loads thrust upon Scobie until in his mere humanity he can no longer bear them.

The complex and closely knit plot makes it difficult to extract any summary of the action from our grasp in detail of the characters and their inter-involvement. Scobie no longer loves his wife Louise who has become neurotic and irritable after the death of their child, but he feels pity and responsibility for her; a further blow to Louise is that he has been passed over for promotion. The driving impetus of the plot is his need to obtain sufficient money to enable her to go to South Africa for a time where he thinks she will be happier. It is wartime; there is much diamond smuggling

from the interior to neutral ships passing through the port.
A new commercial clerk, Wilson, is really an undercover
intelligence agent sent to investigate the smuggling. He
becomes romantically infatuated with Louise who finds him
a diversion from boredom since they can discuss poetry
together; meanwhile Wilson is watching Scobie. Scobie
accompanies the field security police to search a Portuguese
ship in the harbour, the *Esperança;* he finds a letter from the
captain to his married daughter in Germany hidden in the
lavatory cistern. The contents of the letter are innocuous
and Scobie destroys it, feeling an obscure sympathy for the
fat, sentimental captain who would lose his right of entry to
the port if his offence against regulations were discovered.
This episode is important because although Scobie's departure from duty may seem a minor one, it is the beginning of
a descent down a long slide and this is how he sees it:

> The scrap went up in flame, and in the heat of the fire
> another scrap uncurled the name of Groener. Fraser said
> cheerfully, 'Burning the evidence?' and looked down
> into the tin. The name had blackened: there was nothing
> there surely that Fraser could see — except a brown
> triangle of envelope that seemed to Scobie obviously
> foreign . . . Only his own heart-beats told him he was
> guilty — that he had joined the ranks of the corrupt
> police-officers.

Remaining righteous, Scobie is not corrupted by money:
he is corrupted by sentiment. The next step is when he is
refused a loan by his bank manager and has recourse to the
dubiously honest Syrian trader Yusef whom he suspects of
dealing in contraband diamonds. He has in the past always
refused the gifts Yusef has pressed upon him, and this is a
perfectly proper arrangement on the surface, tied only to
four per cent interest, but again his moral status has
altered; the descent continues. He goes on an expedition up
country to inspect the pathetic belongings of Pemberton,
the young District Commissioner who has committed
suicide. At the beginning of his own moral decline the
reader is thus given a premonition of the final disaster in

the death of an undeveloped boy who has left a pathetically schoolboyish letter of apology addressed to his father. Pemberton had been in debt to a shopkeeper who was an employee of Yusef: here and elsewhere the threads of the plot are kept extremely taut. As Scobie discusses the suicide letter with the local Catholic priest, Father Clay, the question of divine forgiveness is already raised, as it is again after Scobie's suicide at the end of the novel:

> He handed the letter to Father Clay. 'You are not going to tell me there's anything unforgivable there, Father. If you or I did it, it would be despair — I grant you anything with us. We'd be damned all right because we know, but *he* doesn't know a thing.' 'The Church's teaching . . . ' 'Even the Church can't teach me that God doesn't pity the young . . . '

It is because Pemberton had been young, unformed, that Scobie would forgive him and believes that God would forgive him; in a similar way he makes a concession for the Portuguese captain because he loves his daughter: 'That had been the turning point, the daughter'. Pemberton and the unknown daughter are shadows cast before; the ultimate and disastrous recipient of his pity is to be a young woman, unformed in character like the one, and appearing to him as a substitute for his lost daughter.

The novel is divided into three books which present, as in a tragedy, the inevitable stages of a rounded action. At the end of the first, Scobie, having obtained the money, is able to see his wife off on the boat to South Africa. At the beginning of Book II he goes to Pende to receive the survivors from the torpedoed ship. He sits in the hospital by the bedside of a dying child and comforts her last moments by making the shadow of a rabbit's head on the wall with his hands. He meets Helen Rolt who has lost her husband in the open boat; he helps her, they become friends, and then lovers. After a quarrel caused by his limited, secret visits, he slips a letter confessing his love under the door of her hut. It is taken by Yusef's servant. He is now in Yusef's power and the inevitable blackmail follows: he is asked to take a packet of diamonds aboard the same Portuguese ship. This act closes on the unexpected return of Louise with the vague explanation that she is no longer worried about his being passed over for the Commissionership and that she must be there to keep him up to his religious duties.

The drama now moves inevitably to its close. Louise wants him to go to communion with her; in the confessional the priest, Father Rank, will not give him absolution since he will not promise to give up his adultery. He must at all costs keep up appearances as lover and husband to serve, in his view, the happiness of both women, and he goes to the altar with a clear-sighted expectancy of his own damnation. His betrayal of God coincides with the final stage of his corruption as a policeman. Before delivering the diamonds he has come needlessly to distrust his loyal servant Ali; Yusef promises in ambiguous terms to draw Ali away and in fact has him murdered. In an atmosphere of nightmare threat, drinking whisky with Yusef, it is an open question whether Scobie dimly understands the full implication of Yusef's reassurance, 'You will not have to worry, I will see to that'. What is sure is that when he finds the body under some petrol drums near the quayside he believes he is totally responsible on account of his lack of trust, a deficiency in the virtue on which his whole way of life is based, and that this betrayal is intimately connected with his betrayal of God. He sees Ali's body as 'like a broken piece of the rosary . . . a couple of black beads and the image of God coiled at the end of it'. Convinced that he has failed to give happiness to either of the two women with whom he is involved, as well as in his career, he carefully plans a suicide that will look like natural death, for the sake of Louise's reputation and the insurance. He feigns the symptoms of angina and obtains from his doctor the drug Evipan (he has picked up a hint for this method from a woman doctor at a dinner party); he then writes faked entries in his diary about his pains and the regular doses he is taking, reserving enough tablets for a massive overdose. Ironically, while he is putting his plan into action he learns that the Commissioner-to-be has been posted to Palestine and he will therefore be offered the coveted job after all. If he had known this at the start there would have been no need specially to comfort Louise, no need to place himself in Yusef's hands, no opportunity to sleep with Helen: the closeness of the dramatic construction is nowhere more apparent than at this point. But Scobie goes through with the suicide. The enigma of the last few minutes of his life is passed on to the reader; as in the last night of the priest in *The Power and the Glory* clues are offered which reflect back on the course of his behaviour as well as pointing forward to his spiritual future.

This is not the end. The end comes with the repercussions of his death on the two women. Louise and Wilson talk about Scobie as they examine his diary; they will probably marry, but not yet. Wilson's training enables him to detect that some of the entries have been made later in a different ink; and he knows that Scobie has been receiving money from Yusef. We now learn that Louise came back because she had been informed by a neighbour of the affair with Helen; she can only tell Wilson that she thought he squared it with his conscience by 'going to confession and starting over again'. This reveals a complete misunderstanding of that moral scrupulosity, or, if one likes, urge towards self-destruction, which prompts Scobie to damn himself in preference to lying or to abandoning either of the women to whom he feels obligation. Louise's only concern is that he may, as Wilson guesses, have committed the unpardonable sin of suicide: 'In spite of everything, he *was* a Catholic'. When she takes her suspicion to Father Rank he sums up in the manner of the old priest who confesses Rose at the end of *Brighton Rock:* 'The Church knows all the rules. But it doesn't know what goes on in a single human heart'. He adds that he thinks Scobie really loved God and when Louise breaks out bitterly, 'He certainly loved no one else', he replies that she may after all be right.

The last we see of Helen is when she has come back slightly drunk from the beach with the crass Air Force officer Bagster who makes a crude attempt to seduce her. Her total apathy dissuades him and on his departure she is left vaguely thinking about God and trying to pray:

. . . the wish struggled in her body like a child: her lips moved, but all she could think of to say was, 'For ever and ever, Amen . . . ' The rest she had forgotten. She put her hand out beside her and touched the other pillow, as though perhaps after all there was one chance in a thousand that she was not alone, and if she were not alone now she would never be again.

As with the whisky priest's arousal of generosity in the dying American gangster, the effect of Scobie on other people is a testimony to his spiritual rightness. Helen had scoffed at his scruples about the sacraments, but she now enjoys an intimation of the presence of God, and it is as if his disinterested love has achieved the caring for her he desperately desired in his lifetime. This brief episode immediately precedes the interview between Louise and Father Rank. It is just as important in its way and carries more conviction: Father Rank's words have the finality of a pronouncement, even within the open, situational terms of Greene's moral theology, and therefore have, certainly for many non-Catholic readers, too much the air of imposed interpretation: the straight account of Helen's state of mind, from barren isolation to recognition of a reassuring otherness, is the best insight into what has gone on in Scobie's 'single human heart' and its living effect.

What he lacks and what he most desires is peace. His sense of the word is so profound that he is angry when his wife says he would have peace if she went away to South Africa:

For he dreamed of peace by day and night. Once in sleep it had appeared to him as the great glowing shoulder of the moon heaving across his window like an iceberg, Arctic and destructive in the moment before the world was struck: by day he tried to win a few moments of its company, crouched under the rusting handcuffs in the locked office, reading the reports from the substations. Peace seemed to him the most beautiful word in the language: My peace I give you, my peace I leave with you: O Lamb of God, who takest away the sins of the

world, grant us thy peace. In the Mass he pressed his
fingers against his eyes to keep the tears of longing in.

The wish for release of the conscientious administrator and
husband is carried on to a different level by the language of
the Mass; the peace offered by Christ is a positive, however
unimaginable, not a mere release from human cares; we are
reminded of the heaven of the sermon in *The Power and the
Glory* which was something more than the absence of pain
though the priest did not have the time to say what that
something more might be. The search for an unattainable
peace provides a counterpoint to the unrest in the fore-
ground of the novel: Scobie finds it only in death when in
his own mind he has inexorably cut himself off from
Christ.[1]

Scobie comes nearest to finding peace when he goes into
the bush with his servant Ali to investigate the suicide of a
District Commissioner. For this episode Greene draws on
his first experience of West Africa, the arduous journey he
made through Liberia with his cousin Barbara in 1935
described in *Journey Without Maps* (1936). Apart from this
episode the setting of the novel and the white colony in
Freetown are drawn from his experience in Sierra Leone in
the war years as an intelligence agent (1941–3). On his
journey up country Scobie dreams peacefully as he never
does at home in Freetown:

> . . . a dream of perfect happiness and freedom. He was
> walking through a wide, cool meadow with Ali at his
> heels: there was nobody else anywhere in his dream, and
> Ali never spoke. Birds went by far overhead, and once
> when he sat down the grass was parted by a small green
> snake which passed on to his hand and up his arm
> without fear, and before it slid down into the grass again
> touched his cheek with a cold, friendly, remote tongue.

In the travel book Greene describes

> . . . the moments of extraordinary happiness, the sense
> that one was nearer than one had ever been to the racial

source, to satisfying the desire for an instinctive way of life, the sense of release, as when in the course of psycho-analysis one uncovers by one's effort a root, a primal memory, should have been counter-balanced by the boredom of childhood too, that agonizing boredom of 'apartness' which came before one had learnt the fatal trick of transferring emotion, of flashing back enchantingly all day long one's own image, a period when other people were as distinct from oneself as this Liberian forest. I sometimes wonder whether, if one had stayed longer, if one had not been driven out again by tiredness and fear, one might have relearned the way to live without transference, with a lost objectivity.

The sense of peace and release from care is here compared to the repossession of the primary self achieved in psycho-analysis (no doubt with a side-glance at Greene's analysis under Richmond) and this in turn is equated with the state of childhood, when people are seen as wholly other, so that the painful and misleading transference of one's emotions to others which characterizes maturity is avoided. Scobie transfers his own emotion of devouring pity to others; he suffers in his person their immense need as he imagines it and in so doing fails to grasp the facts of the case.

The novel is problematic unlike either of its predecessors: there is nothing problematic about Pinkie's corruption — only over his final end does a question mark stand; the indications of the whisky priest's sanctity are there though muted — he is doubted only by himself and by the Pharisees, like the woman in the prison cell. But Scobie has a question mark not only over his spiritual destiny but also over his character as a man. Critics have judged him to be a moral failure, an inferior person, or a self-destructive neurotic.[2] Or he has been described as 'a good man, who loves too well but not wisely',[3] a fairer and less captious reading of the story. The possibility of different points of view on the character shows how far Greene has entered a new type of fiction. While occupying opposite ends of the moral spectrum, Pinkie and the whisky priest are united as representative figures bearing the cross of humanity under stress, endowed with a sense of the terror of life and the possibility of damnation. Scobie is a man in a realistic fiction with particular problems which each reader is free to analyse for himself; whatever post-structuralists may say of the writer's manipulation of the point of view in the classic realist text, this has never prevented certain readers from finding Fanny Price in *Mansfield Park* unbearable or entertaining a sneaking sympathy for Becky Sharp in *Vanity Fair*. So the conduct of Scobie may remain open to different interpretations, and to an even greater degree than in classical realism, since as a twentieth-century man he has a problematic relationship to his social environment. He may seem irritating, or neurotic, or endowed with a certain nobility, or merely the victim of circumstances.

Life for the English officials in West Africa is seen under the metaphor of sickness: 'For fifteen years he had watched the arrival of a succession of patients: periodically at the end of eighteen months certain patients were sent home, yellow and nervy, and others took their place'. The metaphor of sickness continues in Greene's work though the climate that provides it may change: it alters to the dangers of death and betrayal in wartime London, and then back to Africa and the Congo in *A Burnt-Out Case* with a real sickness, leprosy, as a metaphor for the progressive degeneration of life. However much Scobie is presented as a man with particular problems and a certain bent, the novel yet retains a representative character on account of Greene's habitual insistence, through imagery and authorial reflection, on the universality of his setting. The inference is, as the trap Scobie has partly prepared for himself closes upon him, that elsewhere other traps are preparing, constructed of different materials. The critics who condemn his moral and psychological weakness fail to see that, as character is fate according to Novalis, so other characters may have other fates. Like *The Mayor of Casterbridge* among Hardy's other work, *The Heart of the Matter* is the most purely Aristotelian tragedy when set alongside Greene's other novels. Scobie's nobility is balanced on a fatal flaw and to dismiss him as an inferior human being is to allow oneself to forget within the academic pressure chamber that outside it both inferior and superior minds may succumb utterly to circumstances.

The environment that closes in so as to drive men to the breaking-point and to search for a peace that is denied are not the only themes that are repeated with variations from earlier books and are to occur again. Scobie is an interesting variation on the type of the just and weary policeman, the Assistant Commissioner of *It's a Battlefield*, for whom the prototype is Conrad's Commissioner in *The Secret Agent*. Scobie has the same asceticism, the same fear of retirement as these characters, and his chief calls him 'Scobie the Just'; but in the variation his fatal flaw of pity manoeuvres him into the position where he can be corrupted. The theme of the significant pathos of children or the innocent is also developed with variation. We have seen it first in *The Power and the Glory* in the precocious intelligence of Coral who has to die, in the priest's child who is lost, and in the dead Indian boy, an innocent victim. These children seem to be chosen to illustrate the utter proneness of human beings and the disparity between merit and reward. In *The Heart of the Matter* Scobie and his wife have a dead child, Catherine, who died in England before his wife came out to join him. Then there is the child who dies in the hospital at Pende after forty days' exposure in an open boat; Scobie is at the bedside and it is the most moving episode in the book.

The most dreadful of questions for the Christian, the infliction of physical evil on the innocent of the world, is here fully engaged. It has been a crux of European ethics since the Lisbon earthquake in the eighteenth century, but in the twentieth century it has acquired a peculiar import- ance in liberal Western society: the declining belief in an after-life leaves nothing to compensate for the ills of this one, and tender sentiments towards the weak and helpless seem to have been developed in order to offset the appalling cruelties of the age towards many of the fit (so improved provision for the handicapped goes hand in hand with failure to suppress terrorism). In another novel, humanist not Catholic, but equally important as a moral barometer, Albert Camus's *La peste*, the death of a young child in agony from bubonic plague brings together Rieux the sceptic and the priest Paneloux in their common inability to understand why this should happen.[4] Nineteenth-century writers were more inclined to treat the frequent early deaths of Paul Dombey and his contemporaries as a blessed return to an eternal home from which they had come trailing their clouds of glory. But if Greene shares with Camus a twentieth-century concern he also introduces a personal strain into the theme of the innocent child unnecessarily made to suffer. Scobie clearly identifies the six-year-old girl at Pende with his daughter who died at that age. He prays, 'Father, give her peace. Take away my peace for ever, but give her peace'. His whole dedication to serving the right is concentrated in this single act of will; by the same act he surrenders the hope of peace which only release from duty could give. Helen Rolt, whom he is to love, has survived the same open boat and at Scobie's first glimpse of her she is starved and immature-looking and clutching a child's stamp album; she enters his life at the salient moment of the death of the child, and his love and pity are transferred from daughter to strange child to her: she is the first of a number of child-women who are appealing in their immaturity and who involve those who love them in disasters of which they are not the direct cause. Finally, on the theme of the pathos of children, Ali, Scobie's 'boy', though a grown man, is a child in his trust and innocence, and his death is deliberately associated by Scobie with the death of his daughter Catherine and the expiation he feels he must make for that death and for all the other suffering for which he assumes responsibility. This act of expiation for Catherine, Ali, and the others leads up to the climax of the novel, and, in accordance with Greene's customary moral paradox, Scobie's act of atonement is one and the same with the supreme act of despair — suicide.

Is Scobie's suicide, whether humanly or in Christian terms, a sin and a failure? We must look at the whole course of Scobie's behaviour, not just his taking his own life, in order to see how the melodramatic crisis grows naturally out of the contradiction implicit in his whole life.

It is not easy to understand what constitutes the danger of

pity, a danger that is continually stressed both in authorial comment and within Scobie's stream of consciousness. To be sure, we are shown, in the fashion of drama, how precise actions both in the Yusef plot and in the Louise-Helen plot produce a chain of events leading to a tragic outcome. But they might have done so had the spring of action been unscrupulous ambition in one case and romantic lust in the other. What is the nature of this pity that destroys — 'this automatic terrible pity that goes out to any human need — and makes it worse', as Scobie says to himself when he begins to think that the emotion over-rides in him any real love for either woman? There is a perverse and idiosyncratic side to the presentation of how pity works: in regard to women it is excited by ugliness and failure, never by attractiveness:

> The greying hair, the line of nerves upon the face, the thickening body held him as her beauty never had. She hadn't put on her mosquito-boots, and her slippers were badly in need of mending. It isn't beauty that we love, he thought, it's failure — the failure to stay young for ever, the failure of nerves, the failure of the body. Beauty is like success: we can't love it for long.

If this pity has a perverse element about it, it always exonerates itself by dismissing its own cruelty in the very act of making a cruel judgment: 'His wife was sitting up under the mosquito-net, and for a moment he had the impression of a joint under a meat-cover. But pity trod on the heels of the cruel image and he hustled it away'. But how extraordinary to retreat like this from the pitilessness of style to the prepared pitifulness of response. The most dangerous heart of the book, its heart of the matter, lies in its projecting on to Scobie, the honest policeman, a painful sense of separation from other people which is disguised by his steadily maintained life of pitying service. The guilt produced works both ways: Scobie can treat the subjects of his love as inferiors, and yet feel, after all his day-to-day support for them, 'the enormous breach pity had blasted through his integrity'. When he and Helen come together as lovers for the first time there is this same sense, from the prime actor's point of view, of an enemy lying in wait at the gates of love: 'What they had both thought was safety proved to have been the camouflage of an enemy who works in terms of friendship, trust and pity'. The enemy here is much more than passionate love which serves merely as a vehicle: the suggestion in both passages is that it is commitment to other persons which is ultimately destructive of the isolated self and its integrity. It may seem a paradox in Greene as a Christian writer that the supreme virtue of the Christian West, Shakespeare's 'naked new-born babe', should be viewed as dangerous.[5] The paradox lies in his abrupt division between the true Christianity of his characters and conventional codes of right and wrong which we have already met: a Christian morality involves sacrifice and this means the abandonment of the coded compromises by which the lonely self tries to exist in society.

The danger of the commitment to others brought by pity lies in our ignorance of other selves and therefore of their true needs. Scobie's bleak knowledge of the limits of human understanding makes him an unusually intellectual police-man — it should really be he, not Louise, who reads modern poetry; this aspect of his character comes perilously near to inhibiting the decisive actions he undertakes:

> If I could just arrange for her happiness first, he thought, and in the confusing night he forgot for the while what experience had taught him — that no one human being can really understand another, and no one can arrange another's happiness.

As he says to Louise of Pemberton's suicide, 'We'd forgive most things if we knew the facts'. But man never knows all the facts: Scobie's loyalty to the promises exacted by pity, to cherish Louise, to comfort Helen, bring despair into his heart long before the final realization of despair in suicide:

> Despair is the price one pays for setting oneself an impossible aim. It is, one is told, the unforgivable sin, but it is a sin the corrupt or evil man never practises. He

always has hope. He never reaches the freezing-point of knowing absolute failure. Only the man of good will carries always in his heart this capacity for damnation.

So Scobie's plans are doomed from the outset since pity is blind to consequences and cannot see into the inner life of those whom it loves.[6] It is a bitter joke that while he is at such pains to keep his affair with Helen secret his wife should know about it and take it in her stride, rejoining him from South Africa and hurrying him off to Mass with her, thus engineering his blasphemous communion and setting in train his suicide plan. Pity has more luck with children, and perhaps with Helen who is treated like a child. In children there is only a slender barrier between the inner and outer lives and therefore less room for inaccurate analysis. To use Greene's words in *Journey Without Maps*, they are distinct beings and do not flash back one's own image. Scobie's most vital and clearly judged act of pity is also his most disastrous: it is his prayer that his peace may be taken for ever if the dying six-year-old child may have peace. He certainly loses his peace for he has just met Helen Rolt, clutching her child's stamp-album, and the Yusef plot is closing in. To lose one's peace for ever is to be in hell and according to the law of the Church he has chosen hell when he takes communion in mortal sin and then again when he ends his own life. But an act of gratuitous sacrifice for a human being with whom he has no special ties (except the echo of his relationship to Catherine) is a purely Christian act. Furthermore his selflessness is persistent, not a sudden emotional volition: he had come to the hospital to be of use and had wanted least of anything to be left with a dying child; similarly, his care for Louise is expressed not by a single gesture of sacrifice (the loan from Yusef for the passage money) but by a steady effort in small things like prevailing upon her to nibble at her lunch. It now becomes apparent that what from the prudential human side is dangerous blind pity is from the religious side charity, a selfless and spontaneous love which resides in Christ and has therefore no need to calculate consequences.

If pity is really charity it is a character flaw only in human, prudential terms, and the moral and religious levels of the story are one and the same. But there yet remains a problem for many readers, Catholic and non-Catholic, in Scobie's ability to combine Christian charity with offences against moral and religious law, his adultery and his bad communion. The criticism usually is, not that he is a moral monster, but that he is an incredible character. The difficulty is best put, with the incisive common sense we expect, by George Orwell:

> If he were capable of getting into the kind of mess that is described, he would have got into it earlier. If he really felt that adultery is mortal sin, he would stop committing it; if he persisted in it, his sense of sin would weaken. If he believed in Hell, he would not risk going there merely to spare the feelings of a couple of neurotic women.[7]

But although Orwell's points sound impressive none of them stand up. They make Scobie seem an impossible character by ignoring the features which he shares with a tragic hero. The charge that he would have got into a mess earlier ignores the nature of tragedy, and of the novel, which is to be about extraordinary, or at least outstanding events, and to begin at a certain point in time. Orwell's common sense is betrayed by his agnosticism when he falls into the inaccuracy of assuming that adultery is only committed by enlightened liberals; and Scobie precisely does not persist in his adultery.

Orwell's last point is a shrewd one, but it fails to take account of the impossible position into which Scobie has manoeuvred himself, any more than it recognizes the charity which drives Scobie into accepting risks, in regard to his wife, and then on behalf of the dying child, long before he resigns himself to damnation. Orwell's reading, though perverse, does at any rate bring before us the full strain of the paradox by which virtuous intention commits sin and sin demonstrates saving love.

In fact Scobie is a man of good will who sins; it is not that he is unbelievable that upsets us: it is the extent of his goodness and of his sin that we, like Louise and Wilson find alarming: he is indeed a moral monster, but then, in Greene's view Christian morality, losing life to save it, is a monstrous form of behaviour.

The intimations which link Scobie's actions with the sacrifice of Christ do this in an obscure way so that at some times he seems to be sharing the lot of the victim, at others to be inflicting pain on Christ or joining in his betrayal. This serves more than anything to sharpen the paradox of the virtuous sinner. When he has returned to his own house after the first night spent in Helen's quarters he reflects on the impossibility of his dual responsibility and the falsehood that will ensue: it is the interpretation of his action as treachery to God that is uppermost now:

> He had sworn to preserve Louise's happiness and now he had accepted another and contradictory responsibility. He felt tired by all the lies he would some time have to tell: he felt the wounds of those victims who had not yet bled. Lying back on the pillow he stared sleeplessly out towards the grey early morning tide. Somewhere on the face of those obscure waters moved the sense of yet another wrong and another victim, not Louise, not Helen. Away in the town the cocks began to crow for the false dawn.

Yet the echo of the cock crowing for Peter's betrayal is not allowed entirely to dominate the paragraph which forms the conclusion of the first part of the second book. The other wrong and the other victim move 'on the face of those obscure waters', and the Biblical allusion here adds to the crucified God the creative spirit of the first chapter of Genesis moving on the face of the waters. If Scobie's act is likely to inflict fresh pain on God it is also a part of God's creative plan; the confused images of creation and sacrifice suggest a fictional resolution of the perpetual problem of reconciling freewill with divine predestination.[8]

At another time Scobie's desperate course seems to him the right one and the terms of ordinary morality are deliberately and paradoxically reversed. He thinks, as he walks toward her hut, that he will not go to Helen, his

mistress, he could write to Louise and go to confession in
the evening, and thus go to God: 'He would be at peace . . .
Virtue, the good life, tempted him in the dark like a sin'.
When he first begins to contemplate suicide he reflects that,
though the Church teaches it is the unforgivable sin, yet it is
also taught that 'God had sometimes broken his own laws,
and was it more impossible for him to put out a hand of
forgiveness into the suicidal darkness and chaos than to
have woken himself in the tomb, behind the stone? Christ
had not been murdered: you couldn't murder God: Christ
had killed himself: he had hung himself on the Cross as
surely as Pemberton from the picture rail'. The strident
tone of this passage reflects the distraught state of Scobie's
mind and is not a direct statement of the author's theological opinion. However, when this obvious and necessary
reservation is made, it still remains true that moral and
theological judgements form the reflective consciousness of
the whole novel and are not simply confined to Scobie's
attitude; both the Portuguese captain and Yusef pronounce
Scobie to be a good man, the latter on several occasions. It is
particularly significant that the gross and slightly sinister
Yusef, who is always depicted shifting his weight in the
chair from one thigh to the other, should show a peculiar
respect for Scobie; it is different from his superior officer's
humorous regard for his professional probity: it is the
unerring ability of wickedness to recognise the heart of
goodness. But the theme of the virtuous sinner who may be
saved at the last minute achieves its fullest exposition in the
remarkable dialogue between Scobie and God which occurs
after he has collected the package of Evipan:

I am going to damn myself, whatever that means. I've
longed for peace and I'm never going to know peace
again . . . No one can speak a monologue for long alone:
another voice will always make itself heard: every monologue sooner or later becomes a discussion. So now he
couldn't keep the other voice silent: it spoke from the
cave of his body: it was as if the sacrament which had
lodged there for his damnation gave tongue. You say you
love me, and yet you'll do this to me — rob me of you for

ever. I made you with love. I've wept your tears. I've
saved you from more than you will ever know; I planted
in you this longing for peace only so that one day I could
satisfy your longing and watch your happiness. And now
you push me away, you put me out of your reach. There
are no capital letters to separate us when we talk
together. I am not Thou but simply you, when you speak
to me; I am humble as any other beggar. Can't you trust
me as you'd trust a faithful dog? I have been faithful to
you for two thousand years. All you have to do now is to
ring a bell, go into a box, confess . . . the repentance is
already there, straining at your heart. It's not repentance
you lack, just a few simple actions: to go up to the Nissen
hut and say good-bye. Or if you must, continue rejecting
me but without lies any more. Go to your house and say
good-bye to your wife and live with your mistress. If you
live you will come back to me sooner or later . . .

So long as you live, the voice said, I have hope. There's
no human hopelessness like the hopelessness of God.
Can't you just go on as you are doing now? the voice
pleaded, lowering the terms every time it spoke like a
dealer in a market. It explained: there are worse acts. But
no, he said no. That's impossible. I love you and I won't
go on insulting you at your own altar.

We are struck by the intense poignancy of simple
language that somehow avoids sentimentality, as it does at a
different level in the episode of the dying child. But also
remarkable is the attempt to dramatize God's totally loving
relationship to his creation. Again the strange com-
plementarity of divine purpose and individual freedom is
touched upon; Scobie's sin would be arrogance in trying to
arrange other people's lives as if he himself were God, were
it not for the revelation in this passage that he acts only in
obedience to the impulses planted in him by his creator.[9]
God lowers the price he asks and will presumably lower it
still more; because he is a man of good will and wants only to
safeguard others he may be saved from the impasse in
which he has placed himself. But though the treatment of
God's regard for the soul, his suffering on its behalf, and

the intimate union the soul enjoys when it accepts the divine love, is theologically tactful and spiritually sensitive, the passage does not avoid the more subversive implications of the theme of the virtuous sinner. Thus the reference to the sacraments comes dangerously near to treating them as mechanical tokens of obedience rather than vehicles of grace ('the repentance is already there, straining at your heart'). And since, if the clues are to be followed, Scobie is apparently saved at the end, then the Catholic sacramental system, if it is not to be abandoned to the *faux dévots*, must be viewed as a sort of framework of reference *pour encourager les autres*. This would be an alarming conclusion, but less alarming than to conclude that Scobie is abandoned by God and not saved.

A solution to the difficulty is to be found if we follow the hints of the story and perceive that total responsibility assumes total risk in treading the tightrope of Christian moral action and that when Scobie takes the overdose he enters a sphere where rules are no longer applied, but where exceptions are made, as they have to be made for other erring individuals. We are in the realm of the reasonable gamble where alone human behaviour can be lifted beyond mechanical response. All are individually lost, and all may be saved individually through no virtue of their own. This is suggested by the lines of Rilke which Scobie reads in Louise's book when he has said goodnight to her for the last time:

> We are all falling. This hand's falling too —
> all have this falling sickness none withstands.
>
> And yet there's always One whose gentle hands
> this universal falling can't fall through.

The lines sound to him like truth but he rejects them as sounding too comfortable; he cannot pray or trust and is as doubtful of his own future as the whisky priest: 'I slip between the fingers, I am greased with falsehood, treachery: trust was a dead language of which he had forgotten the grammar'. But when he has taken the drug and tried unsuccessfully to say an act of contrition while remaining on his feet, he has the same experience as Pinkie in his last hour of a presence from outside striving to enter in. 'It seemed to him as though someone outside the room were seeking him, calling him, and he made a last effort to indicate that he was here.' Someone appealing for help, someone has need of him, and 'automatically at the call of need, at the cry of a victim, Scobie strung himself to act'.[10] From the depths of his consciousness and, most characteristically, from the depth of his isolation, he responds to the cry of suffering as he had done with the human beings he could not understand, and brings himself with a great effort to say aloud, 'Dear God, I love . . . ' When he falls to the floor the medal of the obscure Portuguese saint given him by the captain comes away. This last touch is no mere item of piety, since whatever intercession is involved the medal takes us back to the moment in the cabin when the whole course of events began; then Scobie acted with disinterested generosity towards the captain who responded with the spontaneous gesture of a simple man: the medal stands for all that, and sums up the continual work of pity which Scobie brings to completion by pitying God himself in his unfinished prayer.

The older Greene has not handled Scobie as gently as I have done, and as many readers would wish him handled. Nor is his later opinion of the novel as a whole at all sympathetic. On his own work a writer is merely one more critic, but Greene's afterthought on *The Heart of the Matter* not only runs counter to the present approach but is illustrative of a wholly different point of view from that implicit in the Catholic novels.

The scales to me seem too heavily weighted, the plot overloaded, the religious scruples of Scobie too extreme. I had meant the story of Scobie to enlarge a theme which I had touched on in *The Ministry of Fear*, the disastrous effect on human beings of pity as distinct from compassion. I had written in *The Ministry of Fear:* 'Pity is cruel. Pity destroys. Love isn't safe when pity's prowling round.' The character of Scobie was intended to show that pity can be the expression of an almost monstrous pride.

In *The Ministry of Fear,* the most fantastic and the most personal of the 'entertainments', Arthur Rowe kills his wife to relieve her from agonizing pain. Yet later he suspects that it was his own pain in watching her, not hers, he was relieving. All his conduct is governed by 'that sense of pity which is so much more promiscuous than lust'. But the rhetoric here would brand pity as a personal indulgence while admitting that it is, in a Christian and Kantian manner, extended to all regardless of personal interest. Whatever Greene says of the inner man, the ghost in the machine, we can only judge Rowe and Scobie by their actions, and their actions are disinterested, which is why they are sometimes disastrous.

Greene is more persuasive when he speaks of technical faults in *The Heart of the Matter* which allow the reader to think of Scobie as a good man hounded by the harsh demands of his wife; we only see Louise through his eyes, and a concession in the narrative to her point of view (apparently present in the original draft) might have shown her in a more favourable light and Scobie in a less. Louise is undoubtedly a narrow character, narrow in her religious and aesthetic stock responses, and in the scope given to her by the novelist. But the great drawback to accepting Greene's reading of his own novel is that there is only one character to express the emotion of compassion as distinct from pity and that is the God who hovers on the edge of the narrative in the dialogue with Scobie already quoted. Since Scobie's point of view is dominant we are obliged to believe that no loving understanding of other human beings is possible: everywhere a moral mosquito netting occludes our vision. However if God can both love and understand, and thus turn pity into compassion, this surely is enough for the whole world of separated monads. It gives us a strange sort of novel, one in which God is felt not simply as an influence but as a character, though a partly hidden character, at the climax of the book. To employ Northrop Frye's nomenclature, Greene at this point departs from the customary limitations of the novel (ordinary men and women as characters, formal realism) and passes over into romance, the form he had practised in his first incursions into prose fiction and to which he had always been attracted: *The Ministry of Fear* is sprinkled with allusions to Charlotte M. Yonge's *The Little Duke*. The characters of romance tend to become psychological archetypes: the final step has been taken when the Form lying behind all archetypes is introduced, for then fiction must come to an end. Or to put it in another way, God cannot be a character in realistic fiction since he is the One and fiction is an imitation of the Many.

The presence of God, or at least of the voice of God, in this single episode breaks into the narrative realism of *The Heart of the Matter* and is more startling than it might have appeared against the black-and-white morality pattern of the two previous Catholic novels. For realism is of its nature the semblance of this world and cannot therefore admit divinity except as the intimation of presence, as in Pinkie's perception in *Brighton Rock* of something outside the car windows. But Greene's criticism of *The Heart of the Matter* concentrates only on what he considers to be technical faults, such as the partial treatment of Louise and the sketchy characterization of Wilson. He concludes:

> Maybe I am too harsh to the book, wearied as I have been by reiterated arguments in Catholic journals on Scobie's salvation or damnation. I was not so stupid as to believe that this could ever be an issue in a novel. Besides I have small belief in the doctrine of eternal punishment (it was Scobie's belief not mine). Suicide was Scobie's inevitable end; the particular motive of his suicide, to save even God from himself, was the final twist of the screw of his inordinate pride. Perhaps Scobie should have been a subject for a cruel comedy rather than for tragedy . . .

But Scobie's immediate response to an appeal for help is not on my reading either ignoble or comic; one can understand the author's objection to criticism which has treated the book as a theological essay, but his account applies more to intention than execution. Scobie does not appear as inordinately proud in his behaviour to any of those he is associated with; salvation and damnation are issues kept in the forefront because Scobie, the dominant 'point of view', keeps them there after his desperate

decision: Greene admits that Scobie is based on nothing but
his own unconscious, and if he is a monster it is not through
monstrous pride but on account of his absurd attempt at
pure moral action in a fallen world: this involves the
breaking of codes, the fall into sin, and ultimate pardon.

Greene in his later novels, from *A Burnt-Out Case* onwards, has become a predominantly comic writer, as he
states in 1974 preface to that novel; so, looking back, he has
little sympathy for his Christian tragedy. His remarks
framed in the terms of comic art, technique and moral
comment, help to isolate by contrast the special quality of
the five Catholic novels which subordinate the moral life to
a religious standard based on the four last things — death,
judgement, heaven and hell. His objection to theological
criticism is primarily directed against the purely rational
approach that would turn human behaviour, real or
fictional, into precisely demarcated issues and solutions.
The human heart moves in ways of which reason knows
nothing; so does God. God comes to Scobie unexpectedly at
the end, as He had come to the whisky priest. It is like
Greene's description of the death of his admired Rochester,
the subject of his one historical biography: 'If God
appeared at the end, it was the sudden secret appearance of
a thief, not a State entrance heralded by the trumpets . . . '[11]
So the later comic Greene, anxious to disclaim the role of
theological propagandist imposed upon him by over-
enthusiastic Catholic critics, has this at least in common with
the author of the Catholic novels written between his
thirty-third and forty-sixth years: he believes with Pascal
that *le coeur a ses raisons que la raison ne connaît point* ('the
heart has its reasons which reason does not recognise') and
that God and man both move in mysterious ways.

Comedy was always waiting in the wings of the drama of
extreme religious commitment or extreme denial. It is
already there in the earliest novels, in Minty in *England
Made Me* with his seedy and secret life, in the episode of the
medical rag during a gas practice in *A Gun for Sale* which
results in the deflation of the pathetically hearty Buddy
Ferguson; it is refined in the treatment of the Lehrs in *The
Power and the Glory*; in *The Heart of the Matter* it flickers

uncertainly, its critical spirit on the edge of the central absolutes. Wilson and Harris, the two new colonial officials, pass the time in cockroach-killing contests and plan to organize an Old Downhamians annual dinner at which they will be the only members of the school. Uncertainty is declared by the element of farce here. Wilson is a draft for a character, one whom Greene admits in retrospect obstinately refused to come alive when the novel was being written. Wilson's love for Louise is romantic and immature; he publishes in the *Old Downhamian* a poem in which he sees himself as Tristram in the legend. In a scene which has no organic relation to the story he goes to a native brothel and waits for a girl to be brought to him. The implication is that his mawkish idealism and half guilty lust are two sides of the one coin; he is an undeveloped personality, and in spite of, or perhaps because of this scene, and his mastery of the techniques of secret intelligence, he carries throughout an air of spoiled innocence: Louise will be able to manage him as she could never manage Scobie. There hangs over him a statement about the failure of innocence and the undeveloped English public school heart which never quite gets made.

Greene's critique of false innocence has its origins in the introspection of the hero in *The Man Within;* Anthony Farrant in *England Made Me* is a variation on the theme; it is developed most fully and successfully in the study of Pyle in *The Quiet American.* The belief in ideals having a reality quite apart from the facts of experience is always a target for Greene's serious comedy; it is the prime mark of false innocence, and is allied to the religious dogmatism which has no respect for life as it is lived which is also a constant target. This and other comic themes are handled more expansively in the novels of the next decade.

If Louise is too narrowly presented and Wilson is too inconclusive (an outline of a problem rather than a man), Yusef is powerfully realised, and it is no wonder his creator was still pleased with him when he wrote the preface for the Collected Edition. The germ is a certain sinister villain of popular fiction who is a big man physically (a Sidney Greenstreet role in film thrillers of the period). Quite beyond the shiftiness of a man living on his wits he is endowed with a psychological depth and a remarkable sensitiveness which responds to Scobie's humanity even while he perceives his weakness. The combination of wiliness and sensitivity gives him more control over events than any other character; he can say with authority to Scobie: 'One day you will come back and want my friendship. And I shall welcome you'. Scobie sees in his blackmailer 'his only companionship, the only man he could trust'. His progressive surrender is indicated by the places they meet in, Yusef's car, his own house, Yusef's house, and finally Yusef's private office. The diction of an intelligent under-educated man to whom English is a second language is unerringly caught without attempt at pidgin or broken speech (it foreshadows the skill in rendering Wordsworth's speech in *Travels with My Aunt*):

> The Royal Ordnance Corps have very fine actors and they have made me appreciate the gems of English literature. I am crazy about Shakespeare. Sometimes because of Shakespeare I would like to be able to read, but I am too old to learn. And I think perhaps I would lose my memory. That would be bad for business, and though I do not live for business I must do business to live. There are so many subjects I would like to talk to you about. I should like to hear the philosophy of your life.

Yusef is drawn with remarkable verbal economy. There are few physical touches other than his hairy chest and his habit of shifting from one huge thigh to the other when sitting. He has less scenes than Wilson, and does not function as a consciousness in the narrative, as Wilson does in the brothel scene and for a few minutes with Louise when his declaration of love is interrupted by a humiliating nose-bleed. Yusef rises above the indecisiveness of the other minor characters because he is Mephistopheles to Scobie's Faust, the cruel servant to one who is the constant servant of others.

In *The Heart of the Matter* the expressionist poetry of the earlier novels has been largely dried out. Similes are

subdued, less frequent, and more functional: 'Thin black
bodies weaved like daddy-long-legs in the dimmed head-
lights'. The focus on particular recurring images is likewise
more purposeful, less surreal. The rusty handcuffs hanging on the wall behind Scobie's desk are the symbol of his
job and also of his imprisonment by pity which finally
immobilizes him. The stamp albums clutched by Helen Rolt
on the stretcher focus on her childishness which excites his
pity; it also works in terms of plot, allowing him an excuse to
continue his visits by bringing stamps to her. Wilson's
ill-fitting tropical suit of peculiar hue speaks of something
unsuitable and inwardly false in his nature. Together with
the less obtrusive imagery a new vein of detached moral
comment is opened which anticipates the authorial wisdom
of the later comic novels; in this book however the comment
is expressed, sometimes incongruously, through the consciousness of Scobie. Believing miserably in a moral solipsism which leaves pity as the only bridge to other human
selves he reflects: 'Point me out the happy man and I will
point you out either egotism, selfishness, evil — or else an
absolute ignorance'. But it is the man of good will who is
ignorant of what goes on in other minds and who wonders
painfully whether, if only he knew the facts, he would have
to feel pity even for the planets, 'if one reached what they
called the heart of the matter'. In the novel that escaped
Greene's intention it is only God who can effectively pity
and succour the creation he has left so calamitously broken.

II

This study tries as much as possible to concentrate on the
unique quality of each novel of Greene, since each designs a
life in fictional time with a beginning and end and does not
conceive of further existence outside the limits it has
prescribed. Of course this attention to the individual work
must be betrayed into consideration of an *oeuvre* since
Greene, like other writers, may seek the separateness of
each new creative idea while surrendering all the time to
repeating variations on the theme of his own compulsions.
At least in his case there is a major check on the operation of

the evolutionary fallacy: Greene's achievement cannot be interpreted as a growth towards a Catholic period, since, on the contrary, he grows out of one. In his next book *The End of the Affair* (1951) the process of growing away may be said to begin, although the subject and to a great extent the *dénouement* are emphatically Catholic and thus associate the novel with its immediate predecessors.

The setting is London in the war years and immediately afterwards. The peculiar atmosphere, especially of the period of the blitz when ordinary life and personal relations co-existed with sudden death is brilliantly evoked in Greene's *London Journal* based on his experience as an air raid warden at a post in Bloomsbury: the barrage balloons, concerts at the National Gallery, the descent into the tubes at night, alerts and all clears. Under the threat, and the fact that flesh could be torn by fragments of metal, flesh responded by learning Russian, reading Trollope, and making love. Two distinguished reactions of the imagination to that instant of time and place are Henry Moore's *Shelter Sketch Book* and Henry Green's novel *Caught* (1943) and it is in the latter that a character remarks: 'War is sex'.

Greene's narrator Maurice Bendrix is also an air raid warden in the blitz. It was a formative time for anyone living through it but perhaps it held a special significance for Greene; bombs encouraged speculation on the chances of death or survival, compacts and wagers, and this must have appealed to the man who in adolescence had played Russian roulette, to the writer who invites speculation on the eternal chances of Pinkie and Scobie, 'between the stirrup and the ground'; also appealing must have been the urban landscape of the blitz where bombardment abolished the demarcation between the domestic and the phantasmagoric: the green baize door is torn away. The first use of this material had been in *The Ministry of Fear* (1943) written during his West African service, where the plot turns on the fact that Arthur Rowe is blown up by a bomb and loses his memory. Returning to the blitz again after the war Greene hinges his story on a vow.

Maurice Bendrix, a novelist, cultivates Henry Miles, a civil servant, because he wants to put a civil servant into his

next book. He and Henry's wife Sarah become lovers and
she visits him in his house opposite theirs on the other side
of Clapham Common. On one of the first flying bomb raids
in the summer of 1944 they are together and Bendrix is
buried under the front door but only slightly grazed. Sarah
makes her vow: if Bendrix lives she will believe in God, and
she will give her lover up for ever. She keeps the vow and
avoids him; he, insanely jealous, can only think that she is
going with another man. He hires a private detective to
watch her, and a fragment of a letter salvaged from her
wastepaper basket seems to confirm his suspicions. He
reads: 'I know I am only beginning to love, but already I
want to abandon everything, everybody but you: only fear
and habit prevent me. Dear . . . ' She is making weekly visits
to a man called Smythe who lives with his sister in a
neighbouring house and has a hideous birthmark on one
side of his face. Bendrix confronts him out of morbid
curiosity, going to the house with the private detective
Parkis's little boy. Parkis insinuates himself into a party at
the Miles' house and manages to purloin Sarah's diary. The
diary is reproduced in full and reveals what has really
happened: she has kept her promise to God and stays away
from Bendrix in unwilling agony; equally grudgingly she is
drawing nearer to God, going into churches and buying a
crucifix. Smythe turns out to be a militant atheist of the old
school who addresses the crowd on the Common and hands
out tracts. Sarah goes to him in the hope of shaking the
unwanted faith that is making inroads into her life.

Bendrix is relieved to find that Sarah has not taken
another human lover: he feels confident he can compete
against a God in whom he does not believe. He visits her in
order to persuade her to go away with him; she escapes
from him and enters a church where he follows her. She is
tired out and already sick from an earlier wetting; he agrees
to stop badgering her. This is the last time he sees her. A few
days later Henry rings up to say she has died of pneumonia.
After her death the two men are drawn closer together
(Henry already knows of Sarah's unfaithfulness) and Bendrix goes to live in the Miles house. They learn from a
Catholic priest, Father Crompton, that Sarah had been

receiving instruction; he had advised her she must not leave Henry and marry Bendrix, though she desperately wanted to, if she wished to become a Catholic. Bendrix, in his bitterness, advises Henry against a Christian burial and Sarah's body is cremated. At the cremation Bendrix meets Sarah's mother, Mrs Bertram, and has dinner with her. He learns from her that she is a lapsed Catholic and had had Sarah baptized, mainly in order to spite her second husband. Now the coincidences that lead to the edge of miracle begin to build up.[12] They involve both the subsidiary persons outside the triangular drama, Smythe and Parkis, the private detective. Parkis's boy Lance is severely ill with an undefined stomach complaint and running a high temperature; he dreams of Sarah to whom he had become deeply attached and in order to please and calm him Parkis borrows one of her old children's books from Henry. In the morning the fever has gone and the child says that Sarah came and touched him and took the pain away. He also says she had written in the book for him. It remains an open question whether the childish scribble Bendrix reads in the book when it is returned was there before or not:

> When I was ill my mother gave me this book by Lang.
> If any well person steals it he will get a great bang.
> But if you are sick in bed
> You can have it to read instead.

The other coincidence is much more startling. During Sarah's visits to Smythe he had fallen in love with her. His disgust at his own deformity provides the incentive for his evangelizing rationalism. He confesses this to Sarah and in pity she kisses his deformed cheek. After her death he visits the house and takes away a lock of her hair. Soon afterwards his face clears up in a single night; at first he is too embarrassed to tell Bendrix when he meets him and pretends that he has had electrical treatment; but later he rings up while Bendrix is with Henry entertaining Father Crompton, and tells him the truth:

He said with an awful air of conspiracy, 'You and I know how. There's no getting round it. It wasn't right of me keeping it dark. It was a . . . ' but I put down the receiver before he could use that foolish newspaper word that was the alternative to 'coincidence'.

So the word 'miracle' is never heard though it would have been if Bendrix had not rung off. But the inference is there and the evidence is greater than that of these two 'cures'. Father Crompton and others speak consistently of Sarah's goodness, and among the others is Parkis who does his job of spying with reluctance, and who always contributes the voice of common human decency since Bendrix, the chief witness, is so bitterly biassed. Then there is the evidence of Sarah's journal, quite apart from its record of her developing trust in God: her unselfishness is shown by her staying with Henry when he needs her, against her own happiness and when her suitcase is already packed; she describes her emotion towards Smythe as envy, rather than pity, of one who carries the mark of pain around with him reflecting the suffering of Christ. Finally there is something peculiarly selfless and unworldly about Sarah's complete neglect of her own health which brings on her fatal illness. The incidents and her behaviour combine to furnish corroborative evidence of supernatural intervention. Greene's later judgment is that every so-called miracle should have had a completely natural explanation and to that end the coincidences should have continued over years in a vastly extended novel 'battering the mind of Bendrix' so as to force on him at last a reluctant doubt of his own atheism. It is uncertain whether this would amount to the attenuation or the prolongation of a miracle: perhaps Greene is simply voicing an awareness that the novel form has from its beginnings been restricted to human actions, and that having come to the limit of those he has in this book crossed the limit. In any case, in the novel as we have it Bendrix is still hating but now hating the God he has come to believe in.

The subject then is a miracle which is rejected by the two men who best knew Sarah's goodness, and which is resisted by the author, not only afterwards, but in the course of writing the book, since apart from Sarah's journal, which precedes the miracle, the point of view is limited to the consciousness of Bendrix. However this subject only emerges after the death of Sarah. Until then the ostensible subject is an illicit love affair. It is a natural history of love concentrating on the psychology of passion in a manner that is more French than English. The highlighting of the three participants and the close analysis of emotion recall *La princesse de Clèves* or *Adolphe* rather than they do any work in English. A few years after *The End of the Affair,* and at about the same time, there appeared Iris Murdoch's *The Sandcastle* and Françoise Sagan's *Un certain sourire:* both novels deal with a love affair between a young girl and a much older man, but their approaches are wholly different. The English novel sees the lovers in their moral and social relations with other people, family and community; Françoise Sagan studies only the biological growth of passion, its burgeoning and its decay. Greene's approach is more akin to the latter: his trio of protagonists are isolated and if Henry has a slightly comic external life of Whitehall committees and the expectation of honours it only emphasizes his separation from the intense core of the lovers. Greene too depicts the love affair as endowed with the vitality of an organism and Bendrix, with his intense jealousy, fears and anticipates the death of love. But he does not know till it is too late that his rival for Sarah's affection is divine and that there is to be a regrouping of the trio after the death of Sarah: still eaten up with jealousy he has God for a rival while Henry remains as comfortably unconscious of this new contest as he had been in the past of his friend's deceiving him.

The betrayal of unique art work into *oeuvre,* or literary history, or individual psychological history means that every book is transitional. On the one hand, *The End of the Affair* might be thought to be the most uncompromisingly Christian of all its author's novels because its incidents include some that approach the very edge of miracle: though it might be argued that no law of nature has been suspended, the coincidence of two exceptional recoveries from physical illness with the loving intervention of one character is bound in the Catholic context to appear to the reader as miraculous evidence of sanctity. Indeed the reader who is not a Christian may feel that by introducing these incidents the author is forcing the issue of belief in a manner that is not acceptable in the novel (the Christian reader of course may also be upset for much the same reason — he may feel that the Christian novelist should render a picture of Christian life and sensibility and that to introduce the slightest suggestion of the supernatural is to abrogate this duty in favour of a dogmatic appeal to 'evidences of Christianity'). On the other hand, the story is the first-person narrative of an unbeliever, so the suggestion of a Christian point of view and of a supernatural reality is, as it were, filtered through a highly unsympathetic consciousness. This consciousness makes for something very different from the presiding atmosphere of *The Power and the Glory* or *The Heart of the Matter;* the religious mind is once again embattled, but now not against persecution, not against the invincible ignorance of a mistress (Helen in the latter book) but against the infidelity of every character: even the one person who is an exponent of the religious attitude is an unbeliever who is seized violently and unwillingly by divine grace. This curious juxtaposition of the near-miraculous to the dry routine infidelity of the modern world is the factor that proved a handicap to many Catholic readers, more than the frank treatment of sexuality by the narrator. This too is the factor which makes the book both a climax and a work of transition.

The frequent comedy and occasional pathos of ordinary repetitive human life assert themselves much more because there are no great issues of life or death to impose a dramatic shape, only an adultery and an unhappy love affair. The descent from melodrama, to be carried still further in the later novels, means that Greene's sheer narrative accomplishment and verbal dexterity have greater freedom. In the preface of 1974 he plays down the miraculous element and seems to regard the chief value of the novel as being the training it gave him in the use of the first person. The narrator (Maurice Bendrix) is, like the principal characters in the preceding books, an imperfect human being flawed by particular vices and driven by an obsession; it is to have the whole story told from his point of view, the closing of any distance between the writer and his world, that introduces a new element; and with the removal of the author's free indirect comment on the edge of consciousness the use of imagery is still more curtailed.

A great part of the descriptive work in the Catholic novels goes into imagery of pain and discomfort. The subject of *The End of the Affair* is unhappy jealous love: if there are fewer similes of pain it is because the emotion is expressed through direct physical sensation: each of the protagonists on separate occasions presses the nails into their palms so that real pain may diminish the pain of thought. It is very much a book about bodies, grappling in sexual congress, made ugly by a huge birthmark, or racked by feverish coughing after exposure to rain and cold. The narrator, in pursuit of his former mistress through the streets of Clapham, is held up at a crucial point on account of a lame leg: it is as if we are never far away from the animal joys and the animal limitations of the body; sometimes pain and pleasure is simultaneous: the chief warden embraces Susan in the deep shelter her husband is inspecting, and she responds: 'He twisted me round against a bunk, so that the metal made a line of pain across my back, and kissed me'. When we do encounter one of the large, metaphysical similes Greene had been accustomed to employ, its vehicle is one of the most terrible pains that can be inflicted on a human body: 'The enormous pressure of the outside world weighs on us like a *peine forte et dure*'. Even daily worry is visualized in terms of wear and tear on the body: 'I could see the bald patch on the crown of his head: it was as though his worries had worn through'. It is not surprising in this world of bodies that God should enter it as another suffering naked body sharing all the animal attributes of a man:

And of course on the altar there was a body too — such a a familiar body, more familiar than Maurice's, that it had never struck me before as a body with all the parts of a body, even the parts the loin-cloth concealed. I remem-

bered one in a Spanish church I had visited with Henry,
where the blood ran down in scarlet paint from the eyes
and the hands. It had sickened me. Henry wanted me to
admire the twelfth-century pillars, but I was sick and I
wanted to get out into the open air . . . A vapour couldn't
shock you with blood and cries.

The 'vapour' of the last sentence is the idea of disembodied
spirit which seems less believable to Susan in this world of
flesh than the doctrine of the resurrection of the body.
Thinking of a scar on her lost lover's shoulder she reflects:
'That scar was part of his character as much as his jealousy.
And so I thought, do I want that body to be vapour (mine
yes, but his?) and I knew that I wanted that scar to exist
through all eternity.'

The first-person narrative achieves a new hardness and
clarity of outline. People who exist primarily as bodies,
desiring and repelling, are shown in fleshly concreteness;
much of the narrative is presented as the frustrated
memories of Bendrix, but they are usually sharp in physical
recall and dwell on details of the act of love with Sarah: 'the
brown indeterminate-coloured hair like a pool of liquor on
the parquet, the sweat on her forehead, the heavy breathing as though she had run a race and now like a young
athlete lay in the exhaustion of victory'. There is no 'vapour'
of romantic idealism about this love any more than there is
about the form of the bleeding suffering God who is a rival
to it; in the world in which Bendrix can betray his friend
ideals lack reality or become extinct: at Sarah's funeral Mrs
Bertram makes nothing of the pantheistic platitudes of the
clergyman and mishears 'the great All' as 'the great Auk'.

The narration also rearranges the fairly simple course of
events. In so doing it does much to enliven what Greene has
called 'the tedium of the time sequence'. Bendrix begins his
story two years after the end of the affair when he meets
Henry again on the Common and goes home with him to
encounter Sarah. From then on the story moves on two
levels of time: on one, the 'present', Bendrix tries to renew
contact with Sarah and takes her to lunch while at the same
time he hires Parkis to watch her; on the level of memory he

goes over their time together since their first meeting at a party at her home on the eve of the war. The first time sequence leads up through the false clue of her visits to Smythe to the discovery by Parkis of the apparently incriminating letter and finally of the journal. The second traces their affair to its climax in the bomb incident and Sarah's vow. Then Sarah's journal takes over and provides the link between the bomb incident in June 1944 and the 'present' in February 1946, thus joining the two sequences. The journal constitutes Book Three, and in Book Four Bendrix recounts his unsuccessful attempt to persuade Sarah to go away with him, when he dogs her to the church. At the end of that book he hears of her death from Henry. The fifth and last book completes Bendrix's narration with the account of his going to live with Henry, the funeral, and the events following on her death. The skilful recasting of the time sequence and particularly the dovetailing of the journal into the whole scheme is technically proficient in a manner that again makes one think of French rather than English parallels. Greene cannot command the precision of the French past tenses, as they are employed, for instance, in the early chapters of Flaubert's *Les confessions d'un jeune homme*, but he does what he can: we are reminded that the sections recalling the past are inserted into a narrative of the immediate past, the 'present' of the novel, by sentences like the following: 'Sarah and I used to have long arguments on jealousy'; 'It must have been some time in May 1940 when this argument broke out'; 'That evening I was still full of my hatred and distrust when I reached Piccadilly'.

The use of a journal (that of Édouard) together with the idea of a novel about a novelist who is writing a novel are found in André Gide's *Les Faux-monnayeurs* (The Counterfeiters, 1925), a work perhaps more admired by Greene's generation than it is today.

Since Bendrix, the narrator, is a novelist and also a man torn apart first by jealousy and then by loss, invention is, by the convention of the book, confined to his own creations which we do not read, and thus the text which he presents speaks all the more by the authority of pain and the licence of private confession than a novel not his novel affords him; it is of course a privileged licence to the *voyeur* reader who has the double assurance, that he is reading a report of something which might have happened (the promise for most novel readers), and that the report is by a specially informed and reliable witness. The taut immediacy of the narrative does not need to appeal to style because its appeal is directly to the only standard of the *voyeur* reader: something else he has seen. The obsessive hate and jealousy and sadness is no longer directed along metaphysical channels by an imposed imagery: when there is imagery it simply asks to be acknowledged as images of this life. Thus in the episode when Bendrix picks up a prostitute and then discovers that love for him has paralysed casual desire the image only extends observation to comprehend the basic sensual truth of youth in a face: 'I got a glimpse of something young, dark and happy and not yet spoiled: an animal that didn't yet recognize her captivity'. How different this is from the soaring melodramatic phrase that transmogrifies life, as when the morality pattern closes in on Scobie's vision and he sees the contents of Yusef's room as having 'an eternal air like the furnishings of hell'.

Bendrix speaks, then, with the authority of his pain and the often brutal directness of uninhibited confession. But he is in a novel, not his novel. He is the opposite of being an omniscient author: his jealousy and his ignorance of Sarah's motives lead him into a plot which is not of his willing; as the plot progresses through the engagement of the private detective and the consequent misunderstandings it slowly becomes apparent that Bendrix's point of view is a false perspective and that it must give way to that of another, an omniscient Author. Bendrix had sought out Sarah at first in order to obtain the stimulus to write a book; from the time when he fears that the love affair is drawing to an end he begins to see himself as a character who is being manipulated in a plot by someone else. In this plot it is inferred that only the saints come fully alive, like those characters who seem to an author to take charge of the story with a life of their own, and Sarah is such a character:

The saints, one would suppose, in a sense create themselves. They come alive. They are capable of the surprising act or word. They stand outside the plot, unconditioned by it. But we have to be pushed around. We have the obstinacy of non-existence. We are inextricably bound to the plot, and wearily God forces us, here and there, according to his intention, characters without poetry, without free will, whose only importance is that somewhere, at some time, we help to furnish the scene in which a living character moves and speaks, providing perhaps the saints with the opportunities for *their* free will.

In contrast to Sarah, Bendrix is selfish, demanding, and jealous in love. From the start her openness and natural kindness to others is stressed,

> All I noticed about her that first time was her beauty and her happiness and her way of touching people with her hands, as though she loved them. I can only recall one thing she said to me, apart from that statement with which she began — 'You do seem to dislike a lot of people'.

He, on the other hand, can feel no complete trust. He had demanded superiority in love and is alarmed by Sarah's beauty: 'I have always found it hard to feel sexual desire without some sense of superiority, mental or physical'. ' . . . in the act of love I could be arrogant, but alone I had only to look in the mirror to see doubt, in the shape of a lined face and a lame leg — why me? . . . Distrust grows with a lover's success'. He is bitter over the earlier lovers Sarah has had and when he learns from her journal who his real rival is he can only think of fighting with this illusion in order to win her back. She has been faithful to him with a 'sweetness and amplitude' of disposition, while he always lacks 'the winning cards, the cards of gentleness, humility and trust'.

Yet in spite of all these contrasts the moral level of the book, as distinct from the religious, somehow fails to come off. After reading the journal Bendrix's selfishness and

Sarah's goodness should stand out in glaring relief, and this is not so. There are several reasons. The sensual intensity of their love affair is one. They begin it in a dubious hotel room in Paddington rented by the hour; on another occasion they make love on the floor when Henry is ill in the room above; Sarah had had other lovers and realizes, in her period of deepest unhappiness when her vow keeps her from seeing Bendrix, that she could easily slip into prom-iscuity. Her abandonment to the flesh is shown as a sign of her goodness, her generous acceptance of others on their own terms, but this plays havoc with any moral judgment of Bendrix: we see them together as equals in a sensual embrace. Also, in spite of the fruits of her goodness in the cures of Smythe and Lance after her death, her sainthood does not appear to be something into which she grows but as an unsought agony forced upon her. What has antici-pated this painful surrender is the total abandonment of their passion: in a highly unplatonic way their bodily excess has prepared them for the total love of an incarnate God: as Sarah says in one of the last entries in the journal, the pages that Bendrix reads first:

> I might have taken a lifetime spending a little love at a time, eking it out here and there, on this man and that. But even the first time, in the hotel near Paddington, we spent all we had. You were there, teaching us to squander, like you taught the rich man, so that one day we might have nothing left except this love of You. But You are too good to me. When I ask You for pain, You give me peace. Give it him too. Give him my peace — he needs it more.

But two days later in the last entry she is writing: 'I'm tired and I don't want any more pain. I want Maurice. I want ordinary corrupt human love'. It is this sharing which unites them beyond moral distinctions, the sharing in ordinary corrupt human love which may put off corruption by wholeness of surrender. So that the miracle of change is like that described by Yeats in 'Easter 1916': 'And what if excess of love Bewildered them till they died?'. The sexual word 'spent' is audaciously successful if their love, and other human loves, bear a relation to what the theologians call *kenosis*, God's emptying of Himself.

Sarah's sainthood is ardent self-surrender rather than the habit of perfection though the last entries of the journal reveal her preparing painfully for the latter. In parallel fashion Bendrix's selfishness is qualified by the sheer domination of his point of view, the eloquent honesty of his frustration and rage (David Lodge has remarked on how the words love and hatred occur in close conjunction on nearly every page)[13]; and on the last page he is still the same man, moving without joy to a grudging recognition of his divine rival: 'O God, You've done enough, You've robbed me of enough, I'm too tired and old to learn to love, leave me alone for ever'. He may be in many ways an unappealing man, but a moral judgment like this applies only outside the possibility of fiction. Sarah loves him, Henry feels an affection for him, Parkis respects him, and, above all, the nervous intensity of the point of view he shares with his creator (just as he shares his working habits) blunts any critical sharpness in the rendering of his weaknesses, which are inseparable from his total nature. It is the same with the whisky priest and Scobie. The reader is so identified with their points of view that he takes little account of the former's drunkenness or the latter's capacity for knowing always what is best for other people.

Thus beyond all traits of character Sarah and Bendrix are involved together in bodily desire which cancels all other value. As he says at the end when he wonders whether to destroy her journal and decides to keep it: '. . . I was tired to death of the mind. I had lived for her body and I wanted her body'. When Sarah makes her vow after the explosion of the bomb downstairs, praying out of the doubt and disbelief she shares with him, she does it to protect Bendrix's body:

Let him be alive, and I *will* believe. Give him a chance. Let him have his happiness. Do this, and I'll believe . . . I love him and I'll do anything if you'll make him alive. I said very slowly, I'll give him up for ever, only let him be alive with a chance.

To pray out of doubt like this is to gamble. It is again to wager the wager of Pascal in which nothing can be lost and everything may be gained. Greene has shown an interest in the wager since the day on Berkhamstead Common when he span the chambers of a revolver pressed to his head, although he never felt the need to play Russian roulette again. Scobie's prayer that the child might have peace and his own peace be taken is another example. *Loser Takes All*(1955) involves comic variations on the ancient theme that the winner does not gain emotional happiness. To gamble is to resist the huge boredom of modern life; it is to escape from its apparent blind determinism. The gambler inserts a wedge into the deterministic mechanism and by choosing one colour rather than another, by venturing on a prediction, asserts his individuality. He stakes a claim to freedom, even within the absurdly narrow range of choices represented by numbers or counters, and at the same time he is asking to act in harmony with the purpose of things, the throw of the dice. By his gamble of guessing at the pattern he is maintaining the existence of the pattern; by seeking happiness as a free person choosing the world he implies his complementary relationship to a personal and loving creator. Sarah's action is not so peculiar because all gamblers pray when they throw the dice, 'give me a five to keep me alive', and such like. Her prayer is a natural continuation of the gamble of love. Michelet writes that 'Love is a lottery. Grace is a lottery'. He makes this statement when discussing the difference between the novel and history: the novel deals in individual destiny, the realm of chance, while history traces the long, slow, regular process of great collective interests.[14] Love and grace operate in Greene's novel as sudden *coups de foudre* and it is difficult to see how his afterthought of rewriting it as a long cumulative chain of coincidences could have avoided imposing on the beauty of individual chance the stately inevitability of history.

The wager staked by Sarah in the sudden impulse of total love that must, since the wager is successful, be also the moment of grace, has an exceptional feature. Gamblers usually predict the future. But Sarah's offer of belief to a hidden God in whom she does not yet believe is contingent on that God 'making him alive'. She has just seen his hand protruding from under the fallen front door and she thinks with the instinct of her love that he is dead:

> I touched his hand: I could have sworn it was a dead hand. When two people have loved each other, they can't disguise a lack of tenderness in a kiss, and wouldn't I have recognized life if there was any of it left in touching his hand? I knew that if I took his hand and pulled it towards me, it would come away, all by itself, from under the door.

Her prayer is that either he lives or that he may be restored to life — 'make him alive'. The latter presumption, like the later presumptions of miracles, is left open with the evidence ambiguous, in this case simply the strange blank state of mind experienced by Bendrix as he recovers consciousness under the door. ' . . . I was completely free from anxiety, jealousy, insecurity, hate: my mind was a blank sheet on which somebody had just been on the point of writing a message of happiness'. The suggestion is that Bendrix is for some instants dead and that Sarah's prayer works retrospectively to bring him back to life. There is a close parallel with Greene's play *The Potting Shed* (1957) in which Father William Callifer offers his faith for the life of his nephew James who has hanged himself. James, who had been pronounced dead, is revived, and the priest loses his faith and becomes an alcoholic. It is Sarah's situation in reverse. Her wager has another feature that is different from the usual simple stake of the gambler on this number or that card: she asks not only for her lover's life to be preserved or returned, but for him to have his happiness and to be given a chance. Bendrix has hardly any happiness after the flying bomb and it can be inferred that his chance is to come in the future with what he makes of the evidence of God's purpose in Sarah's leap into faith and self-denial and the cures of Smythe and Lance. Old and tired, he may still unlearn hatred and take a chance on the being he has come to acknowledge to exist.

The leap of faith, a desperate bid for life in Sarah's case, a bitter forcing of his ingrained prejudices in that of Bendrix, is as far removed from rational proof as it is from religious sentiment. Religion is a total existential choice which operates on a different plane from consecutive reasoning. Hence the futility of Smythe and his like grubbing away with rationalistic objections. The decision for Sarah is not to discriminate between different elements in Biblical or traditional doctrine, but to submit as to a person. Like the respectable bourgeois Catholic the Catholic intellectual has usually been a target for Greene; a systematic theology can be an obstacle to the inquirer as well as a diversion to the believer: on this topic Greene quotes his own story *A Visit to Morin* (1957) in the 1974 introduction to *A Burnt-Out Case*: 'A man can accept anything to do with God until scholars begin to go into details and the implications. A man can accept the Trinity, but the arguments that follow . . . I would never try to determine some point in differential calculus with a two-times-two table. You end by disbelieving the calculus . . . I used to believe in Revelation, but I never believed in the capacity of the human mind'. The winning cards that Bendrix said he lacked were, as well as gentleness and humility, trust. Humanist pride in the mind's capacity for understanding the world ends in 'vapour'. If there is hope for Bendrix at the end it is because he has become 'tired to death of the mind'. When Sarah submits she wishes to take all on trust with the abandon that the theologians call fideism:

> I believe there's a God — I believe the whole bag of tricks; there's nothing I don't believe; they could subdivide the Trinity into a dozen parts and I'd believe. They could dig up records that proved Christ had been invented by Pilate to get himself promoted, and I'd believe just the same. I've caught belief like a disease. I've fallen into belief like I fell in love . . . I fought belief longer than I fought love, but I haven't any fight left.

Like its predecessors *The End of the Affair* follows the French Catholic tradition in its presentation of an extreme religious situation, the co-existence of sin and grace, the challenge to God, and the theme of sacrificing one's entire happiness for that of another; and yet it makes a very different impression from the earlier Catholic novels. This is partly because of the narrative and stylistic innovations already described. It is also owing to the humanity of Sarah's husband and of Parkis. These two exist outside the charmed duo of love and grace. Their ordinary humanity is respected and the respect foreshadows the understanding comedy of the novels that are to follow. Henry is seen through the eyes of Bendrix and initially through his contempt for the man he is deceiving. His conventionality and innocence are unobtrusively sketched. But a personal impression grows in spite of the fact that he is not identified by any of those easy marks of feature, dress or gesture to which the novelist sometimes resorts. More subtly, the behaviour selected draws towards the emotional centre of a quiet man of fixed habits and enlists sympathy even while Bendrix is supposed to be mocking him. There is for instance his dislike of being under obligation as a guest and his unease when he is taken out to lunch. 'I remember Henry chose a Vienna steak — it was a mark of his innocence. I really believe that he had no idea of what he was ordering and expected something like a Wiener Schnitzel. Playing as he was away from the home ground, he was too ill at ease to comment on the dish and somehow he managed to ram the pink soggy mixture down'. Gradually his real affection for Sarah emerges, and so does his fondness for Bendrix. After her death he asks him to stay the night and then invites him to move across the Common and share the house. The sense of their sharing her continued presence is conveyed all the more effectively by the unimaginative Henry: 'I don't know how to express it. Because she's always away, she's never away. You see, she's never anywhere else. She's not having lunch with anybody, she's not at a cinema with you. There's nowhere for her to be but at home'.

The fondness between the two men grows. When they entertain Father Crompton and discuss the coincidence of the inscription in Sarah's children's book and Lance's recovery, Bendrix breaks out in a rage, cursing Sarah and insulting the priest. In bed at night he feels remorse and performs a small act of solicitude for Henry that is not in his character:

> I was sorry I had spoken like that about Sarah in front of Henry. The priest had said there was nothing we could do that some saint had not done. That might be true of murder and adultery, the spectacular sins, but could a saint ever have been guilty of envy and meanness? My hate was as petty as my love. I opened the door softly and looked in at Henry. He lay asleep with the light on and his arm shielding his eyes. With the eyes hidden there was an anonymity about the whole body. He was just a man — one of us. He was like the first enemy soldier a man encounters on a battlefield, dead and indistinguishable, not a White or a Red, but just a human being like himself. I put two biscuits by his bed in case he woke and turned the light out.

As usual a small action, only superficially analysed by the actor, represents a large movement of spiritual force. Bendrix has attained a degree of self-knowledge and with it a recognition of another human being under the mask of the suburban civil servant. If Bendrix is to take the chance Sarah had claimed for him in addition to his life, it will be in company with Henry. At the end when the coincidences are closing in on them he is steering Henry protectively towards the pub, lover and husband reconciled: '. . . I put my hand on Henry's arm and held it there; I had to be strong for both of us now, and he wasn't seriously worried yet'.

Parkis, the private detective, a decent man dedicated to the etiquette of his profession and determined to bring up his son to it, is a Dickensian creation. He is given the idiom of his trade, long-winded but careful in detail: 'Forgive all the details, Mr Bendrix, but in my profession we are trained to put things in order and explain first things first, so the judge can't complain he hasn't been given the facts plainly'. Professional idiom is given a touch of fine whimsy that shades into sentimental pathos; Parkis is totally devoid of prurience or seediness: he is devoted to Sarah who is always 'a very fine lady' or 'a lady of great kindness'. He only oversteps the rules of his profession when he asks to borrow the children's book from Henry and that is because of his love for his son Lance. 'So that was why I bothered Mr Miles and deceived him of which I am ashamed there not being a professional reason, only my poor boy'.

The serious comedy of Henry Miles and the 'character' comedy of Parkis are closely enough involved with the main story of Bendrix and Sarah to make the element of the mysterious and the inexplicable less abrupt (as it is thrust forward, for instance, in the discovery of Sarah's baptism). Ordinary goodness and decency have their way so that the warfare against complacent materialism is not confined to an élite of converted *âmes damnés*. The broadening and mellowing of values is to be still more pronounced in subsequent novels.

Smythe and Father Crompton are more lightly sketched. In the former case this is perhaps a disadvantage on account of his importance in the plot: he illustrates the mysterious working of Sarah's charity, and it is his experience which decisively shakes Bendrix's scepticism. But he is too much a model figure of an atheist whose rationalism is, literally, skin deep, being dependent on the trauma of his birth-mark. There is a difficulty, too, about his being a handsome man *in spite* of the birth-mark: we should expect his good looks either to cause people to overlook the deformity or to be nullified by it. This imperfect realization of a character makes the scene in which Sarah kisses the birth-mark merely a text-book illustration of her charity, though it is almost redeemed when Smythe says that he will not see her again because he cannot bear her pity. Father Crompton is harsh, ugly and without social manners. He completes the gallery of priests who at the climax of each of the Catholic novels remind characters and readers of the profound mystery of God's actions; he joins the priest with a catarrhal wheeze, and Father Rank. He pronounces harshly and dogmatically on man's incomprehension: 'St Augustine asked where time came from. He said it came out of the future which didn't exist yet, into the present that had no duration, and went into the past which had ceased to exist. I don't know that we can understand time any better than a child'.

As in *The Heart of the Matter* reason is imprisoned within its own constructions and only the heart can find out the truth. Extreme scepticism goes along with fideism; it was the same with Rochester on his death-bed and Dryden in *Religio Laici* during Greene's favourite literary age, the Restoration. If it be asked of *The Heart of the Matter* or of *The End of the Affair* why persons like the protagonists should choose a Church so organized in structure and so committed to reasoned exposition of faith and morals, the answer is that Catholicism in the twentieth century, by its retention of the whole deposit of faith, represents the extreme rejection of the modern world on behalf of the religious sense, and the drawing up of battle lines on two fronts, against materialism and against liberal philosophizing, 'vapour'. The intellectual origins of this brand of Catholicism go back to the Decadents and beyond them to the Romantic movement. But ten years after the publication of *The End of the Affair*, the debates of the Second Vatican Council produced an *aggiornamento*, an attempt by the Catholic Church to come to terms with the modern world. The result was, in liturgy and in much else, to make the Church less distinctive and therefore a less suitable vehicle for that extreme separation of the mysterious from the mundane which the alienated intellectual demanded as the solvent for his alienation. But before the Second Vatican Council met Greene had stopped writing Catholic novels like those he had already written.

III

The 1950s were described by Greene as for him a period of great unrest. Physical restlessness he certainly demonstrated. In the years immediately after the 1939–45 war he visited Vienna, gaining material for *The Third Man* (published 1950), his film script for Carol Reed, and he was in Prague at the time of the Communist takeover of Czechoslovakia. He was then successively in Malaya during the

Emergency as a correspondent of *Life* (1951); four times in
Vietnam (1951–55) reporting the French war there for
the *Sunday Times* and *Le Figaro*; in Kenya reporting the Mau
Mau rebellion for the *Sunday Times* (1953); briefly in
Communist Poland (1956); in a leper colony in the Belgian
Congo when the struggle for independence was beginning
(1958–9); and at various times in Puerto Rico, Haiti and
Cuba, the two latter countries both in a state of oppressive
or revolutionary violence (at various dates between 1954
and 1963). He has described these journeys as escapes from
a manic-depressive temperament designed to recapture the
insecurity he had enjoyed during the three blitzes on
London. None of these expeditions was made in search of
material for novels but they brought it all the same. It was
not until the mid–1960s that Greene was to establish a
permanent home outside England, but the travels were to
continue.

There are no more Catholic novels after *The End of the
Affair*. Ten years later *A Burnt-Out Case* (1961) is his farewell
to that phase of his work. His experience of the dangers of
success and the misinterpretation of his work, especially *The
Heart of the Matter*, as if it were a crusading tract, is described
in the 1974 introduction to *A Burnt-Out Case*. Priests and
laity, American and of other nationalities, besought his
advice on the most intimate personal problems. He declares
how used and exhausted he felt by these victims of religion:

> The vision of faith as an untroubled sea was lost for ever;
> it was more like a tempest in which the lucky were
> engulfed and lost, and the unfortunate survived to be
> flung battered and bleeding on the shore. A better man
> could have found a life's work on the margin of that cruel
> sea, but my own course of life gave me no confidence in
> any aid I might proffer.

It was in this period, he says, that the characters in *A
Burnt-Out Case* were born — Querry, the artist who has left
the Church, and Father Thomas, the priest who is obsessed
by his spiritual problems; and he admitted in a letter to his
friend Evelyn Waugh, who had been troubled by the book,

that although there was no crude identification of the author with Querry he shared some of his reactions: 'I suppose the points where an author is in agreement with his character lend what force or warmth there is to the expression'. The intention of the book was, he claims, to render various states or moods of belief and unbelief. Even on these terms the change from what has gone before is enormous; for the novel is a study of a man who has lost his faith and lives in a condition of spiritual indifference; and it includes another character, Dr Colin, treated with approval, who represents 'a settled and easy atheism'.

In the 1974 introduction, and elsewhere, Greene has vigorously disclaimed the role of a teacher; he quotes the passage in *The Idea of a University* where Newman argues eloquently that there cannot be a Christian literature since this would mean a sinless literature of sinful man, a contradiction in terms. However Newman's argument is beside the point. It applies only to Christian literature in the sense of idealized images of behaviour, as it might be envisaged by pious nineteenth-century reviewers, or by readers who approved of Richardson's *Clarissa* and condemned Fielding's *Tom Jones*. Greene on the contrary had depicted sinful man with the sin left in; so had Fielding and Dostoyevsky, and both have, at different times, been regarded as great Christian writers. So while his caution against being considered as a preacher or a theologian has been necessary for some readers it cannot be denied that the novels from *Brighton Rock* to *The End of the Affair* are dominated by their presentation of sin, individual responsibility, and the relation of man to God. In *A Burnt-Out Case* this imaginative pressure seems to be relaxed, or rather to work in reverse, the intellectual Catholic Rycker being seen to misinterpret everything in terms of fashionable theology. The novels of the preceding decade had already exhibited this relaxation and in them we no longer find the *extreme* religious situation: the damnation, the challenge, the sacrifice, the vow, the wager, the miracle. This is the case with *The Quiet American* (1955) and *Our Man in Havana* (1958), as well as the 'entertainments' *The Third Man* (1950) and *Loser Takes All* (1955).

Irritation with the manner in which his work was misinterpreted may be a contributory, but not a sufficient reason for a decisive change in direction. Greene admits that new elements were now introduced into his fiction. He has always been inclined to stress the unconscious level at which most important literary decisions are taken; it is largely on account of a belief in the serious preliminary work of the unconscious that he can repel religious or philosophical questions and prefer to discuss his work purely in terms of the construction and technique imposed on given material.[15] At the end of the introduction he throws out an observation that is both revealing and tantalizing. After referring to Unamuno's *Life and Death of Don Quixote*, he speaks of his own passionate interest in works of theology in the period when his Catholic novels and the plays *The Living Room* and *The Potting Shed* had offended many Catholics. He then states in conclusion:

> . . . at the end of a long journey, without knowing myself the course I had been taking, I found myself, in *A Visit to Morin* and *A Burnt-Out Case*, in that tragi-comic region of La Mancha where I expect to stay. Even my Marxist critics shared a characteristic with Waugh — they were too concerned with faith or no faith to notice that in the course of the blackest book I have written I had discovered Comedy.

The statement is elliptic to say the least. It offers a clue rather than a revelation about the reason for his discovery of comedy and his conception of the comic. The clue derives from Cervantes: the essence of comedy in *Don Quixote* is the pairing of significant opposites who complement each other's qualities: they divide the world between their mutual obsessions. Quixotism rejects the world of appearances in favour of the ideal; Sanchism tries to limit its vision to the concrete and the visible. In the course of their unending dialogue they each undergo subtle conversions to the contrary point of view as well as fierce confrontations. The sacrificial absolutism of the protagonists of Greene's Catholic novels already has something in

common with the Quixotic ideal;[16] for Scobie and Sarah
Miles their duty means the rejection of the standards
prescribed by common sense and common prudence, even
of life and health. The Quixotic dialectic is also potentially
there before its full emergence in the region of La Mancha.
It is present in the dualities Pinkie/Ida and Priest/
Lieutenant, even in the rivalry for Sarah between the
aggressive and amorous writer Bendrix and the stay-at-
home public servant Henry Miles. The change that comes is
the granting of fair play to either side of the equation so that
in place of the tragic climax which changes everything there
is substituted comedy or tragi-comedy: some characters are
left on the scene the wiser, and if some die, death comes not
as a grand consciously chosen climax but as the last
inconsequential incident in a life that is makeshift and
accidental. For the full explanation of the Cervantes hint we
have to look at Greene's last book *Monsignor Quixote* (1982)
where the theme becomes explicit. But in the work of the
1950s and 1960s talents were released which had previously
been restricted. Idiosyncratic and ambiguous creations like
Mr Prewett, the expatriate dentist, Captain Fellows, Yusef,
and Parkis are dominated by the obsessive core of the
novels in which they occur, as moths hover round a lamp;
now they are given a freer space in which to grow.

Reaction against his own reputation and the wish to
develop a talent for comedy cannot furnish the whole
reason for Greene's abandoning the formula of the extreme religious situation and with it the Catholic phase of
his fiction. In ceasing to portray struggles of conscience
which had been so feelingly enacted he indicates that the
writer has passed beyond the struggle. The underlying
reason is psychological and spiritual. Greene's evasiveness
about his personal life, his short-hand minor disclosures
which usually fabricate a major withholding, are elevated
into an art form in his two 'autobiographical' books. The
critic is uneasy because, apart from suspecting a profound
cause for the change in direction, his attempt to analyse it is
likely to be doomed. Greene has preferred to talk like
Conrad or James of problems of construction and to brush
aside theology; the introductions to the Collected Edition

are mines of information on milieux, materials and a craftsman's problems from book to book, but they also constitute a smoke-screen. Greene is so apparently frank in recounting his opium-taking in Indo-China, so apparently intimate with the reader in mentioning his love affairs (but really so hugely general) that to suggest that the most important things are left out seems an intrusion on privacy. The critic does not want to be cast in the role of a religious sentimentalist like Rycker or an investigative journalist like Parkinson; these characters are savagely handled in *A Burnt-Out Case*. And if the critic guesses at some personal crisis of faith he is liable to elicit the reply Marie Rycker receives from the author's hero: 'I warned you not to attach real characters to my story'.

Greene was converted to Catholicism in 1926 when he had only lately left Oxford and was working in Nottingham on a local paper. He was planning to marry a Catholic and began undertaking instruction in the thought that he should learn the nature and limits of the beliefs she held. The unusual features of his attitude, as he describes it in *A Sort of Life*, were his total disbelief in the supernatural and a consequent absence of any form of religious emotion or inclination. The broad Anglicanism of his parents and school had easily departed leaving no deposit. In the course of his instruction he argued to defend his atheism and finally became convinced on intellectual grounds of 'the probable existence of something we call God'. At the same time he realized that after admitting even the possibility of the existence of a supreme and omniscient power 'nothing afterwards could seem impossible'. From one aspect his was a purely intellectual conversion; but from another, on account of his distrust of rational and philosophical grounds, it was an act of total commitment, a wager in the spirit of Pascal. In the terms of the latter he had given his reasonable assent: now this was to be followed by the practice of the faith (*la coûtume*), and for *l'inspiration* he was to wait until later; the Christians of the novels — Rose, the whisky priest, that *anima naturaliter* Sarah — certainly exhibit the humiliations which Pascal says prepare the soul for divine inspiration. But the reasonable assent was always tempered by a sense of the limitations of the intellectual steps leading up to it and a corresponding recognition of the mystery of the existence of God. He was affected by the gloomy neo-Gothic cathedral of Nottingham because it represented 'the inconceivable and the incredible'. He could have said with Pascal

> C'est le coeur qui sent Dieu, et non la raison. Voilà ce que c'est que la foi: Dieu sensible au coeur, non à la raison.[17] (It is the heart that perceives God, not the reason. There lies the essence of faith: God responsive to the heart, not to the reason.)

The scepticism is integrated into faith as it was for Pascal; the God is a hidden God but he is none the less believed in:

> Dieu étant ainsi caché, toute religion qui ne dit pas que Dieu est caché n'est pas véritable; et toute religion qui n'en rend pas la raison n'est pas instruisante. La nôtre fait tout cela: *Vere tu es Deus absconditus*.[18] (God being thus hidden, all religion which does not say that God is hidden is not true; and all religion which does not offer a reason for it is incapable of teaching us. But our religion does just that: *Truly thou art a hidden God*.)

The sceptical strain in Greene's thought on religion and the manner in which it is integrated into faith recalls Pascal's *Pensées*; it is a state of mind which is powerfully described in the conclusion to T.S. Eliot's essay 'The *Pensées* of Pascal' in a passage which might have been designed to render Greene's temperamental blend of doubt and existential commitment (the critic who wrote of 'the boredom, the horror, and the glory' must have been congenial to Greene in the period before the war as a mind, and not only as a Christian apologist):

> For every man who thinks and lives by thought must have his own scepticism, that which stops at the question, that which ends in denial, or that which leads to faith and which is somehow integrated in the faith which trans-

cends it . . . the demon of doubt which is inseparable
from the spirit of belief.

   . . . those who doubt, but who have the mind to
conceive, and the sensibility to feel, the disorder, the
futility, the meaninglessness, the mystery of life and
suffering, and who can only find peace through a
satisfaction of the whole being.[19]

Ideas apart, the double claim here to intellectual severity
and to sensibility generates a particular brand of poetic
emotion as does Greene in his novels. The influence is
Pascal, but also Newman: the last paragraph with its
rhetorical catalogue of human disorders echoes the reso-
nances of the famous passage on our 'aboriginal calamity'
used as an epigraph to *The Lawless Roads*. That disorder is
evident in human life as suffering. If the scepticism leads to
faith, the suffering may become meaningful, and it is the
matter (not the message) of Greene's fiction which contains
such meaning. Either everything is absurd or the void must
be filled by a God with a final end in view. This is
particularly the matter of *A Burnt-Out Case*. Thus the vision
of disorder does not serve merely as a critique of optimistic
liberal attitudes; it leads directly to an acknowledgment of
the hidden God who lies beyond human reasoning. Later
statements that seem startlingly lax in their disregard for
orthodox formulations simply represent a return to this
original Christian and individual scepticism, as for instance
when Greene expresses dislike of the word God on account
of its anthropomorphic associations, or declares that 'with
the approach of death I care less and less about religious
truth'. The wager is all: the leap across the gap into belief in
the reality of the hidden God shows up the limitations of
philosophical and religious language. Behaviour is all, and
so Greene comes eventually in his fiction to the leap of total
surrender, which is faith, being made by those outside the
Church; he arrives at the problem which the middle ages
had conceived as that of the virtuous pagan: was Trajan in
heaven? But the twentieth-century obverse of the problem
is, if he was saved, then why the Church and the sacraments? A rewording of the question is to ask why there are

many religions in the world instead of one religion. Pascal's answer to this question seems to be that the existence of other faiths (with which should be included secularism or atheistic humanism) is evidence of the disorder of a fallen world. The disorder is the cause of God's being hidden, or at any rate partly hidden, and the other faiths are false because they proclaim gods which are wholly and impossibly revealed.

The writer who has passed beyond the stage of writing about struggles of conscience and spiritual crises thus remains consistent to his earliest insights; the continuing use of the evidence of dreams shows an approach from the human side to a partial revelation of the hidden God: a recognition of the authority of the unconscious which was there since the Kenneth Richmond analysis and which is in its aspirations towards a reconciling source more Jungian than Freudian, in spite of his stated preferences for the latter school.[20]

The giving up of novels about struggles of conscience has, however, also a more purely technical cause. By *The End of the Affair* it is to be suspected that a cycle of novels had written itself out. From *Brighton Rock* to *The Power and the Glory*, and on to *The Heart of the Matter* the pack was dexterously reshuffled (an unfair metaphor now for the transmuted pain that goes into these books) and then with the daringly trans-fictional approach to the hidden God in *The End of the Affair* the cycle was over. Writing, and even suffering, must in future take a different direction.

A Burnt-Out Case is built on two metaphors. In the course of the book they come to reflect each other and finally to coalesce. The first is the pathology of leprosy. When the disease has run its course and the smear-tests remain negative, even though fingers and toes may have gone, there is no more degeneration of tissue and no possibility of infecting others. Querry has reached a stage of spiritual and emotional atrophy which is like this: he is a famous Catholic architect who is utterly disillusioned with his career and who has ceased to design buildings. He is also at a crisis in his personal life and can no longer love or feel interest in other people. We encounter him on the river steamer travelling down a tributary of the Congo to bury himself away in the leper colony. But Querry's loss of creative power is itself a metaphor, and not only of the author's disenchantment with his Catholic readers and critics. It stands too for the crisis of writer and man looking back in late career on his achievement and feeling nothing but emptiness of spirit; only he is in the position to savour fully the barrenness of his own ego, and in this way the second metaphor also has application to any creative mind in the modern age when artistic achievement is measured not in works but in individual biographies. The reader is likely to equate Querry, the Catholic architect, with Greene, the Catholic novelist (as has been pointed out by Frank Kermode[21]). Both are dissatisfied by the reputations thrust upon them by the world; both suffer from a vast boredom and are prepared to run to the end of the earth to escape it, though Querry's escape is into complete isolation, not like Greene's into dangerous action.

More important than the autobiographical element, which Greene prefers to call sharing 'reactions of mine' with a character, is the fact that he is now dealing with problems created by his earlier work. He has passed beyond a phase of imaginative inventiveness in character and situation just as he has discarded the earlier descriptive technique which was poetic and expressionist. By the standard of realistic observation he is writing better novels and is confronting the real world, Catholic and secular, more directly without the intervention of a religious idea. In the climax of the story the gamble of faith is only present as a remote conditional clause. But a gamble there is all the same: Querry chooses his life and death at an airport by arbitrarily selecting a destination like a roulette player putting a stake on a number. With only a razor, a toothbrush and a letter of credit from an American bank, he asks for a flight to Tokyo and then switches to an African flight when he sees African names on the indicator.

In Africa man cannot deceive himself or avoid the fate prescribed by his own character. So far the background functions as it does in *The Heart of the Matter* but the Congo of *A Burnt-Out Case* is a much less oppressive and exhausting region than the Coast in that book or the Mexico of *The Power and the Glory*. In his early days at the *leproserie* Querry begins to find something like peace in the country and there is that suggestion of an idyllic primitive life which we have seen in a reflection in *Journey Without Maps*. He takes a book and sits on an old tin barge by the bank of the river and contemplates a scene of natural contentment:

> The cold grey trunks, unbroken by branches, curved a little this way and a little that, giving them a kind of reptilian life. Porcelain-white birds stood on the backs of coffee-coloured cows, and once for a whole hour he watched a family who sat in a pirogue by the bank doing nothing; the mother wore a bright yellow dress, the man, wrinkled like bark, sat bent over a paddle he never used, and a girl with a baby on her lap smiled and smiled like an open piano.

The birds and the family in the pirogue had been seen by Greene on his journey to the Congo in 1959 when the book was being planned. Like the pink laterite roads of the Coast in the evening, this Africa is attractive and comforting; as he had said in an earlier African journal; 'The hot sweet smell from the land . . . it will always be to me the smell of Africa, and Africa will always be the Africa of the Victorian atlas, the blank unexplored continent the shape of the human heart.'[22] As the name Querry suggests, he is a man who asks a question of life concerning its meaning or absence of meaning but also one who goes on a journey of exploration into the dark continent, journeying to find himself where the Victorian travellers had looked for the source of rivers. Greene has some comments on Conrad's *Heart of Darkness* in *In Search of a Character*. He disapproves of that very universalization of the episode of Kurtz which has so captured the majority of twentieth-century critics: 'It is as if Conrad has taken an episode in his own life, and tried to lend it, for the sake of "literature", a greater significance than it will hold'.[23] The detached, almost casual treatment of Querry and of the 'reactions of my own' he shares with him deliberately stops short of this sort of metaphysical straining.

The African background is also less oppressive and more attractive because it throws into relief the abnormal world of the lepers. The description of their symptoms affords a complete image for human suffering and degradation. The preoccupation with deformity now finds a single comprehensive expression;

> One of the catechists, a man who had reached the limit of mutilation, having lost nose, fingers, toes (he looked as though he had been lopped, scraped, and tidied by a knife), fathered a baby with the woman, crippled by polio, who could only crawl upon the ground dragging her dwarfed legs behind her.

As when he gives a wooden leg to the old man living underground in 'Under the Garden' and a cleft palate to his wife, what Greene has to state is that mutilation and deformity provide the natural condition for mankind. But it is also natural for human beings to resist disease and help the mutilated; as with the desperate humanism of Rieux and the others fighting the plague in Camus' *La peste*, the fathers of the community pursue their work in their different ways: they furnish a cross-section of human types, the simple but competent superior with a cheroot always in his mouth, the neurotic discontent Father Thomas, 'with eyes sunk like stones in the pale clay of his face'; most important of all there is the lay medical officer Dr Colin who is an atheist and a courageous enemy of leprosy. His philosophy of life is not hostile to Christianity seeing it as a necessary stage in evolution. Even the expression of a sympathetic interest in such a character is a great innovation in Greene and it removes us wholly from the atmosphere of the Catholic novels:

> 'I want to be on the side of change . . . if I had been born an amoeba who could think, I would have dreamed of the day of the primates . . . Evolution, as far as we can tell, has lodged itself finally in the brains of man . . . We can't avoid it. We are riding a great ninth evolutionary wave. Even the Christian myth is part of the wave, and perhaps, who knows, it may be the most valuable part. Suppose

love were to evolve as rapidly in our brains as technical
skill has done. In isolated cases it may have done, in the
saints . . . in Christ, if the man really existed'.

The idea of evolutionary development continuing in the
human brain suggests an acquaintance with the writings of
Teilhard de Chardin,[24] but the hint of the supremacy of
love recalls one of Greene's favourite early poets, Browning. It comes close to the intuition of a loving creator by
Karshish the Arab physician:

> The very God! think, Abib; dost thou think?
> So, the All-great, were the All-Loving too—[25]

Querry comes to the *leproserie* thinking he is one of the
mutilated; he is wrong about himself as is demonstrated
when in two ways he shows himself capable of human
feeling and interest. First, he feels a close sympathy for his
servant Deo Gratias, a burnt-out leper without fingers or
toes who can nevertheless hop about and perform simple
tasks. Deo Gratias goes off one night, presumably to attend
a pagan ceremony of his tribe, and does not return. Querry
goes after him and finds that he has sprained his ankle and
fallen in a shallow pool; he stays by him all night and brings
him back in the morning. 'Interest began to move painfully
like a nerve that has been frozen.' During the night Deo
Gratias had uttered the word 'Pendele' and Querry extracts
from him that it means the village where he grew up with
his mother, where they danced, where there was a waterfall
and where they were happy. It is like the moment of peace
in the jungle found by Scobie; Querry tells the Doctor that
he will know where to look for him if he should be missing
and the Doctor realizes that he has perpetrated a joke and is
therefore in hope of recovery.

The other sign of the revival of life in him is his agreeing
to be of use to the *leproserie* by designing the new hospital.
He collaborates with Colin and the fathers and is gradually
being restored to the human community. He feels 'as
though he were on the verge of acceptance into a new
country' when an absurd chain of grotesque incidents and

misunderstandings deprives him of his chance of happiness. The impact on his life of the journalist Parkinson and of the Catholic intellectual Rycker and his young wife is more pathetic than tragic, an affair of inflated news exposure, a bedroom meeting, an unfounded suspicion, a drama constructed from the ingredients of French farce but leading inexorably to the death of Querry. It strikes one that the real life of the book is the steady dedicated work of the *leproserie*, as it should have been for Querry, repetitive but with the hope of better cures in the future without mutilations; outside the community in the brittle *colon* life of the Europeans, everything, including love and sanctity, is turned into a news story or an affectation. Rycker is an odious prig who has failed a vocation with the Jesuits and feels badly done by for that. He calles Querry 'the Querry' and thinks that his whole attachment to the *leproserie* and especially his charity in staying the night with Deo Gratias show the self-denial of the saint. However much Querry assures him that he has long stopped praying or going to Mass, he refuses to take his conduct as affording anything but further signs of aridity and saintly humiliation.

Then Parkinson arrives from reporting the civil disturbances in another part of the country. He is a burlesque, but a very funny burlesque, of the conventional hard-drinking journalist with an insufficient respect for truth. His huge body is carried from the river-boat sweating with malaria, as he drops inaccurate quotations and misinformation. ' . . . three weeks by boat to reach this wild territory. Struck down after seven days by the bites of tsetse flies and mosquitoes I was carried ashore unconscious. Where once Stanley battled his way with Maxim guns, another fight is being waged — this time in the cause of the African — against the deadly infection of leprosy . . . woke from my fever to find myself a patient in a leper hospital.' He produces a ridiculous article on Querry, the first of a series, which is translated in *Paris Dimanche*, 'An Architect of Souls, The Hermit of the Congo'. He has obtained his information from Rycker, and Querry decides to confront Rycker and prevent any further attacks on his privacy. Rycker's wife Marie prevails on him to drive her into the provincial capital so that she can consult a doctor about her possible pregnancy. He is compromised by being in her room at night when Parkinson is on the same corridor but he does not touch her. To him she is a mere child but he does not know that she is both completely egoistic and mischievous. She will use Querry in order to get away from a husband she cannot bear and return to middle-class life in Brussels. She therefore tells Rycker that she is pregnant by Querry and sets off to the *leproserie* pursued by her husband.

Arrived at the mission where there is a special celebration for the completion of the hospital, she has a brief interview with Querry; she is wholly unabashed by her lie which has ruined him and his conclusion afterwards is 'God protect us from all innocence'. It is noteworthy that the usual theme of the love of an older man for a young and unformed girl for whom he feels an unbearable pity here takes a different character: Querry has some pity for Marie in her unhappy marriage, but there is no love on either side, only the slightest flirtation, and the usual dangerous consequences of pity are really due more to Marie's unscrupulous deception. Rycker meets and shoots Querry outside the Doctor's bungalow in circumstances of black farce. There is a theatrical storm. '"We shall all feel better for a night's sleep. And a cold shower in the morning," he [one of the brothers] added, and as though to illustrate his words, a waterfall of rain suddenly descended on them.'

Querry gives one of his strange-sounding laughs: it is not clear whether he is laughing at the farcical coincidence of the rain and Brother Philippe's words, or at himself, as he suggests when he is dying, but Rycker, swollen with jealous rage, thinks he is laughing at him and fires. As Querry dies he is heard saying, 'Absurd, this is absurd or else . . . ' There have been interrupted last words before but never so trivial and ambiguous as these. Querry has tried to be of use. He has rehabilitated himself and even tried to help Marie. He is not guilty in his new life, though Marie has indirectly punished him for the other women whom he has exploited; his death is neither an offering nor a punishment. Perhaps in the world of individual action which, unlike the constructive action of the mission, is wholly comic, it is absurd:

perhaps as ever the way is left open that it may not be so. He
may even have died to save Marie who will get an annul-
ment from her husband who, in turn, will have a light and
happy imprisonment, reading scholastic theology and preparing to re-enter the priesthood. Perhaps he has even died
to save Rycker and if that is not absurd it is certainly comic.

Before the perfunctory drama of the Querry-Marie-
Rycker plot the story moves slowly and out of the six parts
into which it is divided the fifth is almost wholly occupied
with philosophical discussion between Querry and Dr
Colin. The first half beautifully sets the workings and
quality of the leper mission and establishes character, but
there is little incident apart from the rescue of Deo Gratias
and the first abortive visit of Marie Rycker to Querry. There
are however little clues here to her unhappiness with
Rycker and her potential for danger. The action and its
movement into real danger quickens with the arrival of
Parkinson. But at the heart of the farce-like action we are
again halted by the long fable of the king and the jewels
which Querry tells Marie as a bedtime story.

This story is a sardonic fairy tale of a boy living in a far
country where the inhabitants believe in a King living in a
city hundreds of miles away and endowed with the attributes of the Christian God, supreme power, wisdom and
goodness. Stress is laid on the King's ability to reward virtue
and punish wickedness but the boy observes that the
rewards and punishments are rarely seen and must presumably be postponed until the next life. The boy grows up
and becomes a successful jeweller, loving many women,
constantly leaving his wife and mistresses but obtaining a
great deal of pleasure. People are perplexed at his good
fortune since he has broken the King's rules, but they put it
down to the fact that he has a great capacity for love, and
love is the highest virtue promulgated by the King. Meanwhile the jeweller has contrived to prove the existence of
the King by all sorts of logical and philosophical methods;
he achieves an objective existence for the King in his city
hundreds of miles away, while his parents simply *knew* he
existed in their hearts. After a while the jeweller discovers
that he does not love at all, and at the same time that he is

not an artist, only a very clever jeweller. He makes a jewel in the shape of an ostrich egg with a tiny figure inside it with another gold ostrich egg, and so on in the manner of Russian dolls. His mistress kills herself, but 'A long time ago he had got to the end of pleasure just as now he had got to the end of work'. Since his public still demands golden eggs with crosses he takes to designing small obscene jewels for the private parts of men and women: however the critics continue to take him seriously as a true servant of the King ('From Easter Egg to Letters of Marque, the Jeweller of Original Sin'). He realizes that his art and his love-making must have been performed for his own pleasure, not for the King. He ceases to believe but wonders after all if his unbelief might be a final and conclusive proof of the King's existence. 'This total vacancy might be his punishment for the rules he had wilfully broken.'

It is customary for Greene to present the unresolved psychic conflicts of his characters in the form of dreams. But this is a highly controlled and reasoned fable; through it Querry is delivering the last word about his life and as he grows tired over his whisky the dressing of fable becomes thin (he substitutes 'building' for 'jewellery' at one point). Certainly the life of Querry is a vehicle for Greene's problems as a writer: the satire on the connoisseurs who write pretentious books about the jewels and consider the navel-stones to be serious moral criticism of the age is palpable. But there is one apparent discrepancy in inter-preting the fable as an orderly allegory of Greene's prog-ress as a religious novelist. The jeweller has constructed logical proofs for the existence of the King and there are many instances in and out of the novels of Greene's distrust of formal theological speculation. The proximate nature of belief, commitment to sexual love, and artistic creation implied by the fable reflects the attitude of the fiction much more exactly: Sarah gives herself unsparingly to God and to Bendrix. The consistent thing is that God remains hidden in his active power however much logical skill goes into finding proofs for his existence. If the proofs invoked are those of love and sacrifice and of the behaviour of charac-ters who take an idea to extreme lengths then God is still

withdrawn, when the new theology of 'capacity for love' has
become a formal structure in its turn, and the original
satisfaction has died. The jeweller (or Querry), in his state
of spiritual vacancy after the satisfaction has been removed,
is forced back on a new and perverse form of the wager.
This involves a strange mixture of faith and unbelief. The
intellectual disbelief and emotional disinclination which
'the end of his sex and the end of his vocation' have brought
him still leave open the sphere of risk in which the gamble
of faith must be exercised, but so long as he does not take
the risk by returning to the sacraments, the King may exist
and be punishing him. 'I'm told that there were moments
when he wondered if his unbelief were not a final and
conclusive proof of the King's existence . . . it was even
possible that this was what people meant by pain. The
problem was complicated to the point of absurdity, and he
began to envy his parents' simple and uncomplex heart, in
which they had always believed that the King lived — and
not in the cold palace as big as St Peter's a hundred miles
away.'

The regret for his parents' simple faith is not so much an
opposition of Protestant personal experience to intellectual
Catholicism as an acknowledgment of the contrast between
the self-consciousness of the convert and any form of easily
accepted, inherited belief. The drama of the extreme
religious situation can hardly accept the ordinary company
of the faithful even as background: the old woman with a
rosary in *Brighton Rock* had at least to be diseased. Contemporary Catholic teaching is likely to advocate that a self-
consciousness similar to that of the convert is desirable for
all the faithful. In *A Burnt-Out Case* the balance is redressed
in the portraits of the members of the community, all of the
ordinary company, except for the tortured Father Thomas
who stands out among them. Significantly, he wants to label
Querry as a saint for his own psychological satisfaction and
then immediately accepts the voice of slander and de-
nounces him.

The content of the fable is repeated in a short story,
written at the same period, 'A Visit to Morin' (reprinted in *A
Sense of Reality*, 1963). Morin is a French Catholic writer

whose novels specialize in the logic of extreme religious situations: 'it was as though some of his characters accepted a dogma so wholeheartedly, that they drew out its implications to the verge of absurdity'. His relation to his books, at once intimate and yet having something of the dissociation of the designer of a problem, is stressed:

> Morin's technique forbade him to play a part in the story himself; even to show irony would be to cheat, though perhaps we might detect something of Morin's view from the fact that the orthodoxy of Durobier was extended to the furthest possible limits, so that at the close of the book we had the impression of a man stranded on a long strip of sand from which there was no possibility of advance, and to retreat towards the shore would be to surrender. 'Is this true or is it not true?' His whole creed was concerned in the answer.

This partial involvement, the presentation of a scenario of faith, is peculiarly relevant to the relation of the author to Querry in *A Burnt-Out Case*. The narrator of the story is not a believer but has admired Morin's books as a boy. He recognizes him at midnight Mass in a French village and goes back to his house with him afterwards. Morin rejects the scholastic arguments for the existence of God and reveals that for twenty years he has voluntarily excommunicated himself. Again there is the theme of the involvement of religion and sex: 'I had only to sleep with a woman to make a convert . . . I loved a woman too much to pretend to myself that I would ever leave her. You know the condition of absolution? A firm purpose of amendment. I had no such purpose. Five years ago my mistress died and my sex died with her.' This death of sex is what Bendrix experienced after the death of Sarah and she after cutting herself off from him. Morin has cut himself off from the sacraments and his belief has withered: so long as he does not put it to the proof he can believe that what the Church teaches is true on account of his own case: 'The wafer must be more than wafer'.

The tortured challenges of the Catholic novels dissolve.

The alienated man remains alienated because in his alienation lies the only guarantee that Christianity may be true. As
Dr Colin says, 'Sometimes I think that the search for
suffering and the remembrance of suffering are the only
means we have to put ourselves in touch with the whole
human condition. With suffering we become part of the
whole Christian myth'. The logic of Querry's fable, like that
of Morin's separation from the Church, cannot avoid the
struggle of belief and unbelief, any more than the artifice of
the theologians can. Below the surface the struggle goes on;
the perceptive Colin sees that Querry is still troubled by lack
of faith. In an anxious dream Querry is a priest visiting
another priest and asking for his confession to be heard and
for wine so that he can celebrate his Mass next morning;
chattering pious women surround the priest and he feels
that he is too late. So the Catholic aspiration runs underground. Meanwhile, for the unalienated of the ordinary
company, the frontiers of charity are extended further and
further: it is the paradox of Christianity that if it is true it
seems to have no need for an institutional form and its
necessary claim is that of a spiritual rhetoric drawing
attention to the essential human condition. The Superior
preaches a sermon in pidgin to his lepers on this point:

'Now I tell you that when a man loves he must be Klistian.
When a man is merciful he must be Klistian. In this
village do you think you are the only Klistians — you who
come to church? There is a doctor who lives near the well
beyond Marie Akimbu's house and he prays to Nzambe
and he makes bad medicine. He worships a false God, but
once when a piccin was ill and his father and mother were
in the hospital he took no money. Yezu made love, he
made mercy. Everybody in the world has something that
Jezu made. Everybody in the world is that much a
Klistian . . . There is no man so wicked he never once in
his life show in his heart something that God made.'

Greene is brilliant in the cross-cutting of scenes, a
technique he improved from his study of the cinema; there
is the scene in *The Heart of the Matter* when Scobie listens to

Yusef's dangerous proposals in the intervals of reading a love letter from Helen. In the present scene Colin and Querry are commenting ironically on the sermon at the back of the congregation; Querry says the Superior's argument would make them both Christians and Colin wishes that Christianity could reduce the price of cortisone. Querry dies just when he had begun to serve others, to laugh again, and to recover happiness. The last words of the book are from Colin and they express its main interest in human service which makes the scruples both of the *faux-dévots* and the intellectually alienated seem unimportant. He returns to his clinic and examines a child: 'You needn't worry,' he says to the Superior, 'we shall be able to cure him in a year or two, and I promise you that there will be no mutilations.'

The leprosy of *A Burnt-Out Case* is real, like the bubonic plague of *La peste*, but as with Camus the struggle against disease becomes a metaphor for politics, the struggle for human justice. In *The Quiet American* and *The Comedians*, the novels preceding and following *A Burnt-Out Case*, during the years when Greene was in attendance on the danger points of contemporary wars and revolutions, the political struggle of haves and have-nots takes over from the religious theme, but without any diminishing of the interest in the mysterious continuities and transformations of individuals.

CHAPTER 5

Death and Fear in the Unjust Lands

I

Greene's years of restless travel from 1950 onwards, often on journalistic assignments, continued until 1966 when he made a home in Antibes in the south of France. This date certainly did not terminate his visits to foreign countries but it marks off a period in which, as well as *A Burnt-Out Case*, the postscript to the Catholic novels, books of a different kind are written. They turn from the problems of religious salvation and the integrity or disquiet of the individual life to the great public struggles of the second half of our century: the communist-inspired wars against the former colonial powers in East Asia and the similar revolts against the corrupt and exploiting regimes of Batista in Cuba and Duvalier ('Papa Doc') in Haiti. The latter exemplify the much broader conflict between the haves and the have-nots throughout Latin America. Since these novels still treat of individual men and women, not causes or masses, the theme becomes that of commitment to a cause, its nature and the degree to which it is an obligation, and how such a commitment may be justified or sustained in a revolutionary situation. It can be seen already that Greene has changed the field of interest of his fiction without departing from its essential concern with the agony of moral decision.

The *Quiet American* (1955) is set against the background of the Vietnam war in the period of French occupation which preceded the American involvement. *Our Man in Havana* (1958) deals with Cuba under Batista and before Castro's revolution. *The Comedians* (1966) describes a group of characters responding in different ways to the pressure of the vicious Duvalier regime in Haiti. It is interesting that, with the exception of the novella *Dr Fischer of Geneva and the Bomb Party*, Greene has written no novel since *Stamboul Train* with a European setting although he visited Poland and Czechoslovakia at times of crisis; in eastern Europe the roles were reversed and it was the communist satellite governments which were playing the colonial game on behalf of the Soviet Union. Nor has he shown much interest in the other troubled region of the modern world, the Arab countries, though he visited the Suez Canal in 1967 after the Six Day War and managed to get himself shelled while with an Israeli army unit during a violation of the cease-fire. But one can hardly expect Greene to have been everywhere, and to question like this his neglect of Europe and the Arab world is to take for granted the thoroughness of his exploration of contemporary violence in Asia and America. Even in *A Burnt-Out Case* political upheaval in Africa is a persistent presence on the edge of the story: the journalist Parkinson has come from reporting the civil war in another part of the Congo.

This documentation of real life in fiction has certain consequences which make the author's viewpoint, and perhaps more important, the reader's viewpoint, differ from what it is in *The Power and the Glory* or *The Heart of the Matter* where personal experience of Mexico or West Africa was equally utilized. It is partly, but not entirely, a matter of the relation between journalism and fiction. Greene had reported on the war in Indo-China for *Life* and the *Sunday Times*; where the ordinary foreign correspondent might collect his pieces into a book he distils them into a fiction. As he put it in his reply to a BBC interviewer:

And of course there is no coincidence about Indo-China. I went there because there was a war on and I stayed there every winter for four years to watch the war. And out of that a novel emerged. I suppose it's a relic of one's old journalistic past, but I see no reason today why the novel shouldn't be written with a background of world events, just as a novel in the nineteenth century could be based entirely on a long experience of Warwickshire or Dorsetshire.[1]

Yet in the nineteenth century *War and Peace* was written with a background of world events and it is not, in character apart from stature, like the novels Greene writes in this period. The key to the difference is in the impingement of the world upon persons in the modern period. It is not now as it was with Tolstoy, or even Hardy, who wrote *The Dynasts* on the great world events of the early nineteenth century as well as novels set in Dorsetshire. 'The unjust lands' which Auden wrote of in the Thirties to contrast them with the safe complacent West now comprise more than half the globe and the consciousness of them and of the dangers of the conflicts they engender diminishes the individual life and makes us prone to the journalistic images of crisis and breakdown as never before. In Mexico and West Africa Greene made something obsessively personal out of personal experience. In Indo-China, the Congo and the Caribbean he can only try to snatch something out of the general experience where man as person is subdued by the contemporary image of momentary historical man in the media. Travel, which is personal, has given way to the aggression and tourism of the global village. We may contrast Evelyn Waugh who in an age of travellers before the frontiers were down and the global, democratic, perpetually sanguinary global village declared, said:

> One does not travel, any more than one falls in love, to collect material. It is simply part of one's life. For myself and many better than me, there is a fascination in distant and barbarous places, and particularly in the borderlands of conflicting cultures and states of development, where ideas, uprooted from their traditions, become oddly changed in transplantation.[2]

The traveller makes his experience part of his life; his successor in the global village is made part of the contemporary world of war and crisis. When all are uprooted and reported on the screen or in the media there is no possibility

of observation from within the frame of a settled civilization
of the developments of conflicting cultures: in transplanta-
tion all are oddly changed, including the observer. Whereas
Waugh, the old-style traveller, could bring to bear on the
goings-on in 'barbarous places' a controlled and distanced
intelligence, it is significant that the narrators of these two
novels, Fowler in *The Quiet American* and Brown in *The
Comedians*, are expatriates, respectively a journalist and an
hotel owner, each with a mistress in the adopted country or
region, and the problem of cultural uprootedness is not
observed by them with detachment but present in their own
persons.

Greene has admitted that there is more direct reporting
in *The Quiet American* than in any of his other novels. The
press conference in Hanoi was recorded almost word for
word in his journal at the time; he like his hero had
accompanied a dive-bomber pilot on a mission attacking a
Viet Minh post; and he too had seen the dead bodies in and
near the canal at Phat Diem, all crucial episodes in the book.
If the result is a different sort of book from the others it is
partly because Greene is so good a journalist; but it must
also be attributed to the domination of character by history
in the new fiction of fact. In the dangerously unified
contemporary world the 'novel written with a background
of world events' as a successor to the two epic works of
Tolstoy and Hardy becomes an impossibility. Unity of
experience involves a self-consciousness about participation in history and this pressure struggles to squeeze the life
out of individuals and leave them as historical types. Thus
Pyle in *The Quiet American* is the American liberal idealist
and Fowler the cynical, worldly-wise European. But
Greene's interest in his character fights back and under the
surface of ideology his private obsessions reassert themselves. So in the end the ideological types of the American
and the European are not without a personal colouring;
after all, Ida and Rose, the types of humanism and the
Catholic sense of sin in *Brighton Rock*, did not lack for this.
Even under social and historical pressure the characters
retain their liveliness of being. The chief effect of
documentary fiction is to alter the reader's viewpoint on the

author: once the authenticity of the report is accepted the author as witness of the events described must re-enter his own work, from which as pure novelist he has previously absented himself. The book does not float free like a work of the imagination and the reader is impelled to seek some identification between the narrator Fowler and the author (he cannot help registering their shared role as foreign correspondent, opium smoker, and sceptic concerning the American presence in the Third World). This may become clearer if we compare some comments of Roland Barthes on non-documentary imaginative fiction, the ordinary novel in which even the technique of formal realism is there to create a world and not to be exercised upon our own everyday reality:

> . . . once an action is *recounted*, for intransitive ends, and no longer in order to act directly upon reality — that is, finally external to any function but the very exercise of the symbol, the disjunction occurs, the voice loses its origin, the author enters his own death, writing begins.[3]

Greene's text both reports events directly and by doing so furnishes a statement acting directly upon reality; the imaginative disjunction is mended and the author lives again in his text. Writing, *écriture*, has a doubtful status in such a work; but then this is not a new problem in Greene's fiction: from the start of his mature writing he drew on his own reportage. The relation of *Journey Without Maps* to *The Heart of the Matter* and of *The Lawless Roads* to *The Power and the Glory* are cases in point; as his art progresses the link between document and fiction draws closer, as with the many points of contact between the journals that make up *In Search of a Character* and *A Burnt-Out Case*. As the process continues the author — who had always moved close to his creation, charming away Pinkie's brutish inarticulacy with a Jacobean poetic *frisson*, endowing Scobie's policeman's stolidity with moral epigrams — seems to enter his own fiction, so that the question Querry's name suggests is whether his attitude is that of Greene (it is what Evelyn Waugh was unhappy about).

It has been widely agreed that *The Quiet American* is Greene's most carefully constructed novel. The documentation of recent history has its effects on the reading of the novel but there are none of the weaknesses which might be attributed to the rawness of immediate reportage; instead, in his subjecting the material of reportage to the discipline of art, he has achieved exceptional effects of conciseness and implication. These scraps of history are by an act of metonymy made to indicate the whole weight of instant history upon modern man. Greene as the knowing author-reporter mediates the truth to the stay-at-home reader oppressed by the chilling images of the media. This is apparent in the masterly compression of the press conference episode — four pages to digest questions and answers lasting over an hour. The point is that the French colonel holding the conference is irritated by the oafish American correspondent Granger into making an unintended admission: all the bitterness and frustration of the French who are losing a war without adequate supplies is distilled into a moment of minor drama:

> The colonel suddenly snapped out the information that French casualties had been in a proportion of one to three, then turned his back on us, to stare furiously at his map. These were his men who were dead, his fellow officers, belonging to the same class at St Cyr — not numerals as they were to Granger . . .
> 'You can say,' the colonel said, 'that six months ago we had three helicopters and now we have one. One,' he repeated with a kind of amazed bitterness. 'You can say that if a man is wounded in this fighting, not seriously wounded, just wounded, he knows that he is probably a dead man. Twelve hours, twenty-four hours perhaps on a stretcher to the ambulance, then bad tracks, a breakdown, perhaps, an ambush, gangrene. It is better to be killed outright.' . . . 'You can write that,' he said, looking all the more venomous for his physical beauty. '*Interpretez*,' he ordered, and walked out of the room, leaving the captain the unfamiliar task of translating from English into French.

The skilful economy of this, based as it is on fact, is comparable to Greene's account of his attendance at the farewell dinner of the great General de Lattre de Tassigny in Hanoi, who persisted in the belief that since Greene had once been in Intelligence he must be a spy. The good journalist is, after all, an artist who prunes the messiness of fact into the truthfulness of fiction.

Greene's social conscience had always been active. In his earlier novels he had depicted the idealism of the intellectual socialist Czinner, and, brilliantly, the sheer lack of scope of the socially deprived in Conrad Drover; but it is characteristic that in both portraits it is a personal collapse of values that comes uppermost and Greene avoids the sentimentality of an ideological plea. In this period he is stirred more than ever by injustice and intolerance and the plight of the oppressed; he comes to believe that communism is more likely than Western capitalist democracy to improve the condition of the common people in agricultural economies such as Cuba and Vietnam; he also claims that the communist leaders Castro and Ho Chi Minh had, unlike their capitalist counterparts, succeeded in reaching the hearts of their people and gaining their confidence. Yet Greene's sense of the necessary independence of the artist prevents him from open commitment to the Communist Party or to any other public cause. He practises the kind of detachment he had advocated in *Why Do I Write?* (1948) where he stated that it was the writer's genuine duty to society to be a piece of grit in the State machinery; loyalty was a trap for the artist:

> If artists don't become loyal to a Church or a country, they are too apt to become loyal to some invented ideology of their own, until they are praised for consistency, for a unified view.[4]

Given social generosity and such a degree of scepticism about the institutions controlling political action, the problem becomes that of deciding in what circumstances action is justified. Fowler in the novel declares that he will not be involved: 'It had been an article of my creed. The human condition being what it was, let them fight, let them love, let them murder, I would not be involved'. But in the end he procures the death of the American Pyle and in so doing takes a political and moral decision which is inextricably involved with his personal life.

The peasantry about whose allegiance the war is being fought are rarely seen. A Chinese family Fowler visits in the port of Cholon is described as from the life; the impression is created of an intensely vital and self-contained community existing alongside yet apart from the foreigners and able to absorb them if need be:

> There was one big room on the landing and a whole family sat and lay about it with the effect of a camp which might be struck at any moment. Small tea-cups stood about everywhere and there were lots of cardboard boxes full of unidentifiable objects and fibre suitcases ready strapped; there was an old lady sitting on a big bed, two boys and two girls, a baby crawling on the floor, three middle-aged women in old brown peasant-trousers and jackets, and two old men in a corner in blue silk mandarin coats playing mah jongg. They paid no attention to my coming; they played rapidly, identifying each piece by touch, and the noise was like shingle turning on a beach after a wave withdraws. No one paid any more attention than they did; only a cat leapt on to a cardboard box and a lean dog sniffed at me and withdrew.
>   . . . still no one regarded me, except that one of the women rinsed out a cup and poured tea from a pot which had been resting warm in its silk-lined box. I sat down on the end of the bed next the old lady and a girl brought me the cup: it was as though I had been absorbed into the community with the cat and the dog — perhaps they had turned up the first time as fortuitously as I had.

The Dickensian proliferation of the scene gives a kind of assurance of security and the assurance is sealed by Fowler's slightly surreal joke. The scene defines by contrast the absence of that security in the rest of the book. The war brings death which thins people out instead of cramming them together in a family party, and the fear of death causes human beings to look outwards uneasily on their fellows, not to exist imperturbably within themselves.

Where in fact we do see the peasants in *The Quiet American* is when they are dead. The fiction of reportage, in so far as it wins rather than draws its ceaseless contest with Greene's use of reportage as another fictional technique, works directly on our fear of death and pain like a disaster movie. *The Quiet American* is largely about the fear of death as the story leads up through every kind of violent death, by bullets, by napalm, by bombs, to the assassination of Pyle. The underlying theme of *The Comedians* is the fear of pain, the tortures that the Tontons-Macoutes are capable of inflicting, always recalled by the maimed body of the barman Joseph; and undoubtedly the climactic scene is when Brown, bullied by the Tontons Macoutes, actually urinates in his fear. The parallel scene in *The Quiet American* when fear is stretched to the utmost is that by the canal at Phat Diem:

> The canal was full of bodies: I am reminded now of an Irish stew containing too much meat. The bodies overlapped: one head, seal-grey, and anonymous as a convict with a shaven scalp, stuck up out of the water like a buoy. There was no blood: I suppose it had flowed away a long time ago. I have no idea how many there were . . . I took my eyes away; we didn't want to be reminded of how little we counted, how quickly, simply and anonymously death came. Even though my reason wanted the state of death, I was afraid like a virgin of the act. Twenty yards beyond the farm buildings, in a narrow ditch, we came on what we sought: a woman and a small boy. They were very clearly dead: a small, neat clot of blood on the woman's forehead, and the child might have been sleeping. He was about six years old and he lay like an embryo in the womb with his little bony knees drawn up.

Fowler is the new Greene character of secular despair who, at any rate with his intellect, welcomes death as a retreat from the boredom and betrayals of life; he is of the same tribe as Querry, and Brown in *The Comedians*:

Lose life and one would lose nothing again for ever. I
envied those who could believe in a God and I distrusted
them. I felt they were keeping their courage up with a
fable of the changeless and the permanent. Death was far
more certain than God, and with death there would be no
longer the daily possibility of love dying. The nightmare
of a future of boredom and indifference would lift.

In the fiction of reportage death is not tamed by the
imagination and is accepted by the reader in its full horror
as what lies in store. The image of a stew of bodies has that
bizarre and gratuitous cruelty which seems to have haunted
Greene ever since the dead dog in his pram as a child. In his
memory as a correspondent however it was the dead child
and his mother in the ditch which conveyed the most
shocking sense of mortality: 'The very neatness of their
bullet wounds made their death more disturbing than the
indiscriminate massacre in the canals around'. Fowler's
peculiar despair may not be shared by the average reader,
but in this episode he shows ordinary human fear of the act
of death and thus communicates the fear to others who are
also perhaps more certain of death than of God. The child
with its legs drawn up embryo-like is only too suggestive of
the weakness of modern man without supernatural aid
exposed between birth and death to the extinction that
comes to biological organisms. The diminutive 'little' hand-
les the body gently but without sentimentality.

The progress towards a soured humanism and a ques-
tionable political commitment in place of a religious one is
accompanied in these books by the replacement of the
thriller form. Pure thriller form was last dominant in
Greene's work in *The Ministry of Fear* and retained only as a
skeleton intrigue in the Yusef plot of *The Heart of the Matter*.
In the new world of international terror the thriller has
become commonplace and therefore redundant; in *The
Quiet American* the lethal intrigues of Pyle, and the machinations of Jones in *The Comedians* represent the re-entry into
fiction of a purely contemporary thriller element based not
on artistic probability but on the possibility of fact. Years
later when Greene returned to the spy thriller in *The Human*

Factor (1978), a book which stirs but hardly thrills, he again draws on the factual possibilities of the secret world. Variation on the recounted facts is possible, but not invention. One may compare the development of Eric Ambler who began by writing thrillers in which the imagination of initiation into fear is sustained by verisimilitude of detail and ended with what looks far more like direct transcripts of a *coup d'état* or a terrorist operation: in fact, verisimilitude becomes *verismo*. It can be seen that, in spite of its savage report on the Duvalier régime in Haiti, *The Comedians* is more intent on breaking out of the documentary mould than is *The Quiet American*. The narrative idea of three men called Brown, Jones and Smith, thrown together on a voyage and continuing to cross paths takes us firmly back from the shared media world to the traditional tale where every self is alone in his dream as well as in company with his fellows. At the same time the rococo extravagance of Haitian corruption does not wholly suppress the personal life, but distorts it into strange patterns, somewhat like Greene's cruel images of death and violence.

As a documentary novel *The Quiet American* communicates the fact of the death of the innocent in war and the fear inspired by that fact. It also acts at a political level to attempt to disprove and ridicule the idea that a 'third force' may be fostered in Asia, distinct from the old colonial regimes but able to assist American policy in its opposition to communism. The proponent of the 'third force' in the book is the American Pyle with his disastrous support for the war-lord General Thé. Pyle's actions are carefully related to his personality and style of thought so that what at first appears as a criticism of policy becomes an indictment of a whole attitude to life. Pyle's idealism is a menace because it is derived from books and from an ingrained liberal attitude prompting him to 'do good' to others from a position of entrenched moral superiority; he can never come to terms with the real world which is not black and white but grey, the world described by Greene in his novels. Contemporary reviews were largely devoted to the question of Greene's anti-Americanism; they included many protests from American readers. These ranged from the

hysteria of an editorial in the *Saturday Evening Post* entitled
'To Get Rave Reviews Write an Anti-U.S.A. Novel' to the
more moderate opinion of Diana Trilling who equates
Fowler's neutralism with Greene's own attitude which she
interprets as pro-communism.[5]

Such a straightforwardly political reading from a sophisticated critic is a measure of the extent to which the
documentary novel, by offering knowledge or knowingness
about present-day history in place of the free handling of
fiction, invites a purely political assessment. At this level of
discussion Greene can certainly be charged with substitut-
ing caricatures for real debate, the caricature of a quiet,
cultured American, Pyle, and that of a noisy, bumptious,
boozing one, the journalist Granger; further, he has tipped
the scale still more against Pyle by making him guilty of an
atrocious bomb explosion in the main square of Saigon
which kills and maims innocent civilians: he has supplied to
General Thé the chemical Diolacton to make the bombs.
The charge of rigging the argument may however be met:
Greene relates in his introduction how the novel was
passionately conceived in the wake of just such an explosion
in Saigon connected with General Thé and the dubious
machinations of an American 'third force'. The novel of
fact can only defend its subordinate use of fiction by a
further appeal to fact. But underneath the documentary
and political fiction is an ordinary wilful novel struggling
for its existence.

Where the political novel may be seen to fail is in bridging
the doubtful space between moral criticism and political
action. Neither Pyle nor Fowler could predict the future of
Vietnam. Greene's praise of the leadership of Ho Chi Minh
has not been justified by the conduct of his successors after
their victory if we judge only by the number of those who
have not wished to live under their régime. But if Pyle had
been right in terms of prediction, instead of grievously
wrong, and if General Thé had provided not an explosion
but a new form of stability in the country, the indictment
against Pyle's life-attitude would still stand because it is
existential and total and not dependent on the results of
action. In spite of his stated preference for communist

regimes in preference to capitalist ones Greene's basic attitude is to distrust initiatives supported by theoretical premises and that is the whole point of the book. 'He gets hold of an idea and then alters every situation to fit the idea,' as Fowler says of the writer York Harding, Pyle's mentor. The attack on American attitudes is really the latest phase of the continuing debate in Greene between the forces of innocence and experience, as may be seen if we look at some earlier examples of his so-called anti-Americanism and then at the presentation of Pyle.

Comments hostile to what is taken to be the American way of life are scattered through his film criticism of the 1930s and are notable for the violent comprehensiveness of the onslaught in which no one is spared and there is an unargued connection made between group habits and moral attitudes and even physical appearance. The following might be a very crude draft of Pyle's background (the film under review is a war film *The Road Back* in which the parts of German soldiers are played by American actors):

It might be funny if it wasn't horrifying. This is America seeing the world in its own image. There is a scene in which the returned soldiers all go back to their school. Sitting in uniform on the benches they are addressed by the Headmaster; they start their lessons again where they left off — it may be meant as irony (I'm not sure), but what it really emphasizes is the eternal adolescence of the American mind, to which literature means the poetry of Longfellow, and morality means keeping Mother's Day and looking after the kid sister's purity. One came daunted out of the cinema and there, strolling up the Haymarket, dressed up in blue uniforms with little forage-caps and medals clinking, were the American Legionaries, arm in arm with women dressed just the same — all guide-books, glasses, and military salutes: caps marked Santa Anna and Minnesota: hair — what there was of it — grey, but the same adolescent features, plump, smug, sentimental, ready for the easy tear and the hearty laugh and the fraternity yell. What use in pretending that with these allies it was ever possible to

fight for civilization? For Mother's Day, yes, for anti-
vivisection and humanitarianism, the pet dog and the
home fire, for the co-ed college and the campus. Civilization would shock them: eyes on the guide-book for
safety, they pass it quickly as if it were a nude in a national
collection.[6]

The weakness here lies in the attempt to link a vague satire
on sentimental bourgeois morality and patriotism with a
precise physical and national type: Greene's skill in sketch-
ing a visual impression is betrayed by its extension into an
indictment against a whole people. Yet the passage and the
less strident and more considered criticisms in *The Quiet
American* are likely to provide invaluable material for the
student of the over-riding problem of twentieth-century
international politics: the jealousy and distrust of Americans by English, Europeans, and others. A wartime joke in
England declared that GIs were 'over-paid, over-fed,
over-sexed, over-here',and Greene's disgruntled comment
at least implies the middle two in its picture of comfortable,
prosperous self-regard.

Another crucial text would be the description of the
American border town Tijuana across the Rio Grande from
Mexico in *The Lawless Roads*. The stress here is on American
mechanization, mass production and uniformity as against
the human reality of Mexican backwardness. One recalls
the exposure of the air-conditioned nightmare in works as
different as Céline's *Voyage au bout de la nuit* (1932) and
Lorca's *El poeta en Nueva York* (1929); the latter said to a
Madrid society woman who was praising American efficien-
cy, 'That place is Senegal with machinery'.[7] Declining
Athens perceives the cultural thinness behind the huge
practical success of imperial Rome: the formula might
explain much of the animus behind these and Greene's
criticisms, if allowance is made for his peculiarly English
superciliousness. But Greene has a personal interest in the
European formula. As the artist of failure and guilt he is
diametrically opposed to a civilization which denies them
and in its invincible Protestantism rejects mystery.

His later attacks on the American idea, or rather the

European dream of the American idea, are more convincing because they are delivered in the persons of likeable characters and not stereotypes. In the story 'Cheap in August' (1967) an Englishwoman married to an American academic on holiday in Jamaica is picked up by an older socially nondescript American. He is an unsuccessful and worried man, and this breaking of the formula makes what remain of its criticisms all the more telling:

> It was as though she were discovering for the first time the interior of the enormous continent on which she had elected to live. America had been Charlie, it had been New England; through books and movies she had been aware of the wonders of nature like some great cineramic film with Lowell Thomas cheapening the Painted Desert and the Grand Canyon with his cliches. There had been no mystery anywhere from Miami to Niagara Falls, from Cape Cod to the Pacific Palisades; tomatoes were served on every plate and Coca-Cola in every glass. Nobody anywhere admitted failure or fear; they were like sins 'hushed up' — worse perhaps than sins, for sins have glamour — they were in bad taste. But here, stretched on the bed, dressed in striped pyjamas which the Brooks Brothers would have disowned, fear and failure talked to her without shame, and in an American accent. It was as though she were living in the remote future, after God knew what catastrophe.[8]

At another point in the story the woman thinks of her husband before his marriage in the words of Henry James: 'A man of intellect whose body was not much to him and its senses and appetites not importunate.' With the introduction of James we enter a new dimension of the great question of the American impact on the older world. Instead of the popular gibe about 'over-fed and over-sexed' it is necessary to change the formula to read something like 'too cerebral, over-analytic and over-scrupulous'. Greene's steady admiration for James dates from early on when he had saluted him as the only novelist of his generation with a sense of metaphysical evil. A story like 'Cheap in August' shows that even late in his career he was prepared to write a minor variation of James's great European theme; significantly his American is not one who is successful or morally fine, but a failure, defeated by life, more like the dreadful ghost of what he himself might have become which confronts the returning Brydon in 'The Jolly Corner'.

The story of *The Quiet American* enables us to see that Greene's target is only partly a civilization he, and other Europeans, have regarded as synthetic: more importantly, his sights are trained upon the most sophisticated, high-minded, post-Jamesian representatives of that civilization. They are blamed for their lack of understanding of the real suffering and shabbiness in the world, for their inability to make the necessary human transition from innocence to experience. It is established in an early conversation between Pyle and Fowler that such an uninformed innocence may become dangerous:

> 'The first dog I ever had was called Prince. I called him after the Black Prince. You know, the fellow who . . .
> 'Massacred all the women and children in Limoges.'
> 'I don't remember that.'
> 'The history books gloss it over.'
> I was to see many times that look of pain and disappointment touch his eyes and mouth when reality didn't match the romantic ideas he cherished or when someone he loved or admired dropped below the impossible standard he had set.'

The climactic effect of Pyle's dangerous innocence is when he engineers support for the adventurer General Thé as a suitable instrument for his entirely theoretical concept of a 'third force'; he has acquired his political ideas from an academic authority, York Harding, whom he refers to constantly. The recurring mention of Harding in the novel provides a device common in Greene: the concentrated symbolic emphasis on a phrase, an idea or a person to develop a moral criticism. If his similes had in the first phase of his development provided a tactics of emotional suggestion, now his new type of repetition is incremental; it drives on the plot and points where the emphasis of human interpretation must lie. 'Once, I remember, I caught York Harding out in a gross error of fact, and I had to comfort him: "It's human to make mistakes."' He had laughed nervously and said, 'You must think me a fool, but — well, I almost thought him infallible.' The climax is when Pyle supplies explosive for General Thé's army which is used to create a ghastly explosion in the centre of Saigon. The idealistic Pyle is indirectly responsible for the killing and maiming of many innocent people. An innocent has destroyed innocents. We might apply to Pyle some words from the conclusion of Geoffrey Thurley's sympathetic study of American poetry at mid-century in which he speaks of ' . . . a puritan refusal to accept the world and experience as they really are . . . a sense that there must be some theory to make the experience offered seem more important.'[9]

Innocence is as dangerous as pity was seen to be dangerous in the preceding novels. Yet, apart from what he stands for, Pyle as a man is generously dealt with. He shows great courage. He paddles down the river to be with Fowler in the danger spot of Phat Diem; when they return to Hanoi they shelter at night in one of the watch-towers on the road to Hanoi, watched distrustfully by two sentries whom they fear may be trigger-happy; there is a Viet Cong attack and Fowler is wounded. Pyle insists on staying with him and then finds a patrol to bring him back to Hanoi. Fowler is alternately cynical about him and admiring: when admiring, he shows the envy of the older man for the younger. He can mock Pyle when he imagines him 'boating down the river into Phat Diem with the caution of a hero in a boy's adventure-story'; or he can speculate on whether this boyishness may be superior to his own world-weary selfishness:

All the time that his innocence had angered me, some judge within myself had summed up in his favour, had compared his idealism, his half-baked ideas founded on the works of York Harding, with my cynicism. Oh, I was right about the facts, but wasn't he right too to be young and mistaken . . .

After all, Greene's original sympathy is with the boy's adventure story which had moulded the form of his first three novels; and what is to be seen in much of the later work (particularly *The Comedians*) is its transformation into the terms of contemporary reality and psychological credibility. Likewise 'some judge within myself' in this passage recalls 'the man within' of the novel of that name. It is necessary to revise the estimate of the novel as an account of a plain opposition of personalities and cultures and to understand that there is a deeply suppressed Pyle-character in Fowler struggling to reach out in sympathy.

Bond and tension between the two men is provided by the Vietnamese girl Phuong. Fowler lives with her and would marry her but his wife in England, a strict Anglo-Catholic, will not divorce him. Pyle can offer marriage and he takes her from him; he immediately explains without deception what has happened: that is the reason for his romantic journey to Phat Diem. Phuong is the first of a series of fragile child-women which includes the girls in the brothel in *The Comedians*, the bride found by Henry Pulling at the end of *Travels with My Aunt*, and eminently Clara in *The Honorary Consul*, who is both whore and wife:

> To take an Annamite to bed with you is like taking a bird: they twitter and sing on your pillow. There had been a time when I thought none of their voices sang like Phuong's. I put out my hand and touched her arm — their bones too were as fragile as a bird's.

These women are simple and ignorant ('if Hitler had come into the conversation she would have interrupted to ask who he was'); they are treated as sensual objects, but in their passivity they retain a child-like innocence. The physical type, or something like it, has been encountered before, in Helen Rolt and in Elizabeth of *The Man Within*, but both those have minds of their own and stand up to their men, even, in the case of Elizabeth, exert a decisive influence. Also the note of sensuality is absent: now the body of Elizabeth merges into the role of Lucy the harlot. Phuong is shuttled between the two men; we never hear of her making an independent decision to leave Fowler for Pyle, and she returns quite passively to Fowler after Pyle's death. There is however the implication that the opportunity for marriage is a motive, and the apparent unassertiveness may be put down to a reading, right or wrong, of the Vietnamese temperament. But it seems more important to regard the interest in this sensuous passivity in the light of a growing preoccupation of Greene's total *oeuvre* and not as mere local observation.

Among this trio Fowler, the first-person narrator, presents himself as the cynical reporter who knows life. He has already left his wife for another woman before coming to Vietnam and finding Phuong. Some of his clipped retorts are in the Bogart tradition and recall one of the great influences on Greene, the early cinema and American 'B' movies; but the coarse blustering and womanizing of the American journalist Granger is used as a foil to bring out the greater seriousness and intelligence of Fowler: his interior monologues make the reader aware of his conscious fear of death and his profound desire for a personal peace (in this last respect he is like Scobie): 'From childhood I had never believed in permanence, and yet I had longed for it. Always I was afraid of losing happiness . . . Death was the only absolute value in my world. Lose life and one would lose nothing again for ever. I envied those who could believe in a God and I distrusted them.' Experience, then, sits upon him uneasily, but he does demonstrate an acceptance of the mixed, sinful human condition which Pyle ignores. This comes out most emphatically both in their total sexual attitudes and in their attitude to Phuong:

> 'Oh, but I know you're straight, absolutely straight, and we both have her interests at heart.'
>   Suddenly I couldn't bear his boyishness any more. I said,
>   'I don't care that for her interests. You can have her interests. I only want her body. I want her in bed with me. I'd rather ruin her and sleep with her, than . . . look after her damned interests.'
>   He said, 'Oh,' in a weak voice, in the dark.

I went on, 'If it's only her interests you care about, for God's sake leave Phuong alone. Like any other woman she'd rather have a good . . . ' The crash of a mortar saved Boston ears from the Anglo-Saxon word.

But there was a quality of the implacable in Pyle. He had determined I was behaving well and I had to behave well. He said, 'I know what you are suffering, Thomas.'

Fowler's bitter jealousy leads him to be deliberately and provocatively cruel but in doing so he does recognize the basis of physical love in the real world over which Pyle tends to slide. Pyle, on the other hand begins with his one shocked exclamation to suggest an appealing delicacy and tenderness for the girl of his friend. He spoils this when he proceeds to lecture Fowler and reveals a degree of moral complacency: he claims to know all about life which is the exact opposite of the case.

By now it becomes apparent that underneath the documentary and the political comment the conflict between innocence and experience is the true theme, played out not allegorically but in a real historical situation in a real world. The boy Wilditch in the story 'Under the Garden' and Henry Pulling in *Travels with My Aunt* move from one to the other, from innocence to experience, but the experience is the completion of a continuous development and therefore what Blake called an 'organized innocence'. In *The Quiet American* the two realms are in conflict. As for the anti-Americanism, it is more a vehicle for expressing the nature of the conflict between Pyle and Fowler than intrinsically significant, perhaps even a kind of Freudian slip on the part of Greene as he looks into intimate places of his world: the loss of childhood and the pains of growth.

There is a further element in the carefully balanced rendering of contrasted attitudes in Pyle and Fowler. Fowler's prime criticism of his quiet American is that he is a naif in regard to the country he is working in: he brings Boston with him as a moral envelope, just as he brings the ideas of York Harding, and as he arrives at Phat Diem equipped with the standard travelling kit of 'one of our medical aid teams'. Fowler, on the other hand, has completely adapted to the country; it is not only that he has a Vietnamese mistress but that he has fallen completely in love with the life of Hanoi; this love extends even to an acceptance of the war as he thinks when throwing dice with the French officers:

> We began to throw and it seemed impossible to me that I could ever have a life again, away from the rue Gambetta and the rue Catinat, the flat taste of vermouth cassis, the homely click of dice, and the gun-fire travelling like a clock-hand around the horizon.

What is most extraordinary here is not the almost euphoric tolerance of the gunfire of a war but the adjective 'homely' applied to a game of chance which many would regard as a seedy relaxation for those very far from a home. Like his creator Fowler is a man who has found a home elsewhere, not simply in Vietnam, but away from England and away from the conventional pattern of English society; like his creator, too, in his Vietnamese period, Fowler is an opium smoker: being away, the acceptance of the home that is homeless, go naturally together with indulgence in a practice of oblivion; the oblivion of opium is an ersatz for that personal peace which the hero in Greene is always seeking. As Greene says in the introduction he wrote later for the novel, ' . . . in Indo-China I drained a magic potion, a loving-cup which I have shared since with many retired *colons* and officers of the Foreign Legion whose eyes light up at the mention of Saigon and Hanoi'. Fowler has drained this cup. He is the homeless one who thinks he has come home, full of knowledge of a country not his own, full, too, of worldly wisdom concerning a life he cannot really take seriously; at the opposite pole to him Pyle retains his own roots and his own self-confident moral stance, though in the opinion of his *déraciné* rival the roots are shallow and the stance leans towards danger and destruction.

As a type of the detached reporter Fowler has remained uncommitted, seeking only his love for Phuong and his enjoyment of his adopted world. While he becomes more and more disturbed by the outrages caused through Pyle's blundering intervention, two people on two different

occasions tell him that he must take sides. Vigot, the French
police chief, refers to that continuing theme, the Pascalian
wager, and says: 'You don't follow your own principles,
Fowler. You're *engagé*, like the rest of us'. Later the Air
Force pilot Trouin tells him: 'One day something will
happen. You will take a side'. At last he agrees to give a
signal to the communist agent Heng indicating that Pyle
will be at the bridge near the Vieux Moulin restaurant at a
certain time. It is interesting to note that the situation
corresponds closely to that in *The Heart of the Matter* when
Scobie gives Yusef permission to deal with his servant Ali so
that he will not betray him. As with Fowler and Heng, the
language is ambiguous: 'He has to be restrained . . . We
would talk to him'. There is no open planning of a murder,
but in either case, the betrayer has an intuition that there
will be a murder and that he is a betrayer. So Fowler takes
sides, but with what motivation? He is certainly indignant at
what Pyle has provoked and anxious to prevent any further
intriguing with the irresponsible General Thé; after his
seeing the dead bodies in the square the indignation has led
him to a definite political decision: he is assisting the
Communists, however temporarily. But the means by
which Pyle is removed seems both drastic and underhand.
He is under the bridge because he has received a dinner
invitation from Fowler for a certain time. A miasma of
treachery hangs around the whole episode. Fowler is, after
all, a jealous rival who wants Phuong back quite as much as
he is a man who has at last chosen to support a distinct
political cause. In so far as he offers an example of the
uncommitted finally coming down into the mud of the
common struggle on account of a sense of justice, *The Quiet
American* looks forward to the more explicit expression of
this theme in *The Comedians* and *The Honorary Consul*; in so
far as Fowler is a Judas-figure he acts out a different role: as
the sinner of any kind is near to God, the man who betrays
and then feels guilt is in a fashion a surrogate for the whole
human race which betrays Christ and crucifies him. It is
completely in order that at the end of the book, as at the
close of *The End of the Affair*, the narrator *might* be
interpreted as approaching the threshold of belief merely
through need:

I thought of the first day and Pyle sitting beside me at the Continental, with his eye on the soda-fountain across the way. Everything had gone right with me since he had died, but how I wished there existed someone to whom I could say that I was sorry.

These last sentences of the book provide a key to its complex construction. Fowler lives among poignant or painful memories which are interrupted by the shocks of a violent present, the bodies in the canal at Phat Diem, the attack on the watch-tower, the bomb in the square. He looks back to his first meeting with Phuong and his life with her before the arrival of Pyle (his memories hardly extend at all to England and his estranged wife); upon this memory is imposed the recollection of his first meeting with Pyle and Pyle's first encounter and falling in love with Phuong. The narrative form of the novel corresponds to the play of action and memory in Fowler. Even the episode which might appear a report of pure action, devoid of restrospect and not particularly attached to the main Fowler-Pyle story — Fowler's dive-bombing expedition with Captain Trouin — is revealed on inspection to be closely linked both to memory and the developing action: Fowler as a war correspondent is not supposed to go on a 'vertical' (i.e. dive-bombing) raid; he gets away from Hanoi and breaks the rule as some alleviation for his agony of mind after his loss of Phuong; after the raid he takes a prostitute (ineffectually) for the same reason; and it is in conversation with Trouin that hints are thrown out that he must eventually abjure his neutrality and take a stand as human beings must, thus anticipating what he feels obliged to do later after the explosion in the square.

So there is a carefully conceived double time scheme which serves to communicate the ambiguous relationship between the deposit of past experience and the will in present action: past desire is filtered through memory to influence the course of desire and act in the present. There are four parts of the novel. The first section of the first part deals with the night of Pyle's murder, probably beginning at the moment of his death off-stage, and Fowler's first interview with the police as a suspect. The next two sections go back to the beginning of it all, Pyle's coming, his dancing with Phuong and falling in love with her. The last two sections show the development of the triangular relationship and the whole second part has a steady forward chronology, moving through the night at Phat Diem, the press conference, the Caodist festival, and the night skirmish on the road outside the watch-tower. But in the third part time is again a collage: it begins with his second interrogation by Vigot and then goes on to relate the last stages of the break with Phuong and Fowler's detection of the source of the explosives which go to make the bomb in the square. Part Four begins with his final interview with Vigot and goes back to complete the events leading up to Pyle's death, Fowler's last scene with Pyle (a particularly shocking close-up since the reader knows that at the other time level he is already dead), the fatal conversation with Heng, and finally the scene of reunion with Phuong which follows chronologically on the last interrogation by Vigot ('Has Monsieur Vigot been to see you?' 'Yes. He left a quarter of an hour ago'). In the end is the beginning and the book describes that circle of time which Coleridge called 'a snake with its tail in its mouth'.

The total pattern is a collage: the snips of time would have to be rearranged to provide a chronological continuity. The lessons of Conrad (technical, not stylistic) and of Ford Madox Ford's *The Good Soldier* now begin to bear fruit. But the technique exists not to show itself off but to communicate the tensions of a passionate involvement with the chief character and his setting.

II

Greene's next book, *Our Man in Havana* (1958), is an 'entertainment'. While the gap in tone and treatment between the novels and the entertainments is often almost indistinguishable, *Our Man in Havana* possesses some of the specific 'entertainment' features: less depth of characterization and a more facile thriller progression towards a contrived happy ending. The innovation lies in the fact that the thriller form is no longer being taken seriously; this is a major departure from the solemn cinematic melodrama of *A Gun for Sale* and *The Confidential Agent* where comedy is to be found in distinct fringe episodes like the debagging of Buddy Fergusson in the former book. Now mysterious or violent events are clothed in an atmosphere of irony and black comedy. It is another symptom of the eclipse of the pure thriller in a real world become equally fantastic. As Alfred Kazin has remarked:

> . . . we can see that the Khruschev-Dulles age lends itself not to dread but to farce. Our plight is now so universal and at the same time so unreal that the age of anxiety has turned into the age of absurdity.[10]

The setting is Havana during the corrupt Batista regime with the Castro rebels waiting in the mountains. Wormold, a vacuum salesman in Havana, allows himself to be recruited as a British secret agent in order to provide some extra money for his much loved and extravagant daughter Milly. He sends bogus reports based on a book code taken from Lamb's *Tales from Shakespeare*. After a time his scheme rebounds on him. He has supplied imaginary plans of military installations based on vacuum cleaner designs. An unspecified hostile agency becomes interested in the names of real persons he has given in his reports. His friend, the ex-Prussian officer Dr Hasselbacher, and others are killed, and he himself is in danger. 'He stood on the frontier of violence, a strange land he had never visited before.' He enters into the stream of events and revenges Dr Hasselbacher by killing his assassin. He is not acting for the British Secret Service or for any organization but to assert his individuality: 'If I love or if I hate, let me love or hate as an individual. I will not be 59200/5 in anyone's global war'. However ironically enough the authorities reward him and he happily marries his secretary.

What is of significance in this truly entertaining novel, which fascinates because of its rapidity of pace, is the importance of the moment of transition from ordinary life to a world of fantastic danger and violence; the author describes it in terms of crossing a frontier, and of course it echoes the trauma of the green baize door in the author's childhood and in its fictional version in *The Ministry of Fear*. Also, once again the innocent man demonstrates his power to create havoc, but this time he collects himself to meet the challenge and goes some way to redeem the harm he has caused. As with Fowler, it is individual engagement, not service to a particular cause, that Wormold finds he must choose. In the next novel to be considered, *The Comedians*, the theme of engagement is given a rather different turn.

III

In *A Burnt-Out Case* (1961) the debate on faith became a debate on doubt. That debate is now set aside for a time and in *The Comedians* (1966) and its successor, *The Honorary Consul* (1973) not only is God hidden but his people have retreated further from the hope of his presence; the only value is an embattled humanism which is often aligned with Marxism, not as a new form of belief, but as an efficient contemporary instrument for survival in the face of cruel and impersonal state powers and a general moral confusion. Irony and comedy more and more affect the tone. Meanwhile under the surface the individual's assertion of that other self formed by his personal history is still at work: humanism, or Marxism, as a cause, is ultimately justified as a means for that self to realize itself.

The setting of *The Comedians* is the Republic of Haiti under the dictatorship of the brutal and paranoid Duvalier ('Papa Doc'). Constitutional law is suspended and the dictator rules through the terror inspired by his secret police, the Tontons Macoute, in their sinister dark glasses, who are a law to themselves. It may at first seem that there is here in the cruelty, poverty and corruption of Haiti, one more forcing ground for evil, one more arena for the extreme moral test, of the kind familiar from the background of earlier novels — atheistic Mexico, Indo-China, or Cuba. Yet there is a difference in *The Comedians*, and the difference marks a decisive change in tone and emphasis which is felt in all of Greene's subsequent novels. The scene is open, not oppressively enclosed, and laughter is possible even in the dark night of Haiti; sometimes it is critical laughter, sometimes a quite disinterested sympathetic humour. The comedy that Greene had demonstrated in asides, and in ancillary characters and episodes, and to which he had given fuller rein in some of the entertainments (*Loser Takes All* and *Our Man in Havana* are cases in point), now moves nearer to the centre of the stage in a major novel.

The reason is that the interest is spread over a large group of characters; while there are several characters in *The Heart of the Matter*, they all revolve around the spiritual and dramatic needs of Scobie, the tragic protagonist. Brown, the narrator in *The Comedians,* is another rootless or uprooted person, like Fowler or Querry, who has lost, as he says, 'the capacity to be concerned'. But his state of spiritual dryness and exhaustion is not allowed to monopolize the action, as Querry's problem does in *A Burnt-Out Case*. There are others who do not live simply in his eyes but possess lives of their own; the convincing proof of this is that they act so as to surprise him and therefore to surprise the reader too. The strength of the earlier Greene lies in the dynamic energy generated in the treatment of enclosed, obsessive themes. The strength of *The Comedians, The Honorary Consul,* and their successors, resides in the broad, tolerant range of a vision that is at once comic and intensely serious. To quote Brown again, invoking the absent God in whom he no longer believes, 'all are driven by an authoritative practical joker towards the extreme point of comedy'.

The Comedians begins with an ironic obeisance towards the traditional tale of adventure, like those which delighted our Edwardian ancestors in the pages of the *Wide World Magazine* where Captain Kettle made his appearances: three characters called Brown, Smith and Jones are thrown together on a Dutch ship bound for Port-au-Prince in Haiti. Brown is the owner of an hotel in Port-au-Prince which, in the days before the Duvalier terror and the secret police, the Tontons Macoute, had been profitable and fashionable. Now there are no tourists. He has failed to sell the hotel in New York and is returning because there seems nothing else to do. He is a rootless person, a

British citizen but born in Monaco, the natural son of a flamboyant, life-loving mother, who has bequeathed him the hotel; his life has been wandering and hand to mouth; these facts, however, we are to learn later: life on board ship maintains privacies. Mr Smith and his wife are Americans; they are ardent vegetarians, she believing that abstention from meat will, by eliminating acidity, provide a cure for the grosser human passions. Mr Smith has actually been a candidate for the United States Presidency on a vegetarian ticket. He and his wife have also marched on civil rights marches in the American South. Jones is the dark horse of the three: he calls himself 'Major Jones' and claims to have seen action in the jungle in Burma during the war. He talks in outmoded slang and conveys the impression that he is playing a role, indeed living in the midst of a huge confidence trick, but he has a saving self-awareness of his role-playing: above all he makes people laugh.

The strangely discontinuous world of an ocean voyage where between one port and another the voyagers enjoy a sort of moral anonymity, a life within a life, is brilliantly caught in the first chapter. It is an image of the disconnectedness in human lives that is Greene's prime study. The climax is the ship's party before arrival when the black Mr Fernandez mysteriously weeps and Mr Baxter gives an extraordinary doggerel recitation about the London blitz wearing the warden's helmet which he always carries at the bottom of his trunk. Here may be noted an increasing habit in the later novels: the redeployment of personally significant material from the past, whether themes from life or from Greene's earlier fiction. The echo here is of his time as a warden at a post near the Tottenham Court Road in the raids of 1940–1.

Once the ship berths and Brown goes to his hotel the book appears to start over again. We learn about his past, his mistress whom he re-encounters that night waiting for him in her car in the square where they had usually met in the past, his mother, the history of the hotel. Kingsley Amis has objected to this double start to the novel as 'unnecessary padding which slows down the movement of the story'. On the contrary, the introduction on the Dutch ship is necessary in order to establish other selves as well as Brown, lively and carrying with them much that is yet to be explained, if it ever will be. Brown is not to be allowed to monopolize the psychological interest of the book, like Querry. But he is important and that is why his past is unfolded, but in second place.

After Brown has been reunited with his mistress, Martha, who is the German wife of Pineda, a South American ambassador, he returns to the hotel, now empty and derelict, where he is to welcome the Smiths as his guests. The only remaining servant, Joseph, is crippled after torture by the Tontons Macoute. By the swimming pool Brown finds the body of a former Minister of Social Welfare who has committed suicide by cutting his veins, anticipating arrest and its consequences. He consults his old friend Dr Magiot about disposing of the body; Dr Magiot is a Marxist and also a man of great dignity and integrity. But the body is eventually found and Brown is persecuted by the Tontons Macoute. Meanwhile his travel companions go about their business in Port-au-Prince. The Smiths try ineffectually to start a vegetarian centre and spread their gospel of natural health; for a long time their innocence cannot comprehend the evil and corruption of the place and it is only slowly that their eyes are opened. The final revelation only comes when Mr Smith sees the wilderness of mud that is the new city of Duvalierville and when the new Minister of Social Welfare openly offers him a bribe: he and the other ministers involved are to obtain government grants to pay the construction workers for the vegetarian centre and then dismiss them while continuing to draw the grants.

Jones has some dubious scheme to ingratiate himself with the Haitian government and make his fortune; he begins badly: he arrives carrying letters to the wrong people, is thrown into prison and beaten up. Brown and Mr Smith obtain his release. In a short time he bobs up irrepressibly and is able to pursue his scheme: he is established in a government rest-house and is seen being respectfully escorted by officers of the Tontons Macoute.

His success is however short-lived: his scheme is exposed by the villainous Tonton Macoute Captain Concasseur; with Brown's help he has to seek asylum, first on the Dutch ship which is now back in harbour for one night, then for a longer period in Pineda's embassy. Philipot, the nephew of the dead Minister of Social Welfare, with Joseph and a few others, have formed a guerilla group near the Dominican border; they need arms and, still more, training and leadership. They believe that Jones, who talks so much of his commando days in Burma, is the man to lead them. Martha likes Jones, as everyone does, and Brown, having to leave her with Jones in the embassy and only see her for occasional stolen meetings in his hotel, is morbidly jealous. When asked by Dr Magiot to arrange for Jones to be smuggled out to join the guerillas he is only too anxious to oblige. Jones has said so often that he could teach Philipot commando tactics and that he would go like a shot if he had the chance: speaking in front of Martha he cannot back out now. In an episode of extreme excitement and taut suspense Brown drives Jones down the broken, pot-holed southern highway to a rendezvous with Philipot in a cemetery near Les Cayes; they are surprised by Concasseur and his Tontons Macoute but immediately rescued in an ambush by Philipot and his guerillas.

The end of the story comes in Santo Domingo where all the characters except Jones reappear. Brown has been aided by the guerillas to cross the frontier and leave the country of nightmare. He could never return to his hotel now. Looking fruitlessly for a job he reencounters the Smiths who with their habitual generosity lend him money and help him to find one. It is in the undertaking business of Mr Fernandez, another travelling companion. Martha too is in Santo Domingo since her husband is being reposted to Lima; but the love affair which had been dying for a long time is now at its end. Passing a frontier post Brown meets Philipot and the survivors of his band who have crossed the border into safety. Jones had certainly given them leadership and inspiration though he had to be taught to fire a rifle: only Brown had heard his confession in the cemetery that he was rejected for the army on

account of flat feet and that the nearest he got to the
Burma war was as an entertainments officer attached to
ENSA at Imphal. The book ends with Mr Fernandez
telephoning Brown about his first assignment: the living
and the survivors cannot escape in this text from the smell
of death.

The comedians of the title are those who play a part and
wear the actor's mask; they refuse to come to terms with
themselves, and stay on the edge of life avoiding involvement. Brown says, 'I suppose those of us who spend a
large part of our lives in dissembling, whether to a woman,
to a partner, even to our own selves, begin to smell each
other out'. The theme of play-acting and make-believe
runs through the book. It is first met in the comic turns
and recitations of the last night's concert on board ship;
when Jones shelters on the same ship later he has to escape
from it in woman's clothes to avoid the Haitian police and
it is in this comedian's dress that he arrives at Señor
Pineda's embassy to claim asylum. But of course his whole
career as Major Jones the ex-commando is role-playing.
Philipot was a comedian but has now dropped the mask
and taken the decision to join the guerillas and fight to
overthrow the tyranny of Papa Doc. He replies to Brown
who is wondering whether he and Jones are not both
comedians:

'They can say that of most of us. Wasn't I a comedian
with my verses smelling of *Les Fleurs du Mal*, published
on hand-made paper at my own expense? I posted them
to the leading French reviews. That was a mistake. *My*
bluff was called. I never read a single criticism . . . The
same money would have bought me a Bren perhaps.' (It
was a magic word to him now — Bren.)

The ambassador said, 'Come on, cheer up, let us all be
comedians together. Take one of my cigars. Help
yourself at the bar. My Scotch is good. Perhaps even
Papa Doc is a comedian.'

'Oh no,' Philipot said, 'He is real. Horror is always
real.'

Brown is the isolated man who cultivates non-involvement. If it were not for the human density of the novel it would merely be a variation on a theme familiar in Greene. But the importance given to Jones, his *alter ego* as drifting adventurer, strikes a new balance. Brown's disenchanted preoccupation with himself is exposed to critical comparison with other human beings as was not the case with Fowler (in spite of Pyle) or Querry. Brown has also a vestigial Catholic conscience, a more familiar property in Greene, having been brought up by the Jesuits and believing in youth that he had a vocation. 'My mother had taken a black lover, she had been involved, but somewhere years ago I had forgotten how to be involved in anything. I had lost completely the capacity to be concerned.' He had returned to Haiti at his mother's invitation a little before her death. After her death, Marcel, the black lover, asks to have his old room in the hotel again, and there he kills himself.

This is the first sign given in the book of the involvement which is the alternative to Brown's accidie, a total involvement which means abandoning any fear of death, whether for love or for a cause thought to be just. Brown finds in his mother's drawer the medal of the French resistance: like all such relics of the dead he cannot be sure if it was hers or belonged to someone else, but again, given her passionate and positive temperament, there is a hint of commitments that lie beyond him. His love for Martha is selfish and purely sexual, and accompanied by gnawing jealousy during the long periods when he cannot see her. Even more effectively than in *The End of the Affair* this is a remorseless account of a physical relationship that is burning itself out. Ironically his chief rival is Martha's child Angel to whom she gives all her care; Angel's bleak gaze suggests that he guesses at something going on and resents the intrusion on his own demanding love for his mother. When Jones is sheltering in the embassy his perpetual good humour acts as a catalyst for the nerves of the family and draws them together. He is good with Martha, good with Angel, good with the dog Midge, even the pompous Señor Pineda warms towards him. Brown

can only imagine that Jones has slept with Martha, who
when interrogated by Brown says at last in exasperated
and weary annoyance that she has; it later appears from
what Jones says, in the terrifying night waiting for the
rendezvous in the cemetery, that she has not. But this is a
novel scrupulous in its adherence to the multi-faceted
character of human knowledge. The human monad
Brown in his isolation can only decide on his limited
knowledge of the persons in his life, as with his mother's
medal of the resistance. The independent life of the other
characters is what Brown would like to abolish but cannot.
Martha, a far more generous person, sums up with a ring
of truth:

> We're what you choose to make us. You're a Ber-
> keleyan. My God, what a Berkeleyan. You've turned
> poor Jones into a seducer and me into a wanton
> mistress. You can't even believe in your mother's medal,
> can you? You've written her a different part. My dear,
> try to believe we exist when you aren't there. We're
> independent of you. None of us is like you fancy we are.
> Perhaps it wouldn't matter much if your thoughts were
> not so dark, always so dark.

The sense of love dying into an ineffectual lust is conveyed
through the increasing physical clumsiness of their encounters, a crudely brief attempt in a bedroom in the
embassy when Brown finds anxiety has made him impotent and hastens to a brothel to reassure himself, and an
unsatisfactory episode in her car:

> . . . to disguise my lack of feeling I acted crudely. I
> pulled her body out from under the wheel and thrust
> her across my thighs, scraping her leg on the radio-set,
> so that she exclaimed with pain.
> 'I'm sorry.'
> 'It was nothing.'

However Brown is capable of disinterested respect for
goodness and courage in others, Dr Magiot or the Smiths;

and he is finally redeemed from his moral solipsism when he enters the world of action at last to rescue Jones, to smuggle him out of the embassy under the noses of the Tontons Macoute, and to drive him on the dangerous journey to meet Philipot and his guerillas.

The Smiths are an innovation in Greene's fiction, although a tentative sketch for them may be found in the Lehrs in *The Power and the Glory*. Satire on their foibles and obsessive preoccupation with what are now called health foods is fully outweighed by the recognition that the righteousness they exhale is genuine and supported by extreme and unconscious bravery. The satire involves the actual names of the foods which are played over repetitively in the contrapuntal manner which enables Greene to knit words and character into an indivisible whole:

> 'Excuse me, Mrs Smith,' the captain said, 'but what is that you are drinking?'
> 'A little Barmene with hot water,' Mrs Smith told him. 'My husband prefers Yeastrol in the evening. Or sometimes Vecon. Barmene, he thinks, excites him.'
> The captain gave a scared look at Mrs Smith's plate and cut himself a wedge of duck. I said, 'And what are you eating, Mrs Smith?' I wanted the captain to taste the full extravagance of the situation.
> 'I don't know why *you* should ask, Mr Brown. You have seen me eat it every evening at the same hour. Slippery Elm Food,' she explained to the captain. He put down his knife and fork, pushed away his plate and sat with his head bowed.

The Smiths are a lesson in the distinctions necessary to be made within Greene's conception of innocence. Innocence can be an unfledged ignorance with which goes a sublime inability to learn: this is the innocence of Pyle and it is mortally dangerous to other people. But there is also the innocence of evil of the inviolately virtuous mind and this is what Mr and Mrs Smith have; it is accompanied by the innocence that is ignorance, yet they can unlearn that, though slowly, since they are not enclosed in Pyle's envelope of complacency. One is reminded of the virtuous characters in Fielding, like Allworthy, who of their nature find it difficult to detect when they are being deceived. Mr Smith gives money to a maimed beggar at Duvalierville and it is immediately stolen by another, stronger negro. It is a dry comment on the fate of so many overseas loans. He goes against advice into the Post Office and is hemmed in by beggars ready to pounce on an American:

> Two one-armed men and three one-legged men hemmed him round. Two were trying to sell him dirty old envelopes containing out-of-date Haitian postage stamps: the others were more frankly begging. A man without legs at all had installed himself between his knees and removed his shoe-laces preparatory to cleaning his shoes. Others seeing a crowd collected were fighting to join it.

But the Smith's innocence goes with a good sense that finally sees through the facade of Haiti to its dark night; and their finest moment comes when Brown is being pushed about by Concasseur and his men on his own verandah and Mrs Smith, utterly fearless, stops them with a word, like a Spenserian heroine whose purity of mind is effortlessly effective in the real world: rarely, Greene opts here for the Platonic sentiment that virtue alone is free:

> 'Hit him again,' Captain Concasseur told the man.
> *'Dégoutant,'* a voice said, *'tout-à-fait dégoutant.'*
> I was as astonished as they were. The American accent with which the words were spoken had to me all the glow and vigour of Mrs Julia Ward Howe's *Battle Hymn of the Republic*. The grapes of wrath were trampled out in them and there was a flash of the terrible swift sword. They stopped my opponent with his fist raised to strike.

There is ample recompense here to the United States for the totalitarian criticism of *The Quiet American*. The Smiths are comedians only in the eccentricity of habit, not in anything important. When Mr Smith says, 'Perhaps we seem rather comic figures to you, Mr Brown,' the answer is, 'Not comic . . . heroic'.

Jones's dishonesty, his shady record in Burma, the Congo and elsewhere, is partly redeemed by his innate romanticism. It is a naive innocence that makes him boast of his commando prowess to Martha whom he admires and so fall into Brown's trap. He falls into it so easily because like all romantic myth-makers he secretly desires a test that would enable him to convert dream into reality; that he is no mere fantasist is demonstrated by the fact that he is always ready to modify or withdraw a lie when he becomes aware that his audience have seen through him: such is the case when he has to confess to Brown that his Asprey's cocktail case was not a present from fellow officers during the Burma campaign as the result of a bet. Meanwhile he lives in his myth:

> Give me fifty Haitians with a month's training and Papa Doc would be on a plane to Kingston. I wasn't in Burma for nothing. I've thought a lot about it. I've studied the map. Those raids near Cap Haitien were a folly the way they were done. I know exactly where I'd put in my feint and where I'd strike.

This is the language of a man who wants to convince himself as well as others; Brown's mean and jealous trick to get him out of the embassy affords him his great opportunity for self-realization. He ceases to be a comedian and joins the Smiths, Martha, and Dr Magiot. The latent quality of humanity under his shiftiness is revealed by his reciprocated friendliness to Mr Smith. As he says, 'I always felt that Mr Smith and I had a bit in common. Horses out of the same stable.' When Brown reflects, 'What could a saint have in common with a rogue?' he exposes his moral crassness: a major drive of Greene's fiction is to explain the affinity and the impossibility of precise demarcation. Yet in his last days with the guerillas Jones is in one sense still a comedian since he adheres to the legend of his military experience and they still believe him. He cannot fire their rifles, but that they believe is because they are out-of-date models; they believe his intensely held personal myth that he can detect the presence of water precisely because there is no water to detect in the dried up region through which they are going.

But this surface of a comedian is cancelled by the ultimate commitment of death when Jones stays behind on account of his flat feet and fights it out with their pursuers. One level of the novel reflects upon another, and Brown remembers a letter taken from the dead Marcel's pocket he had read and reread: his magnificent comedian mother had written: 'Marcel, I know I'm an old woman and as you say a bit of an actress. But please go on pretending. As long as we pretend we escape. Pretend that you love me like a lover. Pretend that I would die for you and you would die for me.' Marcel does die for her and therefore gives up his part in the comedy.' . . . so perhaps he was no *comédien* after all. Death is a proof of sincerity.' And Jones is to join him on the final tragic stage where his acting is to assume a new tone in the real and tragic world with Dr Magiot and those who have chosen. It is all summed up in the last letter of Dr Magiot to Brown when he is waiting in Port-au-Prince for the knock on the door:

We are humanists, you and I. You won't admit it, perhaps, but you are the son of your mother and you once took that dangerous journey which we all have to take before the end. Catholics and Communists have committed great crimes, but at least they have not stood aside, like an established society, and been indifferent. I would rather have blood on my hands than water like Pilate. I know you and love you well, and I am writing this letter with some care because it may be the last chance I have of communicating with you. It may never reach you, but I am sending it by what I believe to be a safe hand — though there is no guarantee of that in the wild world we live in now . . . I implore you — a knock on the door may not allow me to finish this sentence, so take it as the last request of a dying man — if you have abandoned one faith, do not abandon all faith. There is always an alternative to the faith we lose. Or is it the same faith under a different mask?

The surprising independent existence of other selves in a world which is a system of monads and no longer dominated by a single, obsessional consciousness is not only maintained by the direct statements of the characters, like Martha's indictment of Brown's solipsism quoted above. It is written into the dramatic turns of the plot. Brown's misplaced jealousy of Jones is one instance; others come with the unexpected shock of new knowledge. Brown learns in casual talk with Pineda that Martha's father had been hanged as a war criminal in the American zone in Germany after the war. Brown registers acutely the personal impact of this knowledge, but characteristically generalizes it into a comment on what the whole of life has become in the aftermath of war and terror: 'I wondered whether the world would ever again sail with such serenity through space as it seemed to do a hundred years ago. Then the Victorians kept skeletons in cupboards — but who cares about a mere skeleton now? Haiti was not an exception in a sane world: it was a small slice of everyday taken at random.'

But the rudest intrusion into Brown's self-limited vision coincides with a major turn in the plot. Jones, who has been exposed and imprisoned, emerges irrepressibly in charge of his destiny and on good terms with the government. At Mère Cathérine's brothel Brown is told by Concasseur of an important state guest whom he is guarding. A man emerges with a girl from one of the booths: 'But Concasseur and she were not smiling at each other, both their smiles were directed at the guest of great importance on whose arm she had entered. It was Mr Jones.' Story-telling skill in the employment of confused expectation is here wedded to that recognition of the substantiality of other lives which is the core of the book.

The theme of the uncommitted and the engaged, and of the former becoming the latter, is strongly present therefore, but not laboured as a thesis. Comedians have their say; they too cherish ideals, but of necessity the ideals lie in lost moments of the past or in an impossible future.[12] Brown thinks of the carnival days when his hotel was prosperous with a good cook and a famous barman; his memories are crystallized in a remembered moment when he saw a naked girl making love in the pool at night: he holds on to the pleasure of the body distilled into nostalgia and regret. The Smiths, only part-comedians, remember as their high moment a civil rights march in Nashville when Mrs Smith had been struck by a policeman. Jones harbours a dream of a great brash golf club on a Caribbean islet which he will run at enormous profit. Even Philipot retains a comedian streak in his new serious role when he goes on and on about the importance of having a Bren, turning the word over and over like a symbol in his Baudelairean poetry. The comedians are even allowed *their* statement of intent, their claim to a kind of negative commitment in a mad world:

We are the faithless; we admire the dedicated, the Dr Magiots and the Mr Smiths for their courage and their integrity, for their fidelity to a cause, but through timidity, or through lack of sufficient zest, we find ourselves the only ones truly committed — committed to the whole world of evil and of good, to the wise and to the foolish, to the indifferent and to the mistaken. We have chosen nothing except to go on living, 'rolled round on earth's diurnal course, With rocks and stones and trees.'

In view of the realistic epistemology of other selves already discussed it is natural that Jones's apotheosis as guerilla leader and his death should happen, as it were, off stage, and be left largely to the reader's imagination. To work on, the reader has only the briefest report from Philipot to Brown ('With him we began to learn, but he didn't have time enough. The men loved him. He made them laugh.') As with his treatment of the thriller, here Greene has polished and refurbished the jaded formulae of the boys' adventure story, the reformed black sheep, the

heroism unto death. The warring dialectic of engagement
and non-engagement, developed throughout the novel,
receives its final statement in the sermon preached at the
Requiem Mass for Jones and his companions. Greene is
good at sermons, as the priest's sermon in *The Power and
the Glory* witnesses; it is not that he is doctrinaire but that,
like a good preacher on the Gospels, he has the faculty of
digesting the implications of a dramatic narrative into
poetic or reflective comment (from being an Eliot of the
novel we have seen him turn in a generation into a fictional
La Rochefoucauld): here, in spite of the background
awareness of the theology of the Latin American liberation
church movement, he seems wholly original, plain and
succinct, and completely and honestly intent on the
reconciliation of Catholicism and social justice which is a
major subject of the later novels; yet there is a highly
personal undercurrent of thought — is it that with the
withdrawal of God, or his distancing in a dominant mood
of scepticism, action *is* belief? For St Thomas, who
provides the text for the sermon, was the doubting apostle
who demanded to see the wounds made by the nails:

> The priest was a young man of Philipot's age with the
> light skin of a *métisse*. He preached a very short sermon
> on some words of St Thomas the Apostle: 'Let us go up
> to Jerusalem and die with him.' He said, 'The Church is
> in the world, it is part of the suffering in the world, and
> though Christ condemned the disciple who struck off
> the ear of the high priest's servant, our hearts go out in
> sympathy to all who are moved to violence by the
> suffering of others. The Church condemns violence,
> but it condemns indifference more harshly. Violence
> can be the expression of love, indifference never. One is
> an imperfection of charity, the other the perfection of
> egoism. In the days of fear, doubt, and confusion, the
> simplicity and loyalty of one apostle advocated a
> political solution. He was wrong, but I would rather be
> wrong with St Thomas than right with the cold and the
> craven. Let us go up to Jerusalem and die with him.

The open denunciation of the Haitian régime had a direct political effect. Duvalier brought an action against Greene in the French courts and was awarded one franc damages (a happier result for the author than that of the Shirley Temple libel case in 1938). He also, in 1967, issued an official pamphlet accusing Greene of all manner of perversities including drug addiction. The incident is significant because it exhibits a twentieth-century writer making effective protest against tyranny in a manner more familiar in the age of Voltaire or that of Byron; Greene, in fact, is a unique successor of liberal romantic poets like Shelley in *The Mask of Anarchy* or Byron in *The Vision of Judgment* who used the pen as a sword. Right down to his exposure of the Nice police he has practised the belief that good writing, being truth speaking, has a function in the public world.

CHAPTER 6

Love and Pity

I

In construction and execution *The Comedians* is a very good
novel and its successor *The Honorary Consul* (1973) is even
better (*Travels with My Aunt* (1969), which appeared between them, is a purely comic novel).

The theme of political commitment and the political duty
of a Christian in an unjust society is even more to the fore in
The Honorary Consul than in *The Comedians*. Father Rivas is a
Catholic priest who has become a Marxist revolutionary,
and his school friend Dr Plarr, the representative of
indifference, takes sides for the sake of Rivas far more
decisively than Brown does for Jones, since he loses his life
in doing so. So if the discussion of the novel seems
restricted, though I admire it as much as any by Greene,
and he himself considers it his best, it is partly because it is a
subtle and accomplished variation on a continuing theme.
It has the tolerance and the mellowed wryness of attitude to
be found in all the later novels; the tiredness of life is no
longer an extreme disease but another mask among many
to be assumed, and there is admission of the existence of a
disconcerting reserve of human freedom enabling the
wearer to put down the masks and be himself to his own
terror and amazement. Perhaps also there is a sense in
which, like Tolstoy's happy families, all controlled, calmly
good novels are alike, and therefore to some extent
immune to critical discussion; they are not, like the great
flawed novels, sustained by dreams and personal obsessions
for example, most of Hardy, or indeed *The Power and the*

Glory and *The Heart of the Matter*. Therefore my restricted discussion will dwell principally on features which cannot be classed as repetition or variation.

The setting of *The Honorary Consul* is a small port on the shores of the great river Paraná in northern Argentina which forms the border with Paraguay. The mood is even more elegiac than that of *The Comedians*, breathing the sadness and the missed opportunities of middle age. In the first scene a plume of smoke on the further shore lies across the red bars of the sunset 'like a stripe on a national flag'; 'It was an evening which, by some mysterious combination of failing light and the smell of an unrecognized plant, brings back to some men the sense of childhood and of future hope and to others the sense of something which has been lost and nearly forgotten.'

Eduardo Plarr, a man in his thirties and a doctor, is, like so many Argentines, of mixed descent, the son of an English father and a Paraguyan mother. The elder Plarr is an opponent of General Stroessner's régime in Paraguay and supposed to be in prison. When Plarr was a boy his father had sent him for safety with his mother down the river to Argentina. The mother 'had mislaid her beauty and become querulous', and lives in Buenos Aires eating too many cream-cakes in fashionable tea-rooms. Plarr feels the guilt of middle-class comfort and is his father's son in his sympathy with the poor: 'In the *barrio* of the poor I am aware of doing something he would have liked to see me do'. Apart from this he is emotionally cold, sleeping without love with a succession of married women, an exile from any community and any form of belief.

Then comes the shocking intervention of chance and danger into the deadening round of his life: his old school friend Leon Rivas, leading a small group of Paraguyan terrorists, plans to kidnap the American ambassador as a publicity stunt and in order to bargain for the freedom of those imprisoned across the border. By their amateurish blunder they capture instead Charlie Fortnum, a very minor British official, not a real consul but an honorary one in the port. He is wounded during the kidnapping and they need a doctor; so Plarr becomes involved and is brought to their hiding-place in the *barrio* of the poor.

The ironies multiply. Plarr is the lover of Charlie Fortnum's wife Clara, a former prostitute in the local brothel. The possible release of his father might have been a good motive for Plarr's assisting the terrorists but he now learns from them that his father has been shot trying to escape. Though the main motive for his helping the terrorists is now removed, he, the egoist and cynic, finds that he cannot abandon his old friend Leon or the friend he has cuckolded, Charlie Fortnum. He goes to Buenos Aires and tries to prevail on the British ambassador to intervene but Fortnum is not important enough for a diplomatic representation. 'The trouble is, Plarr,' says the ambassador, 'Fortnum is such pitiably small beer.' His smallness not only controls the course of the plot: it is the source of the spiritual humility which makes him loving and tender to his wife, the ex-whore, and more interesting than other characters who are sustained by power or self-sufficiency. In fact the others, including Plarr, are comedians in the sense used in the previous novel, and Charlie Fortnum is not, (although he is a figure of fun to all.) Plarr, like Jones, leaves off comedy to die for his friends and possibly also for an ideal he did not know he had entertained associated with the respect he feels for his father.

Still hoping for an intervention at a high level to raise a ransom, Plarr proposes the foundation of a local Anglo-Argentinian society; there will only be two members, himself and a British expatriate Humphreys, but the president will be an Argentinian novelist of some reputation, Jorge Julio Saavedra, who is to write a stirring letter on Fortnum's behalf to national and international papers. Meanwhile Plarr has several interviews with Colonel Perez the chief of police who suspects him of connivance at the kidnapping both because of his father's politics and his known liaison with Clara. The ironies are emotional, too: Charlie loves Clara even when he learns she has been unfaithful to him; Clara, pregnant by Eduardo Plarr, begins to understand that she loves him; Plarr, too resolute in resisting the claims of others really to know himself, does not know where he stands:

If for once he had been aware of a sickness he could describe in no other terms, he would have unhesitatingly used the phrase 'I love', but he had always been able to attribute the emotion he felt to a quite different malady — to loneliness, pride, physical desire, or even a simple sense of curiosity.

Colonel Perez and a paratroop detachment find the hut where the terrorists and their prisoner are hidden and close in. A time limit for their surrender is announced over a loudspeaker. Plarr goes outside the hut to plead for them and is immediately shot. Leon goes to his assistance and is shot down too. Leon says as he is dying, 'I am sorry . . . I beg pardon'. He is presumably apologizing for letting his friend become involved; but Plarr, intending to make the sort of joke they had made as boys against the formulae of the Church, says, *'Ego te absolvo'*. The words of absolution thus uttered take on a serious resonance since a para approaches to finish him off and in a few seconds they are both dead.

Once again Greene has practised the journalistic skill of being the right man in the right place to present an incident which bears within itself the seed of future events. The book shares this prophetic quality with *The Quiet American:* the tactical failure of the French to control the jungle war in Indo-China, emphasized in the latter work, forecasts the futility of the American military effort fifteen years later, just as Pyle's ideas foreshadow the inadequate policies leading to the military débâcle. A year after the publication of *The Honorary Consul* the British ambassador to Argentina, Geoffrey Jackson, was kidnapped by the Tupamaro guerillas and held for several months before obtaining his release, a period in which his unflagging resolution and capacity for engaging in intelligent dialogue gained for him the respect of his captors.[1] Once again Greene is reporter as well as creator, and the imaginative impact of the novel is qualified by its function as interpretation of that frightening public world reflected more coarsely in the mass media.

The Argentine has terrorists, and indeed secret police, but, unlike Haiti, is not at the time of which Greene is writing a terrorist society. It is however a very peculiar society, a country, in its urban centres, of exiles and expatriates, often hankering after their European roots and priding themselves on their superiority to other Latin American nations. Nostalgia for French culture and Europe in general alternates uneasily with a different national myth: the home-grown cult of the *gauchos*, the horsemen of the pampas, as celebrated in the popular epic *Martin Fierro*. This is the cult of male honour and courage, the *machismo* that often finds its expression in a knife fight to the death against impossible odds. It is not too fanciful to suggest that if the Foreign Office had circulated *The Honorary Consul* in the right quarters as an ancillary state paper in the early months of 1982 our commanders in the Falklands might have been better prepared to comprehend the temper of the Argentine pilots who flew their planes to almost certain death over San Carlos Water.

Eduardo Plarr is personally and racially an Argentine, with some roots in another country, fluctuating in the strength of his sense of identity but desperate to establish it. But the chief exponent of *machismo* in the book is the novelist Saavedra: he writes melancholy books, one about Castillo the fisherman who wages an unending struggle with the sea for a small reward, another about passionate love and jealousy which ends in the ritual knife fight. Saavedra is an aging man whose reputation has not grown; he has been deeply wounded by a young critic Montez whom he had helped to get his books published and who has now written a mordant article on his work denouncing the whole cult of *machismo*. He is comparatively poor, living in a tiny room with two suits on hangers and a few books, his own works. Under a surface of sheer comedy Greene exposes his essential dignity, as he had done with the old German doctor Hasselbacher in *Our Man in Havana* or Parkis the private inquiry agent in *The End of the Affair*. He goes to Señora Sanchez' brothel merely in order to prevent inordinate desires coming between him and his work.

The climax of the comedy, involving his total attention to style in life and art, is when he agrees to write the letter to the newspapers for the Anglo-Argentinian society, but, regardless of urgency, insists on correcting the draft and turning it into an artistic work of psychological delicacy:

Do you believe writing is as easy as that? Would you do a delicate operation, on the spur of the moment, on this table? I will sit up all night if necessary. The quality of the letter I write you will more than make up for the delay, even in translation. By the way who is going to translate it — you or Dr Humphreys? I would like to check the translation before you send it abroad. I trust your accuracy, of course, but it is a question of style. In a letter like this we have to move the reader, to bring home to him the character of this poor man . . . It is a situation in which such a man either succumbs to fear or he grows in stature . . . I saw, behind the superficial gaiety, a profound melancholy.

The irony is revealing, because although Saavedra is forcing Charlie Fortnum's character into his own romantic-heroic idiom, he does hit upon the real depth of the latter's nature which underlies his unselfish love for Clara: *machismo*, like Communism or Catholicism, is an interpretative tool that can be applied to all lives. Nobly and extravagantly Saavedra offers himself as a hostage in Fortnum's place, and Plarr thinks that in such a country the scheme might work; Saavedra has of course a personal reason: 'At least I will show young Montez that *machismo* is not an invention of the author of *Martin Fierro*'. C. S. Lewis wrote that courage was the necessary underpinning of all the virtues, and *machismo* is a cultural melodramatization of the quality of courage; in the context of terrorism the other characters tend to fall into the style of *machismo*, Leon and his companions holding out against the whole state apparatus, and Plarr walking out of the hut to face the bullets of the paras. It is inevitable that at the end it should be Saavedra who pronounces Plarr's funeral oration in which the facts are twisted and the sentiment translated into the melancholy national idiom:

You were a friend to each of your patients — even to the poorest among them. All of us know how unsparingly you worked in the *barrio* of the poor without recompense — from a sense of love and justice. What tragic fate then it was that you, who had toiled so hard for the destitute, died at the hands of their so-called defenders.

Only Charlie Fortnum, the survivor, is immune to *machismo* for he displays virtues that are without a cultural solvent: charity and humility.

A far more famous writer than Saavedra is depicted to be must have given Greene material to enrich the ethos of the fictional character. Amongst the great variety and subtlety of his work Jorge Luis Borges has several stories celebrating the moral tradition of *Martin Fierro*, including one which actually celebrates the hero himself. In another a man convalescent from an illness returns to his old home in the rural south of Argentina; some louts pick a fight with him, an old *gaucho* throws him a knife, and he goes out with them on to the plain, 'firmly clutching the knife, which he perhaps would not know how to wield.'[2] It is all there, as in the novels of Saavedra and in the parody deaths outside the hut of men whose private search for identity must be interpreted in terms of the myth of masculine identity embraced in a chosen moment of death. The norm of the myth is typified in the terrorist Aquino, one of Leon's companions, who writes poetry and whose favourite poem is 'Death is a common weed, Requires no rain'.

In a masculine culture like this the authority of the father is a dominant force; fear of the father's anger and disapproval is the spur towards daring action, whether making love to women or risking death with other men. Charlie Fortnum had been humiliated by a father who was a bully, but now he feels lost without him and drinks too much in compensation (his repeated comic tags are that he 'knows his measure' and a reference to his beloved Land Rover as 'Fortnum's Pride'):

> I used to be angry with my father. He didn't understand me, I thought, or care a nickel about me. I hated him. All the same I was bloody lonely when he died . . . I even imitate him. Though he drank more than I do.

His father was always accusing him of cowardice, of crying

too easily. But in his ordeal Charlie shows no self-pity and behaves better than the obvious exponents of *machismo;* in a childhood incident his father had abused him for babyishness in crying over a lizard he had squashed; his reply had been, 'I'm crying for the lizard, not for me'. He alone among the personages of the novel demonstrates a capacity for a truly outgoing love; in the incongruous realm that is human nature he alone, the clown and drunkard, is a fully grown up person:

> He was not crying now for himself. The tears were for Clara and a few of them for Fortnum's Pride, both left alone and defenceless. Loneliness, as he knew from experience, was a worse thing to suffer.

Charlie, then, has finally freed himself from obsession by a father whom he had loved and hated. In comparison Plarr knows himself but slenderly and has never quite come to terms with the loss of a far nobler father whom he had infinitely revered. The relationship is perhaps only fully satisfied when he goes out of the hut to his death; previously he can only try to come near his father's code of justice by working in the *barrio* of the poor, or escape from his unsatisfactory mother in the arms of other women. It is significant that when one of his former mistresses, Señora Escobar, straddles him in a chair while her husband sleeps in another corner of the room, and asks him to go on saying something, he can only remember the nursery rhyme, 'This is the way the postboy rides, gallopy, gallopy, gallopy,' which his father had recited, dandling him on his knee.

His love for Clara begins as mere physical curiosity. She has the thin child's immature body which in Rose, Helen, Phuong and Marie Rycker has provided a magnet to other alienated men. He wonders if a man too rational to fall in love is destined for a worse fate, to become subject to an obsession. But gradually tenderness replaces lust, though he will still not recognize the change in his feelings or in those of Clara. When he comes to her at the beginning of her pregnancy and after the kidnapping of Charlie Fortnum, she touches his cheek and says, 'Do you remember that time at the camp when I told you I was pretending? But, *caro*, I was not pretending. Now when you make love to me I pretend. I pretend I feel nothing. I bite my lip so as to pretend. Is it because I love you, Eduardo?' Her tender and naive question cannot penetrate the protective shell of his cautious egoism; as he goes away he has almost forgotten it: 'It could not have been very important. The only questions of importance were those a man asked himself.' It is only under the stress of the ordeal in the hut that he begins to recognize his own emotion; he is jealous of Charlie's selfless love for Clara, and his jealousy, together with the wish to repay the debt to his father, impel him towards his last gesture: 'I don't know how to love. Poor drunken Charlie Fortnum wins the game.' At the end, after Plarr's funeral, Charlie takes comfort from the fact that Clara genuinely loved Plarr and that he in a fashion came to love her. They will call the child Eduardo. His magnanimity is impressive, a sort of *machismo* in reverse; though Clara delicately denies that she had loved Plarr he knows that this is not true and rejoices:

> Her lie meant nothing to him now at all. It was contra-dicted too plainly by her tears. In an affair of this kind it was the right thing to lie. He felt a sense of immense relief. It was as though, after what seemed an interminable time of anxious waiting in the ante-room of death, someone came to him with the good news that he had never expected to hear. Someone he loved would survive. He realized that never before had she been so close to him as she was now.

A major success of the book lies in its ability to present convincing images like this of the extraordinary range and frequent bewildering incongruity of the relations of men and women. As Leon says, 'When I was a young priest, I used to try to unravel what motives a man or woman had, what temptations and self-delusions. But I soon learned to give all that up, because there was never a straight answer. No one was simple enough for me to understand.' Greene, however, does probe these complicated motives in a prose that is spare and functional now and freer from imagery. Short blunt sentences convey immediate emotional facts; the longer ones, varying the rhythm, explore more tentatively the realizations of intimacy that lie on the edge of consciousness; no wonder Saavedra is treated with sympathy since he helps to define the style of the book:' . . . the opening sentence is the key to the rest. One has to strike the right tone, even the right rhythm. The right rhythm in prose is every bit as important as the right metre in a poem.'[3]

There is an apparent fissure in the novel between the personal motives which guide Fortnum and Plarr, and indeed Saavedra, and the political ideology of liberation as expounded by Leon to Plarr in the hut on their last night alive. This fissure is not an artistic fault, since the division of values is never reconciled and is perpetuated in a constant debate. Even the almost accidental formula of contrition and absolution between Leon and Plarr at their death remains a problematic and ironic gesture in the direction of the Catholicism they have both left behind. The debate between Plarr and Leon is a more mature and telling version of an argument that has existed since the formalized and over-simple morality dialogue of the priest and the lieutenant in *The Power and the Glory*. The perfected version of the debate is to be found in the long conversations of the priest and his friend the Communist mayor in Greene's *Monsignor Quixote* (1982), where there is the leisure of the road in place of prison or siege with a mortal crisis hanging over the participants. Leon's case certainly does not simplify the issues: he has taken a wife, embraced violence, and been excommunicated by the Church, but he considers that, since he follows his conscience against outright hypocrisy and oppression, he is separated from the Church by mutual consent, not divorce. He looks forward to a renewed Church beyond 'the temporary Church of these terrible years'. Many details contribute to the picture of him as 'a priest for ever' attempting to live out his priesthood on a new and strange plane. He breaks eggs over a pan and as he holds the shells the position of his fingers reminds Charlie Fortnum of the priest breaking the Host over the

chalice. The faint trace of the tonsure through the hair that
has grown is 'like a prehistoric camp in a field seen from a
plane'. The debate is also complex because Plarr is not the
exponent of traditional Christianity but of the wickedness
of God, if there is a God, in such an evil world; and Leon
shares something with him and the uprooted comedians of
the novel since he too is trying to resolve an unsatisfied
relationship with his father: in his case he is reacting against
a rich and powerful father who had been a successful
lawyer for the rich and for the ruling party in Paraguay.

The crux of the debate in the hut is reached when Leon
attempts to counter Plarr's belief that the God who has
created this world must be a monster, 'that horror up there
sitting in the clouds of heaven'. He does so by disarmingly
accepting the responsibility of God for man's evil. He made
us in his image — and so our evil is His evil too. How could I
love God if he were not like me?' Responsibility is tempered
by a belief in an evolving universe which recalls the echoes
of Teilhard de Chardin in *A Burnt-Out Case:*

> When you speak of the horror, Eduardo, you are
> speaking of the night-side of God. I believe that the time
> will come when the night-side will wither away, like your
> communist state, Aquino, and we shall see only the
> simple daylight of the good God..It is a long struggle and
> a long suffering, evolution, and I believe God is suffering
> the same evolution that we are, but perhaps with more
> pain . . .
>   . . . I believe in Christ, I believe in the Cross and the
> Redemption. The Redemption of God as well as of Man.
> I believe that the day-side of God, in one moment of
> happy creation, produced perfect goodness, as a man
> might paint one perfect picture. God's good intention
> was for once completely fulfilled so that the night-side
> can never win more than a little victory here and there.

It is noteworthy here that the daring or unorthodoxy lies
entirely in the luxury of speculation, and the speculation is
used to buttress an unshakeable acceptance of the divinity
of God in Christ and his love for men, and to reconcile that

acceptance with 'belief' in the intellectual or emotional sense in the fallen world evacuated by God. Leon, under pressure of his Indian wife Marta, says a Mass for his besieged band, without vestments or an altar. Before the *Domine, non sum dignus* the loudspeaker blares out its last message, 'You have exactly one hour left to send out the Consul to us and save your lives'. This again recalls the hurried Mass in the village in *The Power and the Glory* before the arrival of the police. In the circumstances of contemporary violence the rites of a religion of hope are celebrated, without ecclesiastical trappings, without intellectual assurance, but persisting along the road of choice and the assent of will. The apogee of this Christianity made naked is to be found in *Monsignor Quixote* when the absent God is sacrificed and worshipped through the mere motions of the Eucharist.

II

The love that is described in *The Honorary Consul* and the next novel, *The Human Factor* (1978), is, unusually for Greene, happy, or, at any rate, living, married love. No doubt this needs some qualification in regard to Clara and Charlie Fortnum: Clara is too passively simple to claim an active happiness, and her passivity is perhaps only stirred by Plarr; but the moment of communion Charlie feels with her at the end suggests a more harmonious future. It is a highly traditional realist novel ending in that it obliges the reader to think forward into continuing existences outside the text; yet the openness of Greene in handling the decisions of his characters in the course of the text precludes any dictatorial control by the author over what the future holds. The reader can only know that the text is not closed in upon itself but has referents in an imagined world of which it is merely a partial report, that Lady Macbeth indeed had children. Will Charlie go on drinking? Will Clara again be unfaithful? Even so, will the new bond between them somehow persist? (There will be the child of course, the conventional cementing of a marriage in so many stories, another instance of how Greene adapts and transforms the formulae of novelistic convention and of poor human nature.) The questions are as easy or difficult to answer as it is to decide the balance between selfishness and altruism in Brown's engineering Jones's escape in *The Comedians*. The printed pages of the text and the white pages of futurity are equally open, equally random in the strain they put upon human volition.

We do not encounter this degree of openness in *The Human Factor*. In the forefront of the book is a happy and equal marriage between a white man and a black woman of comparable intelligence and education with a child to whom they are attached. They are Greene's happiest couple, but their treatment by the plot is of the cruellest, leading to their apparently permanent separation in circumstances inimical to the peace of mind of each. One is bound to reflect that Greene is more inclined to favour the twisted and the fallen, a drunk and an ex-prostitute, than the normally happy; it is the same in the novella *Dr Fischer of Geneva or the Bomb Party* (1980), where an idyllic marriage is shattered by the girl's early, fortuitous death in a skiing accident: but on the author's behalf it should be remembered that poor nature and traditional wisdom afford sufficient instances of such early deaths. What does emerge from what I call the 'normality' of Maurice Castle and Sarah in *The Human Factor* is a certain externality of treatment: it is the divided, those at odds with the man within — Plarr, Brown, Querry, Fowler, Scobie — who enjoy the dubious luxury of a rich inner life.

Sarah is normal, or more ordinary, in another way. She is not a thin-boned waif-like child like so many of Greene's earlier women characters, Rose, Helen, Phuong and Clara. The temper of these women moves along an arc between two poles: at one pole they represent a challenging purity, as does Elizabeth in *The Man Within*, at the other extreme they offer the passive promiscuity of the whore to the men who are obsessed by their physique. The men are the isolated ones who have lost countries and beliefs, exiles from their own identity, and their obsession leads to the dangerous form of love that is pity. At this other pole the passivity of the child-women extinguishes their individuality and they move in flocks, chattering together like birds, as do Phuong and her sister, or the well-behaved girls in Mère Cathérine's brothel or in that of Señora Sanchez. For the permanently exiled the brothel becomes a home, a place for a pure and basic sexuality without the corruptions of any social superstructure, a nostalgic attempt to recover infantile joys. The primal scene of this regained domesticity is the table at which the girls quietly sit with their madam talking and sowing. We meet the scene again in *Monsignor Quixote* but there with a still more extraordinary viewpoint: the scene, which the exiles had found almost innocent as a point of rest amid the disturbance of their lives, is now seen through truly innocent eyes and from a life that is not disturbed. Maurice and Sarah live in a different emotional world: they do not need to recover childhood innocence: their son Sam (her child by another man before her marriage) can do that for them.

Maurice Castle works with his friend Davis in Section 6A of the Intelligence Services which deals with the affairs of Southern Africa. There is a suspected leak of information to Soviet Russia and a new head of security, Colonel Daintry, begins to investigate. The spy is in fact Maurice; he has been supplying secrets to the Russians for years, not for ideological reasons but to discharge a personal debt of his own estimation. He had worked under cover in South Africa and been assisted by Sarah and a Communist, Carson. When Maurice and Sarah become lovers the affair becomes known to the South African security police and the law moves against them. Maurice has to flee to Mozambique, leaving Sarah behind, but Carson is faithful to his promise to smuggle her out of the country to join him. This is the moral obligation, to a man and not to a party, which drives Maurice to disloyalty. His every clandestine act is a sacrifice to the freedom and safety of Sarah and Sam: the assumption is that states and organizations do not really exist as moral entities deserving obedience. The old man under the island's advice to cultivate disloyalty (in 'Under the Garden') is now put into practice in a strangely manufactured situation. Humaneness and sentiment condone Maurice's action; so do the madness and unpleasant-

ness of most of those in the organization he is supposed to
serve: but his conscientious betrayal leads only to misery for
the wife and child he loves. Since Maurice is a quiet man and
happily married, suspicion over the leaks falls on his
colleague Davis: Davis drinks too much, gambles, and is
hopelessly in love with one of the girls in the office, Cynthia.
The unpleasant Dr Percival, who is ostensibly a medical
man but in actuality has an executive post in the service,
undertakes to remove Davis by means of a new poison
Aflotoxin, the symptoms of which may be confused with
those of cirrhosis of the liver. It is noticeable at this point
that Maurice must have become aware that Davis is suspected and under surveillance; the poison is being adminis-
tered in gradual doses by Dr Percival and he is experiencing
weakness in his legs and arms.

Is there here another instance of the betrayal of a friend
by a man of sensitivity caught in a trap of conflicting
loyalties, Scobie betraying Ali, Fowler sacrificing Pyle? It is
not possible to give a positive answer to the question since
Maurice does not apparently begin to suspect poisoning
until after Davis's death. Maurice realizes that danger is
coming near to him and wishes to resign but it is impossible
at this stage.

A new operation is being planned, Operation Uncle
Remus: it involves the close co-operation of the U.S. and
Britain in the defence of the South African Republic by
early warning systems and tactical nuclear weapons.
Though Maurice has sent what purports to be his last
report by a secret 'drop' in a hollow tree on the common
near his home, he considers that his Soviet masters must
hear about Uncle Remus. He resorts to his usual channel of
communication, a book code; the book he uses is Tolstoy's
War and Peace; he has bought it, as he has bought other
books, from Mr Halliday's respectable second-hand shop in
Soho, opposite Mr Halliday's son's shop which is a porno-
graphic establishment. He had always understood that it
was the son who was his letter-box and he now gives Mr
Halliday an urgent message for him; the son is picked up by
the police on account of his business and Maurice waits for
what he thinks must be certain arrest. Muller, the South

African security officer who had been his opponent in the past and who is now connected with Uncle Remus, has an intuition of his treachery and informs Colonel Daintry. The latter visits Maurice and questions him but takes no immediate action. When 'they' act to get him out of the country, their representative is the totally unexpected Mr Halliday, an underground Communist since his time as a Soviet prisoner after the post-World War I Archangel campaign. He is disguised and put on a plane to Paris as a blind man. His final destination is Moscow.

The epilogue is unrelievedly chilling. There is an account of Maurice's early days in Moscow, 'under wraps' in almost complete isolation, of his reunion with his old contact Boris and of his beginning to learn Russian. Meanwhile Sarah is miserable in Surrey with her snobbish and narrow-minded mother-in-law. She learns from Dr Percival that since Sam is not on her passport she would never be able to rejoin Maurice unless she went alone: mother and son would not be allowed to go together. In Moscow Maurice has learned the same and the book ends with a desperately frustrated telephone conversation between husband and wife in which they exchange unconvincing hopes for reunion in the future until the line goes dead.

The Human Factor is not a novel of the high, confident distinction to be met in *The Comedians* and *The Honorary Consul*. It does however possess valuable qualities which are liable to be overlooked on a first reading. This is because of the book's relation to the genus of the spy thriller. Though light years away from James Bond, Greene clearly invites comparison with practitioners of the secret service romance like Len Deighton and John Le Carré. The comparison is very much to his advantage. It is as if an old cat had come away from the fireside to show that he can catch mice too as well or better than the frisking kittens. All the appurtenances are there, the drab realism of office routine, exposing the fact that most secret service work is deadly boring; the chief always called 'C' (like the wartime chief of SIS); the oblique, fencing conversations of the principals over lunches at the Travellers or the Reform; the arcane vocabulary of 'traces', 'drops' and 'covers'; the ultimate bestiality underneath the routine in the shape of the slow murder of the feckless and attractive Davis. Moreover, the plot of intrigue and eventual exposure is complex but not too complex; Greene does not indulge in the wanton obfuscation which some of his would-be rivals have substituted for subtlety, any more than he practises the exaggerated use of the 'metaphysical' simile, modelled on his own earlier imagery. The whole sequence of the escape, from the appearance of Mr Halliday as *deus ex machina* to the safe arrival of Maurice on the Paris flight, is a brilliant achievement of adventure writing comparable to the episode of Brown and Jones on the road to Les Cayes or the account of the night spent by Fowler and Pyle in the watchtower and then in the paddy-field.

The effectiveness of all this has its dangers: it tends to mask the ways in which Greene is transforming the genre he has adopted (he had of course written a secret service thriller before largely for burlesque purposes in *Our Man in Havana*). Greene's major effort is towards humanizing the thriller form. In Le Carré and others this effort remains a pretension rather than an accomplished fact. The prime example of this humanity is the live marriage of Sarah and Maurice. Their life in the home counties moves quite apart from the corridors of power; its lowness of key is conveyed by the fact that Maurice has no car and goes to and from the station on a bicycle; the boy Sam is skilfully drawn, and there is a dog Buller, a rounded character, the epitome of a lovable but stupid animal, and surely a rare intrusion from children's fiction into a serious novel (Buller, like his master and mistress meets a terrible end: Maurice has to shoot him in order to escape quietly). Colonel Daintry does not like his work and he is last seen after the exposure of Maurice preparing his resignation; Sir John Hargreaves — 'C' — is an old African hand who does not like the South African policeman Muller and regretfully remembers times in the bush when his boy was preparing his chop: between them they inevitably recall the Assistant Commissioner in *It's a Battlefield*, and are contrasted with the wholly horrible and contented Dr Percival who enjoys the game for its own sake but wants to be on the side that wins in his lifetime: since he has no real loyalties he is incapable of treachery. Early in the novel, looking at a Ben Nicholson on his host's wall with its boxes of colour, he reflects on the fragmented lives of people who live in their separate boxes:

> 'Take a look at that Nicholson. Such a clever balance. Squares of different colour. And yet living so happily together. No clash. The man has a wonderful eye. Change just one of the colours — even the size of the square, and it would be no good at all . . . There's your section 6. That's your square from now on. You don't need to worry about the blue and the red. All you have to do is to pinpoint our man and then tell me. You've no responsibility for what happens in the blue and red squares. In fact not even in the yellow. You just report. No bad conscience. No guilt.'

But the integrated human beings in the book are those capable of feeling guilt and worrying about what goes on in the blue and red squares, in South Africa, for instance. Reference is again made to the coloured boxes of the abstract picture when Muller tells Maurice that, since they are now on the same side, they had better concentrate on seeing the same picture and Maurice replies 'In fact we're in the same box?'. There is a difficulty here for any more common view of moral obligation. Is not Maurice's conduct very far from being an integrated view of behaviour? Does not his betrayal of country and colleagues make him a partial man like others, concentrating on one box, in his case the red one? Greene would, one imagines, meet these objections by reminding us that Maurice is not a Communist and has not embraced an ideology: he is acting purely on a personal motive. Yet presumably once his choice has been made he can not abstain from weighing the camps against Dresden and Hiroshima, Hungary and Czechoslovakia against the Bay of Pigs, and so on. There is no sign that he does this. As for the ordinary human revulsion from treason, Greene's peculiar consciousness of human failure in relationships allows him to minimize any such shock. As he writes of the double agent Philby whom he compares to an English Catholic working for Spain in the reign of Elizabeth: '"He betrayed his country" — yes, perhaps he did, but who among us has not committed treason to someone or something more important than a country?'[4] He admires Philby for adhering to the faith he has found with 'logical fanaticism' and not allowing liberal qualms to turn him into 'a querulous outcast of the Koestler-Crankshaw-Muggeridge variety'. But Maurice is not such a fanatic, and since his treason is only justifiable on personal and emotional grounds, we are bound to think of his indirect responsibility for the death of Davis.

Greene's peculiar belief in the entirely private valuation of action, as if decisions were taken quite apart from group codes or inherited standards, means that his study of Maurice has no room to examine the tensions and conflicts we would normally associate with the life of a sensitive man acting as a double agent. Maurice is just a good ordinary man who happens to be found out. Is it that his weakness is loving too much, for it is certainly his love for Sarah that launches him on his career as a double agent? The idea of an excessively scrupulous love, a love that becomes a devouring pity, is deliberately excluded. In fact it looks as if the earlier condemnation of pity is in process of revision:

> Why are some of us, he wondered, unable to love success or power or great beauty? Because we feel unworthy of them, because we feel more at home with failure? He didn't believe that was the reason. Perhaps one wanted the right balance, just as Christ had, that legendary figure whom he would have liked to believe in. 'Come unto me all ye that travail and are heavy laden.' . . . It wasn't pity, any more than it had been pity when he fell in love with Sarah pregnant by another man. He was there to right the balance. That was all.

This righting the balance, which excludes the inordinate pride of pitying others and is an imitation of the 'legendary' Christ, is the moral spring of Maurice's action in a world where prescriptive morality is already suspended or tainted by the *Realpolitik* of the Dr Percivals. Righting the balance is a principle that reflects back on the conduct of Charlie Fortnum in *The Honorary Consul;* we might have expected, on the premisses of *The Heart of the Matter,* that in taking Clara out of the brothel his feelings for her would be contaminated by the superiority of pity, but this is not so: a balance has been adjusted, a burden lifted, and the conclusion leaves promise of more equal interchange.

The question remains of the narrow limits placed on human decision in Maurice's case. He is like Scobie in being caught in a trap, and he does not have Scobie's final clutching at faith as a way of release. He picks his last random sentence from *War and Peace:* 'You say: I am not free. But I have lifted my hand and let it fall'. But this freedom, whether in London or Moscow, is so curtailed as to be derisory. Like Scobie again finding peace in the bush, like Daintry and Hargreaves missing a simpler and more expansive past, or Davis wanting to exchange his office for Mozambique, he hankers after a state of things from which the perpetual nagging of detail and choice would be absent:'. . . a city where he could be accepted as a citizen, as a citizen without any pledge of faith, not the City of God or Marx, but the city called Peace of Mind'.

The Human Factor is full of allusions to Greene's past and to his earlier work. Maurice's home is in Berkhamstead where Greene grew up;[5] the story is strongly localized in the station, the canal, particularly the common. Sam plays at hide and seek there with his father and Davis, as Greene had done, and the game corresponds to the adult games of secret service. The poems Sam likes Maurice to read reproduce the intense early emotions stimulated by poetry as they are described in *A Sort of Life*. There is also a confessional episode: Maurice goes into a Catholic church in Watford but encounters an unsympathetic priest who tells him he is wasting his time and that what he needs is a doctor. The theme of the clash between the need of the penitent and the advice received stretches back through the severity of Father Rank towards Scobie in the confessional to Greene's own experience when, planning marriage and afraid that he might be epileptic, he was advised simply to trust in God.

These allusions to recurring themes in the fiction and to crucial experiences in his past endow the book with a special character which marks it off from the common genre of the spy thriller, however excellently written. Greene has indeed humanized the thriller form but he has done something else too. He has written a sort of running commentary on his own kind of novel. Every novelist with each new novel creates a fresh disguise for the single novel he is writing all the time; and the novelist late in his career and at the summit of his skills finds that his remaining subject-matter lies more and more in the fruits of his past inventions and in his experience as a writer. Greene had in *Travels with My Aunt* (1969) already begun the game of literary allusions based on his earlier work; there is a visit to Brighton, and the introduction in person of the elderly crook Visconti who is a humorous reincarnation of the evil Renaissance tyrant who had thrilled the boy Greene in the pages of Marjorie Bowen.

In *The Human Factor* the function of the allusiveness is to bring the writer home to Berkhamstead. The theme of the frontier between custom and moral choice is approached by a return to the psychic origins: the spy-game on the familiar common merges into reality. As Greene quotes elsewhere from AE: 'In the lost boyhood of Judas Christ was betrayed.' A childhood hiding-place becomes a letter-box and a 'drop' for a real coded message. The relating of the past to the present at both the fictional and the personal levels, Castle's and Greene's, makes the drama of espionage the vehicle for a statement about aging. Maurice Castle's treachery is mitigated in its impact on the reader, not simply because he is a decent person and not a political fanatic, but because the real betrayer is time. His loyalty is to his wife, a son, and the memory of a friend, not to Communist ideology; but the past catches up with him and separates him from his wife. He had identified himself with her plight under the 'colour bar' in South Africa: now an even more cruel exile divides them. The son is not his son, and his very growth, the excited happiness of the all too suggestive game of hide and seek he plays with Davis on the common, throws Castle's aging into relief, as all children must do. The friend whose generosity of spirit was his main incentive in his clandestine course, dies, and again the past recedes leaving him stranded by his choices. So the final frustrated telephone conversation with Sarah and the interrupted line have been long prepared.

There is thus an elegiac quality about the book and an isolation of its central character which form its distinctive features. Maurice bears his isolation, even in its final form, with dignity, yet there results from it an inevitable narrowing of the scope of the work, beset as he and his family are by the sinister mad hatter's tea-party of the secret world embodied in Dr Percival and his vision of life as an amoral pattern of abstract squares. Seen in these terms, of time, closed inherited choices, and the ensuing constriction, the novel is a considerable achievement. It lacks however the openness and expansive scope of *The Honorary Consul,* and the contrast enables us to recognize the outstanding merit of the latter book. It is not just that the freedom of the characters, of Plarr, Charlie, Clara and Leon, allows us to hope, and thus provides some humanistic palliative, a guarantee that history can encroach thus far upon us and no further. That is not at all a message to be deduced from a text where history presses hard enough on both sides of the great river, the Parana. We have already seen that the freedom and the hope do not produce certainties, since the future of Charlie and Clara, the survivors, remains problematic. But the freedom, like the vast air, the huge pampas, the thick jungle beyond the river, is a freedom for the characters to grow. Plarr changes as a man, not like Brown in *The Comedians* by making a few right decisions and then resuming the comedian's role, but by learning at least a jealous love in place of indifference; Clara falls in love indeed, while Charlie discovers within his foolish private self enormous reserves of strength and moral tact. It is this growth of the characters within the text which is a new departure for Greene, and which, demonstrated through an assured and transparent technical assurance, communicates to the reader a sense of exhilarating freedom.

CHAPTER 7

Comedy and Beyond

I

In this survey of Greene's novels, which has been constructed largely but not wholly in their chronological order, it has been possible to watch the gradual encroachment of comedy. Greene writes in the introduction to *A Burnt-Out Case* as if he had only discovered comedy in that novel; in reality, it had been there all the time, but as it were waiting in the wings in minor characters and single episodes like the hospital rag in *A Gun For Sale*, or Parkis and his son in *The End of the Affair*, or Pyle seen through Fowler's eyes in *The Quiet American* (but this is comedy that soon turns sour).

Then in *The Comedians* and *The Honorary Consul* the comic characters begin to occupy the higher ground: Jones and the Smiths, Charlie Fortnum and Saavedra. In these latter the delight of their ridiculousness blends with a sense of the nobility in their natures which events reveal. The feckless charm of Davis and the comic cross-purposes of intelligence life in *The Human Factor* are darkened by the prison-like determinism of the novel which seems to present a view of personal need as something that cannot ever be satisfied or even understood. The MI5 men searching Davis's belongings after his death think there must be something highly significant in the recurring letter 'c' in the margin of his copy of Browning's poems; only Maurice can know that it must refer to Cynthia, the girl with whom he is in love. Humour like this, or like that associated with the two booksellers, father and son, goes sour because it emphasizes the ignorance and misunderstanding which surrounds the lives of the chief characters. Even Dr Percival, with his passion for trout fishing and his preference for steak and kidney pudding to steak and kidney pie, is a comic 'character' of a horrible sort. But in *Travels with My Aunt* (1969) the comic spirit is dominant; it is no longer a vehicle for satire, no longer a grotesque distortion within a world of violence and death. Humour and bizarre invention enjoy their own freedom in a world in which moral convention and the life of social habit are flouted at every turn.

In 1966 Greene made his home in Antibes and thus brought to an end a period of extreme restlessness. The prevalence of comedy, the removal of tension, the lessening influence in his work of the depressive side of his tempera- ment, may or may not have been affected by a more settled mode of life. The new mood, sardonic and worldly-wise but not jaded or cynical, is apparent in the stories collected as *May We Borrow Your Husband? and Other Comedies of the Sexual Life* (1967). What is specially interesting is that the greater mellowness of mood is accompanied by a significant formal revolution. It is for this reason that *Travels with My Aunt* is being considered out of its chronological sequence and together with *Monsignor Quixote*.

Both these novels are comedies but both also abandon the tautly plotted thriller construction that is habitually favoured by Greene and which reappears in *The Human Factor;* they are episodic, and the author indulges himself grandly, not sparing extravagance and coincidence, espe- cially in *Travels with My Aunt.* Greene's apprenticeship to romance had been the psychological adventure story as practised by Stevenson and Conrad; the form was then crossed with the early twentieth-century thriller. Now by discarding thriller plot he is returning to the original episodic form of the romance; but the weakness of the form, the risk of complete disintegration as in the old romances of chivalry, is avoided because a unifying princi- ple of interest has been substituted which is maintained through all the episodes. Greene has invoked the august shade of Cervantes himself, the father of the novel: the debt is patent and declared in *Monsignor Quixote,* in *Travels with My Aunt* there is a preliminary essay. The interest is that provided by two contrasting characters and two points of view which divide the world between them. The dialectic of two characters, presented to a great extent in argument in direct speech, is already present in the debates of Querry and Dr Colin in *A Burnt-Out Case,* in some of the discussions of Fowler and Pyle in *The Quiet American,* in Eduardo Plarr's arguments about Christianity and Communism with Leon Rivas in the hut in *The Honorary Consul.* Now it is the primary matter of these two late novels.

Form and emotional tone, then, are new; what look back to the earlier fiction are constant allusions and cross-references to its episodes and characters, usually light-hearted and self-mocking. It has been seen how this tendency to echo the music of his own personal time in a different key has been growing until, in *The Human Factor*, the chief character is set down in the Berkhamstead of his boyhood with a kind of mocking tenderness. There is also one other theme carried over from the past: that of the transition from innocence to experience; serious human insight is never wholly lacking in Greene, but in *Travels with My Aunt* the sheer fantastic energy of pure comedy is dominant.

Henry Pulling is a retired bank manager who lives a blameless and humdrum existence in the suburbs cultivating dahlias. At his mother's funeral he meets again his Aunt Augusta, his mother's sister, who snatches him up into a new life of travel and risk on the seamy side of the law. Her colourful past includes many love affairs and a period in an Italian brothel. In her seventies she is living by currency smuggling and has a negro lover Wordsworth who adores her.

After Henry's first visit to her flat he finds that Wordsworth has hidden marijuana in the casket containing his mother's ashes and he is soon visited by the police. Then his aunt takes him to Paris and after that to Istanbul on the Orient Express; she is now smuggling a gold brick disguised as an ornate Venetian candle. Henry spends the journey with Tooley, an American hippie who induces him to smoke pot; insensibly his stiff personality is changing and he is sorry when she departs for Katmandu to join her lover. Back at home, practically deported from Turkey, Henry seems to be sinking with regret into his old life, and wondering whether to offer marriage to the sedate spinster Miss Keene who is rather fond of him and has gone to South Africa. But Aunt Augusta strikes again and this time his old life is completely shattered.

A first-class ticket to Buenos Aires arrives from her, and from there he goes by river steamer along the rivers La Plata and Paraná to Asunción, the capital of Paraguay. He is the unwitting carrier of a fake Leonardo da Vinci drawing which is hidden under a photograph of Freetown, Wordsworth's old home. On the journey he re-encounters Wordsworth and meets, coincidentally, a CIA agent who turns out to be the father of Tooley. In Asunción on the National Day he has the misfortune to blow his nose on a red handkerchief, the colour of the ruling Colorado party, and spends a night in jail. Aunt Augusta has been reunited with her former lover, the adored Mr Visconti. They plan to buy a share in a plane smuggling cigarettes from Panama and later to own their own aircraft. A ramshackle mansion is hastily furnished and a great party and ball given to local notables. The CIA agent is bought off with the fake da Vinci. By the end Henry has agreed to go into the smuggling business and is planning to marry in two years' time the fourteen-year old daughter of the chief of customs who has good English and reads Tennyson with him.

Travels with My Aunt is an extravaganza, a picaresque string of anecdotes by Aunt Augusta, including that of another former lover, Curran, who founded a dogs' church in Brighton, or of M. Dambreuse, who kept two mistresses in the same hotel in Paris, visiting one at night and the other in the afternoon. It would be crass to read moral lessons into the book. Yet it is a celebration of freedom and vitality; its dismissal of conventional negative morality is not very different from that met in Greene's other work, except that usually the contrast is made with genuine personal moral decision, not with anarchic amoralism. As the reader has suspected all along, Henry is discovered to be his aunt's natural son; his initiation into the world of danger and illegality is partly a variation of the familiar theme of

transition from the child's security to the adult world, partly
a joyous response to his own true nature (the same
combination is found in 'Under the Garden' in the prophetic myth of Wilditch, the restless traveller): 'I felt oddly
elated to be alive, and I knew in a moment of decision that I
would never see Major Charge again, nor the dahlias, the
empty urn, the packet of Omo on the doorstep or a letter
from Miss Keene . . . I think even then I knew there would
be a price to pay for it.'

Apart from the surprises of a picaresque narrative, much
of the work is taken up by the conversation of Aunt Augusta
and Henry; through disjointed anecdotes the reader is able
to reconstruct her disreputable life and her mastering
passion for Mr Visconti. But the anecdotes are not everything: in the course of them she is presenting a view of life
in opposition to the safety-first view of Henry the bank
manager. She flares up when Henry suggests she should
have despised Mr Visconti for betraying her, and Greene's
prose flares up too:

> 'I despise no one,' she said, 'no one. Regret your own
> actions, if you like that kind of wallowing in self-pity, but
> never, never despise. Never presume yours is a better
> morality . . . you, I suppose, never cheated in all your
> little provincial banker's life because there's not anything
> you wanted enough, not even money, not even a woman
> . . . Your poor father didn't have a chance. He was a cheat
> too, and I only wish you were. Then perhaps we'd have
> something in common.'

But in this celebration of the human will for life and
pleasure the mortal note does not remain unstruck. Wordsworth, the negro lover, dismissed by Aunt Augusta, comes
back inconsolably during the ball and is killed in the garden
by a bodyguard. This death for love has been played out
before in the suicide of Brown's mother's lover, another
negro, in *The Comedians*. In the later book the comedians are
not to have it all their own way for, when Henry comes in to
announce the news, he finds his mother and Mr Visconti
rapt, dancing alone in an empty ballroom: they are isolated
in the selfish blindness of love:

A flash-bulb broke the shadows up. I have the photo-graph still — all three of us petrified by the lightning flash into a family group: you can see the great gap in Visconti's teeth as he smiles towards me like an accom-plice. I have my hand thrown out in a frozen appeal, and my mother is regarding me with an expression of tenderness and reproof.

Visconti is named, of course, after the villain of Marjorie Bowen's *The Viper of Milan,* the book which first opened the young Greene's eyes to the existence of pure evil. There is an ironic gesture in the direction of his past as a writer, in revisiting Brighton, and ironies that are not personal in the naming of a policeman John Sparrow and the Turkish police chief Colonel Hakim (a character in more than one Eric Ambler thriller). Evil has now been captured and softened but not entirely tamed: it is a bad accident that leaves Wordsworth dead and Henry's Miss Keene an expatriate spinster in the Transvaal.

II

The two comedies, *Travels with My Aunt* and *Monsignor Quixote*, are separated by a very different sort of comedy, *Dr Fischer of Geneva or the Bomb Party* (1980) which is described by the author as a black entertainment. It is a *conte* or novella, but since it is the longest of all Greene's stories and has been published as a volume on its own it demands consideration here. Not only on account of its length. For once again, as in the *Human Factor* which it follows by two years, a number of themes from earlier books and earlier life are gathered together and woven into a new pattern. The pattern throws into startling opposition a pair of innocent lovers like those in the early thrillers and a figure of the most chilling cruelty. Evil now walks abroad, not with the swashbuckling violence of a Visconti, who has already been tamed into a dream of laughter as the crook who remained faithful after everything to Aunt Augusta, nor with the mean sadism of a Captain Concasseur, but in the form of a total selfishness; this selfishness can make contact with other beings only by possession of them and contempt for them. This is what Dr Fischer does, and through him the reader can understand more fully why Aunt Augusta regarded contempt as the most deadly of the vices. Unlike anger, lust, jealousy, common cruelty, even inordinate pride, it is not a corruption of love, but the denial of the very possibility of love.

Dr Fischer has made his millions by Dentophil Bouquet, a toothpaste which keeps at bay the infections caused by eating too much Swiss chocolate. His home is, suitably, in Switzerland, at the hygienic capitalist heart of Europe where he maintains his neutrality towards all human affections. His wife has found affection and a shared love of music and Mozart with a poor clerk called Steiner: Dr Fischer breaks up their apparently innocent relationship, has Steiner dismissed from his job, and hounds and nags his wife to her death from misery and neglect: he could have borne an adultery with another rich man, but the fact that another individual could excel him in disinterested regard and that this could be reciprocated by his wife is not to be suffered. All this is in the past. There is one daughter of the marriage, Anna-Luise. She too falls in love with a poor clerk, Jones, in a firm of chocolate exporters and marries him; they live without any support from the father. Dr Fischer surrounds himself with toadies ('the toads', as Anne-Luise calls them), whom he delights in teasing and tormenting at his famous parties while he plays on their greed with luxurious presents and the promise of more to come. There is a Swiss army officer who is not a general but is always called General, Mrs Montgomery, the American with blue-rinsed hair, an international lawyer named Kips, a tax adviser Monsieur Belmont, and Richard Deane, a failed movie actor sinking into drink and privately watching his own former successes. Jones is sought out by Dr Fischer and added to his party list, an object of curiosity and jealousy to the 'toads'. These parties are the occasion for every kind of humiliation and insult to the guests: they accept every insult for sheer greed. This time, before the presents are distributed, they have to endure a meal solely of porridge. Only Jones keeps his dignity by refusing to eat it. A curious passage of dialogue between Jones and Dr Fischer at the dinner suggests that we are now back at

Leon's (*The Honorary Consul*) concept of the night side of God which can permit evil:

'What was I saying?'
'That God is greedy.'
'Well, the believers and sentimentalists say he is greedy for our love. I prefer to think that, judging from the world he is supposed to have made, he can only be greedy for our humiliation, and *that* greed how could he ever exhaust? It's bottomless. The world grows more and more miserable while he twists the endless screw, though he gives us presents – for a universal suicide would defeat his purpose – to alleviate the humiliations we suffer. A cancer of the rectum, a streaming cold, incontinence. For example you are a poor man, so he gave you a small present, my daughter, to keep you satisfied a little longer.'
　'She's a very big alleviation,' I said. If it's God who gave her to me I'm grateful to him.'
　'And yet perhaps Mrs Montgomery's necklace will last longer than your so-called love.'
　'Why should he wish to humiliate us?'
　'Don't I wish to humiliate? And they say he made us in his image. Perhaps he found he was a rather bad craftsman and was disappointed in the result.'

There is a development from the theology of Leon. The night side and the day side of God are now being operated by human beings in their acts of will. Dr Fischer chooses to see God in his own image as a giver of presents, bribes, in between the endless humiliations he inflicts on the human body before its extinction. Jones, happy in love, cannot understand the wish to humiliate and is happy at all that is given because of what he has been given – all must be alleviation so far. But Dr Fischer's icy detachment does speak an echo of that idea of an evolutionary God which Leon had sketched, as if some day the craftsman will get it right. Also the idea of God made in man's image, man in God's, sets up an oscillation that recalls two significant episodes in the past of Greene's work: the good humour with which the whisky priest sees through the treacherous character of the mestizo who dares to grumble at the priest whom he is betraying; and the moment when Scobie, having takes the overdose, decides *in his personal sense of justice* that there is something he ought to do for God. The last word, literally the last word, is always with the individual soul irrevocably committed to its own spiritual idiom.

The dark side of God is turning to Jones. Anna-Luise is killed in a pointless ski-ing accident where no error or lack of skill on her part is at issue. At first Jones thinks the body brought down the *piste* cannot be hers because she was wearing a white sweater and this one is wholly red. What has been one of the rarely succesful and tender sexual relations in Greene, a marriage more surely rendered than that of Maurice Castle and Sarah, though in a few dextrous strokes, more seriously tender than that of the pair in *Loser Takes All,* another gambling story, is cruelly shattered. Dr Fischer does not do it. Or is he the malefic God who holds the bank in a world where to love is to risk, as much as to play for money and power?

The conclusion tells us something in answer. Dr Fischer holds a last party; he has shown no emotion at the death of his daughter and no trace of sympathy for Jones who has attempted suicide without success (twenty aspirins drunk fast in a pint of Scotch) and still wants to die. There is a last party and Jones and all the 'toads' are invited. It is Christmas and there is snow on the ground but the dinner is held out of doors beside a great fire. There is a Christmas cracker for each guest to be taken from a bran tub and each cracker but one contains wrapped round its paper motto a cheque on Crédit Suisse for two million francs. The remaining cracker, declares Dr Fischer, contains a lethal device. Of course the guests, except for one, allow their greed to overcome their fear, and Jones is only too ready to embrace the possibility of oblivion. But Dr Fischer has had his last joke: there are cheques for all, but no bomb. At the end of the party Jones, wandering drunkenly by the lake in the grounds, encounters Steiner who feels that he must on his own crushed behalf deliver a final insult to the great insulter, Fischer. 'Now I want to get near enough to him to spit in God Almighty's face." But it is too late. Though there was no bomb there is a shot. And a hundred yards away they find the body of Dr Fisher who has blown his brains out.

Jones lives and only memories of love can remain, for him and for Steiner. The ending of the story sounds remorseless enough: 'Courage is sapped by day-to-day mind-dulling routine, and despair deepens so much every day one lives, that death seems in the end to lose its point. I had felt Anna-Luise close to me when I held the whisky in my hand and again when I pulled the cracker with my teeth, but now I had lost all hope of ever seeing her in any future'. But this is just what Jones says, and he was never a believer anyhow. He has also thought, at the death of the persecutor: 'I looked at the body, and it had no more significance that a dead dog'. This is a strange echo of the childhood episode in Greene's memories when he recollects a dead dog being carried at the foot of his pram in Berkhamsted. The immortality of love has gone, but so has the sting of the fear of death, and there is no more hate left for the persecutor.

It is a Christmas tale and a Christmas tale is necessarily a fairy story. Russian roulette is played for the last time, this time with Christmas crackers, and there is no chamber with a bullet in it. The dead dog is remembered and then forgotten. There are bright colours against the crisp snow, blood and the sparks of the fire and the flash of the crackers. But Dr Fischer has taken his own life in the end, being unable to live with a dead wife whom he killed and a daughter whom he tried not to love. Love suffers and dies from the nature of the world but in this fairy story evil cannot live, and withdraws itself. If we talk of a pattern and a resolution of the pattern we are no doubt indulging in wishful thinking; if we talk of a fruitful tension we are not thinking at all. But in this fairy tale, conceived at the Christmas table of a daughter, some sort of negation has died. The 'toads' are to meet again outside a Spanish church, carrying a holy image plastered with bank notes of high denomination, but while the contest of love and capital and desire goes on, some sort of ogre has departed from the world with the Doctor, some sort of spell has been exorcised, and we are prepared to leave the cold neutrality of the fable world for the large expansive spaces of a different book.

III

Superficially *Monsignor Quixote* (1982) is one of those imitations of Cervantes of which there have been so many. In form it follows its great original: a picaresque journey along the Spanish roads brings into being a loose chain of anecdotes and incidents. The method suggested by *Travels with My Aunt* is now applied more maturely and thoroughly. Even the encounters along the way are less important than the continuing dialogue between two men: it is two flesh-and-blood characters who argue, however, not abstract representatives of two 'points of view', although their debate does concern two differing twentieth-century attitudes to the human condition.

Greene's Don Quixote, descendant of the knight of the sorrowful countenance, is the parish priest of a small village in La Mancha. His friend is the Communist mayor who bears the same surname as Sancho Panza. One day, Don Quixote assists an Italian bishop *ex partibus infidelium* with his car, and gives him a simple lunch which is much appreciated. To show his appreciation the bishop procures his promotion to Monsignor and with this fantastic start the adventure gets under way: personal clues are scattered (as when later, merry from wine, Don Quixote says 'I think I am becoming what they call a whisky priest'), and the otherwise arbitrary descriptive detail concerning the mysterious bishop, that he was so tall he had to stoop to enter the priest's door, appears to indicate Greene himself, the creator who has made Don Quixote a monsignor and so set the whole story in motion. Don Quixote is able to leave his parish and go on leave, taking with him his friend the mayor who has been defeated in the local elections. He drives his little Seat car named after the knight's horse *Rocinante*. They go by Madrid, Salamanca, Avila and Valladolid; they see the Valley of the Fallen, the grandiose shrine built by Franco for the dead of the Civil War, and the simple sepulchre of the man of letters Miguel de Unamuno,

author of *The Tragic Sense of Life*. They stay the night in a
brothel: Don Quixote does not know where he is and can
only say how quiet and well-behaved the servants are (there
is also a repetition of the joke of the misunderstood *bidet*
which originated as another instance of priestly innocence
in *A Burnt-Out Case*). Don Quixote charitably hides an
escaping thief in the boot of the car and from now on they
are in trouble with the Guarda Civil.

As well as the general pattern of knight errantry and the
arguments between idealist and materialist the original *Don
Quixote* provides sources for particular episodes: here the
Monsignor is cast in the role of his ancestor freeing the
galley-slaves and, as on that occasion, there is no gratitude
from the liberated. The robber steals Don Quixote's shoes.
Soon, with another echo from the romance, the Monsignor
is brought home by his doctor and housekeeper and
confined on the instructions of his bishop, an unattractive
example of ecclesiastical formalism, as one who is mentally
deranged. But there is a second part, again following the
example of Cervantes: Don Quixote escapes and he and his
Sancho go on their travels again aiming for the mountains
of Galicia. Here they encounter their last adventure. They
hear much of the 'Mexicans'. These are those locals who
have amassed riches in Mexico and then come home. Some
of them shamelessly bribe the Church in these parts for
influence and indulgences. Don Quixote comes upon a
particularly revolting annual festival in a small town: the
statue of the Blessed Virgin is carried from the church
plastered with banknotes and auctioned to the highest
bidder. Don Quixote interrupts the ceremony at the crucial
point when the statue is born from the church; declaring
'This is blasphemy', he, though the mildest of men, tears the
capitalistic trappings from the image so that it falls to the
ground.

Now he is again pursued by the Guarda Civil, this time —
for blasphemy. Rocinante crashes to a standstill in the
courtyard of a Trappist monastery which gives him and his
friend shelter. He is dying, but before he dies he goes like a
sleep-walker from the guest room to the chapel, followed by
the wondering Mayor and the Guest Master: he says his last

Mass, a fragmentary Latin Mass without the elements of bread and wine, and his last act before final collapse is to place a purely symbolic, non-existent Host on the tongue of the Mayor who kneels in friendship and charity ('Anything which will give him peace,' he thinks). This is Greene's latest dramatic rendering of the problem of belief. It is also his version of the Knight's battle with the windmills.

Many of the themes that make for tension in the later novels are now resolved and there is at any rate an attempt to answer questions that have been left hanging in the air; this coincides with a progression of style towards the simple and transparent, indicating baldly rather than evoking. Background, as usual, is employed as a dramatic factor: from *The Quiet American* onwards broken cultures in revolutionary situations serve to sustain the existential struggles of uprooted characters; both the Monsignor and the Mayor are seeking a rooted support for timeless problems and they do this against the backcloth of a Spain where a journey like that of the original Quixote is still not inconceivable:

'How little Spain changes,' the Mayor said. 'You would never feel in France that you were in the world of Racine or Molière, nor in London that you were still close to Shakespeare's time. It is only in Spain and Russia that time stands still.'

Against this background the likeness of a truly simple and Christian soul, a knight-errant of the spirit, is fittingly portrayed. His obedience is assaulted by doubts, and he is inclined to accept it when Sancho tells him that belief can die, but he wants in his ignorance to believe and he wants others to believe. He has a dream which makes him realize what a spiritual desert would have been created if the whole world had believed Jesus Christ was the Son of God: 'No doubt. No faith'. Absolute certainty would remove faith as well as doubt. In his doubts he can meet the equal doubts of the Mayor who has to reconcile himself to the works of Stalinism, who will not opt out and become a Eurocommunist, and has to agree with his friend that the whole world has grown bourgeois now. They are both survivors, a favourite word of Greene's. Don Quixote can admire as a Catholic the eloquence of the passage in the *Communist Manifesto* lamenting the passing of the beautiful hierarchies and pieties of the past to the money economy; after his death the Mayor feels what is almost a fear that the love he has come to entertain for Don Quixote should continue to grow — 'And to what end?' He is like Bendrix fearing what lies in store for him, just as Don Quixote is following the analysis of Fowler and Brown and Plarr when he prays to be saved from indifference.

In the Catholic novels assurance can only be reached, if at all, through the sins of a fallen world; in the humanist novels from 1955 onwards the limit of assurance is marked off by doubt and downright disbelief, though it may be approached through the commitment to political justice. Now in the dialogue of Mayor and priest the two forms of engagement are drawn closely together even as their cementing friendship clears for them a space of mutual tolerance and understanding. By the last episode of the hostless Mass and the giving and taking of communion by love and will, three major themes are on the way towards elucidation: the remoteness of man from the hidden God without the aid of the dynamic of love, the debate of humanism and Catholicism ending in mutual recognition of a shared commitment, and the problem of the traumatic effect of fallen experience on the innocent mind. Don Quixote has endured doubt and bewilderment but his is an inviolate innocence of the good soul that subdues experience to a purpose directing him from outside. This is what is happening when during his last uneasy sleep fragmentary memories of his strange journey form into a mosaic of wandering speech: the purpose and the meaning lie outside and are to be added to him.

It is a way towards elucidation but to speak of resolution and reconciliation is no doubt too glib. As in his favourite Browning, the vitality of the soul for Greene resides in a continuing doubt and tension. Don Quixote's spiritual integrity after death is wonderfully indicated by his ability to sow these saving doubts in the positive mind of the

Marxist Mayor (is it not the same in the roles after death of Scobie and Sarah?). The forms of Greene's personal thought never neglect difficulties and differences; they provide a valuable point of reference in a world which, in its own jargon, polarizes every issue, temporizes with every pressure group, and sacrifices polity and justice to a pretence of 'caring'.

The achievement of the final scene of *Monsignor Quixote* permits us to look back on the formation and development of a style in Greene. The beginning is in eliminating epithet and finding the verbs of action that will allow narrative to move. But immediately, in his 'morality' phase, in *Brighton Rock* and *The Power and the Glory*, Greene goes on to control the tone of his novels by means of a rhetoric based on expressionist images, while his narrative scenes and transitions are sustained by the forms of the cinema. After this first period, as the Catholic novels languish into the post-war secularized phase, a true realism is achieved, and the role of trains of poetic imagery subdued but not abandoned; the flowering of this second period is found in *The Comedians* and *The Honorary Consul*. But all the time, quite apart from the use of similes or the exchange of melodrama for the believably quotidian, a purging of language has continued to eliminate self-consciousness by utterly bare and natural statement. Such a process can of course be carried out by a writer who thinks there are only phenomena for which the barest physical description will suffice. Greene is not one of these, and his is the far more arduous practice of the plain style by one who uses it to point to experience of which language cannot speak directly. This is what is happening in the scene of Don Quixote's last Mass; the danger of trying to say too much, of falling into sentimentality, is avoided with great skill and self-control; and yet, by adhering to a simple narrative of fact and the simplest thoughts at the surface of the Mayor's mind, something is pointed at: the barest constituents have seeded another narrative that grows between the lines.

If we are to apply to Greene's linguistic development the categories employed by David Lodge and derived from

Roman Jakobson,[1] we could say that he begins like major
writers of the early twentieth-century modernist movement
with metaphor, the imaginative conjunction of image and
idea, especially notable in his use of simile. He develops in
the pure realist novels to the method of metonymy, the
non-metaphoric use of details of action and behaviour to
plot out larger meanings. Philipot's reiterated desire for a
Bren gun spells out a composite sign of his romanticism and
frustration. Metonymy is still at work in *Travels with My
Aunt:* Henry's dahlias and Miss Keene's practice of tatting
carry more than their own weight in their reflection on
character. But the category of metonymy does not seem
wholly adequate to contain the device of transparency
employed in *Monsignor Quixote*. The halts along the road to
eat cheese and drink Manchegan wine, cooled in a stream,
work as a code for harmony and increasing friendship,
when a second bottle is opened, and perhaps a third. But
one is struck by a transcendence of the ordinary by the
ordinary, a ritual aspect. The repeated scenes do not just
operate as a useful shorthand within the convention of
realism: by creating an atmosphere suggesting ritual
celebration they seem to point outside the limits of realism.[2]
In this latest stage of his work Greene can be seen to have
abandoned the narrative of action in which he excels for a
loose dialogue, to have given up all but slightest aids from
imagery, and yet to gain a surprising reverberation of
meaning and feeling through the barest of styles.

Looking back on Greene's long career as a novelist which
has produced over a score of books up to *Monsignor Quixote*
it is possible to draw some conclusions. Only now is it
possible, since this study has no pre-determined critical
approach, though, of necessity, it is spoken with a personal
voice. For the writer or speaker there must be a point of
view: my dialect, like the reader's, is an idiolect: but the
point of view need not, in Newman's phrase, be 'viewy'.
This has been not a theory of Greene's work but a reading
of it or rather a score of readings.[3] Each of those readings
may be attempted without before or after in mind, but as
what has gone before begins to accumulate, and what is to

come after becomes dimly foreshadowed, the unique work
which is an attempt to realize one particular artistic idea
falls into a context: its idea becomes part of a figure in a
larger carpet. One feature of the chronology of an *oeuvre*,
trite but rarely noticed, is that its development corresponds
to the maturing and aging of an individual; not to biography but to that remorseless process akin to the ringing of a
tree which most biographies and autobiographies are
trying to escape from. Seen in this way Greene's later work
enjoys in a large measure the compensations of age while it
also endures the deprivations. From *The Man Within*
onwards one is watching the growth of a professional from
the training period to the great performances and on from
them to the easy, informal relaxation of tension in the latest
book. In the period of training and early achievement up to
The Power and the Glory Greene brought about a fusion of the
mechanics of the thriller with the world of desire and
aspiration represented by romance. The fusion gave play to
his always consistent loyalty to the promptings of the
unconscious, to the wishes and obsessions of the under-self
and the conflicts to which they give rise (we remember how
his creator spoke of Minty as 'coming on board' in *England
Made Me* and threatening the unity of the novel, and how
Brighton Rock, designed as an entertainment, turned out
differently). But the conflicts had to be realized in character
and action. The deep themes are of innocence and initiation, the latter seen as a kind of violation in this earlier
melodramatic phase; of the divided self; and of the guilt or
complicity in guilt which inevitably ensue from the self's
division. These themes are set against a picture of the social
and moral breakdown of the twentieth century world so
compelling in its intensity as almost to constitute a theme in
itself: 'What are the roots that clutch . . . ': the Christian
doctrine of original sin in the form of Newman's 'aboriginal
calamity' could provide an interpretive myth for the slums
of Brighton in *Brighton Rock* or the shiftlessness of Anthony
Farrant in *England Made Me* but so might a purely moral-
political analysis. So what has been distinguished as the
political humanism of *The Comedians* and *The Honorary
Consul*, succeeding the Catholic novels of Greene's middle

period, is present already in his treatment of the plight of Conrad Drover in *It's a Battlefield* and in the social conscious- ness pervading even the first Catholic novel, *Brighton Rock.*

Since melodramatic action had been chosen as the mode for the reflection of moral conflict, romantic language had to be eliminated, adjectives and adverbs had to go, in order to capture the hardly expressible core of a few seconds of fateful near-automatic response. To say that the style was tautened by the discipline of writing would be a correct, but too negative way of putting it. The chief characteristic of the pre-war phase is that together with disciplined narra- tion there goes an extraordinary expressionist poetry, a lurid lighting, working largely through the bizarre, 'metaphysical' simile and the description of persons and places at a certain oblique angle from the norm. The influence of the cinema contributed both to the narrative discipline and economy, to rapid transition and juxtaposi- tion, and to the creation of expressionist imagery. So as with all literary terrorism, the surrealists, for instance, the attack on the stereotypes of literary language results in a new rhetoric. These linguistic features continue into the first Catholic novels of the middle phase, *Brighton Rock, The Power and the Glory* and *The Heart of the Matter,* but are considerably modified in the last book and still more so in that which succeeds it, *The End of the Affair.* So we are enabled to think of a transition to a third phase beginning at this point; in the third phase the rhetoric becomes simpler and less poetic: in place of the startling image the commen- tary tends to employ prose aphorisms, the disenchanted accumulations and distillations of observed wisdom. Mod- ernism seems yet further behind us and the manner is almost that of the classic realist text, though with a much lighter hand at authorial manipulation of the central characters on account of the peculiarly open or ambiguous presentation of the first-person narrator in *The End of the Affair, The Comedians,* and *The Quiet American.*

Language is inextricable from meaning. In the terminol- ogy of semiotics the signifier transforms the signified which in any case must to the communicator, when he approaches it as *content,* be a potential *sign* for something else.[4] Hence the baffled return to origins, the search for meanings in the early stages of a case-history apparent in the introspections of Anthony Farrant, Pinkie, Brown and Plarr on their adolescence; another example would be the search back for the ultimate meaning of the word 'peace' or 'happiness' found in the thoughts of Scobie travelling in the bush *(The Heart of the Matter)* or Deo Gratias spending a night in the jungle dreaming of the mystical joys of the land of Pendélé *(A Burnt-Out Case)*. Hence also Greene's hint of an explanation of his origins as a writer in *Under the Garden* which ends up as a paraphrase of a mystery with a highly ambiguous signifier in the battered tin chamber pot. The linking of signifier with signified at the level of the whole text rather than in particular phrases or statements may be observed precisely in the transition between the middle and later phases of Greene's work. The style alters when overtly religious subject-matter is abandoned. In *Brighton Rock, The Power and the Glory,* and *The Heart of the Matter* the protagonists, poised 'on the dangerous edge of things', holy sinners running against the current of orthodox proprieties, stretch out in an abject realization of their sinfulness towards the God who appears to have withdrawn from his world. Language is desire, and the gap beyond which they cannot see *(Deus absconditus)* is filled by their desire with a language of dereliction and distortion which by reducing human beings to the animal admits their fear for their desire but tries to contain it in imagery. In *The Power and the Glory* the pictures of Senators and Congressmen in the American magazines have 'big clean-shaven mastiff jowls', and the dying gangster is 'like a reptile crushed at one end'. It is in *The End of the Affair* that this type of imagery is first subdued; that book, by its intimations of sanctity and miracle effectively steps outside the boundaries of the novel; at the same time Bendrix, its central character, reciprocates the withdrawal of God by his own withdrawal from belief. He is the first of a line of disillusioned agnostics who ensure a return from imagery to a more neutral prose and from the drama of spiritual struggle to a more classic realism.

Most critics have been ready to acknowledge that Greene

has an unerring power to create what D.H. Lawrence called 'the spirit of place'; but here too the desire to possess the world preceded knowledge of the world, just as the little boy in *Under the Garden*, the young Wilditch, nurses dreams of strange places, like a map of Treasure Island. The expectant eye of the traveller, tutored by experience, moved on to evoke many real settings. There are the early London scenes, before and after the Blitz; there is the squalor of a Mexican town or the bright colours of Haiti; brooding elegiac scenes by the great rivers, the Congo or the Paraná. Too many to choose from, but a modest example can remind us that Greene's descriptions of place are never mere background but settings for human beings: here are a man and a wife who are going to quarrel and part and come together again, standing in the main square of Monte Carlo:

> . . . the little square at the top of the world. To the south there was nothing higher, I suppose, before the Atlas mountains. The tall houses stuck up like cacti towards the heavy blue sky, and a narrow terracotta street came abruptly to an end at the edge of the great rock of Monaco. A Virgin in pale blue with angels blowing round her like a scarf looked across from the church opposite, and it was warm and windy and very quiet and all the roads of our life had led us to this square.
>
> (*Loser Takes All*, 1955)

Like the places, which the potential traveller needed before he could find and describe them, so the characters in the places had to be set in motion by the obsessive drives of the writer before they could attain independent life. Fowler and Pyle in *The Quiet American* are segments of the original unified Greene persona as rendered in Andrews of *The Man Within*, where innocence, guilt and vulnerability all come together, Fowler and Pyle enjoy a fuller being by the division of the composite self. The next step is when these independent selves can communicate one with another, and that comes late. With Pinkie, the whisky priest, and Scobie respectively, nightmare, fever and a solipsistic tendency to project personal problems on to other people, effectively block intercourse with their fellows. The disillusioned heroes of the later books may have grown away from the solipsistic nightmare, but they hide in a protective casing of self-regard: such is the case with Fowler, Brown and Plarr, though voices like those of the French police inspector and Dr Magiot tell them that they cannot for ever avoid commitment. The change, the meeting of persons, comes in *The Honorary Consul* when Plarr cannot quite put out of his mind the question Clara had asked him, the question which told him that she loved him:

> On the stairs (the lift might have been heard by his neighbours) he tried to remember what that question of hers had been which he had never answered. It could not have been very important. The only questions of importance were those which a man asked himself.

Trying to exclude, but not entirely excluding, a new thought about himself as he goes down the stairs, Plarr's situation is not wholly free from the figurative: Eliot had used the figure of the stairs with explicit symbolism to represent the mystical ascent in his conversion poem *Ash Wednesday*. It is significant that Plarr *descends* the stairs, always the return to the origin of selfhood. More pronounced is the fact that the meaning of the passage, the denial of the importance of what Clara has said, which by having to deny cannot exclude, plays around the lines of plain statement. The manner is a stage on the way to the manner of *Monsignor Quixote*. In that novel, supported by the great European critique of the romantic mode by Cervantes, the thriller plot and many properties of self-conscious writing are discarded: much is conveyed through the thinnest of means. The mutual understanding of two personalities in their contrariety grows in the course of the debate about politics and theology; and both men are changed during the debate. The dross of words and of the quotidian is distilled into hope. The Mass said by Don Quixote without the elements of bread and wine, and the non-communion which is a true communion, given to a non-believer, takes the reader back to the hastily impro-vised Mass in the hut in *The Honorary Consul,* said for the guerillas before their death by the non-believer Leon, and further back to the golden chamber which turns out to be a tin pot flecked with yellow paint in *Under the Garden.* These are the attempts the writer makes in the struggle of fiction to bridge the unbridgeable gap between the real and the ideal: or between the ideal and the real.

Graham Greene has admired Henry James whom he has saluted as the only writer of his time who knew about evil.[5] James always wanted to be a popular novelist, as he wanted to be a successful playwright.[6] Greene has been both, but like James he too has pursued in our troubled times the form of the good novel with passion and devotion. James wrote in *The Middle Years:* 'We work in the dark — we do what we can — we give what we have. Our doubt is our passion and our passion is our task'.

NOTES
BIBLIOGRAPHY
INDEX

NOTES

CHAPTER 1

(*pages 11–36*)
1 J.I.M. Stewart, *Eight Modern Writers* (Oxford, 1963) p.208.
2 Kathleen Nott, *The Emperor's Clothes* (1954) pp309–11
3 Wordsworth, *Preface to Lyrical Ballads; Prospectus to The Excursion, Poetical Works of William Wordsworth* edited by Ernest de Selincourt and Helen Darbishire (Oxford, 1949) p.5.
4 Sigmund Freud, *Thoughts on War and Death (1915). Collected Works XIV*, Standard Edition pp.289–90.
5 *The Lawless Roads* (1939; ed. 1950) pp.3–6.
6 W.H. Auden, 'Though aware of our rank and alert to obey orders', *Collected Shorter Poems*, p.59.
7 'The Spy', Introduction to Kim Philby, *My Secret War* (1968).
8 Alexis de Tocqueville, *Democracy in America* translated by Henry Reeve, edited by Phillips Bradley (New York, 1956) ii.62–3.
9 *A Sort of Life*, (1971) p.189.
10 *Ways of Escape* (1980) p.257. Greene is quoting from Miguel de Unamuno's *The Tragic Sense of Life*.
11 A critique of the assumptions of revolutionary Christianity particularly in regard to the Church in Latin America is to be found in Edward Norman, *Christianity and the World Order* (Oxford, 1979) pp.53–6.
12 *The Lawless Roads* (1939; ed.1950) p.3.
13 *A Sort of Life* (1971) p.72.
14 Evelyn Waugh, *Spectator* 10 March 1939.

CHAPTER 2

(*pages 37–78*)
1 Anne Wilson, *Traditional Romance and Tale* (Ipswich, 1976) p.55.
2 Sir Thomas Browne, *Religio Medici* ii.7. (*Religio Medici and Other Writings* edited by L.C. Martin (Oxford, 1964) p.64.)
3 Northrop Frye, *Anatomy of Criticism* (New York, 1967) p.305.
4 The story is told by Jean Cocteau in his *Coq et Harlequin* (translated by Rollo H. Myers, *Cock and Harlequin*, 1926).
5 Graham Greene, review of *Hôtel du Nord* in *Spectator* 23 June 1939, reprinted in *The Pleasure-Dome: The Collected Film Criticism* edited by John Russell Taylor, 1972, p.230.
6 *Odd Man Out* (1947) was a film of Carol Reed who was to direct *The Third Man* with Graham Greene as script writer.
7 *The Pleasure-Dome*, p.39.
8 *A Sort of Life*, pp.198–9.
9 Robert Louis Stevenson, *Kidnapped* (Tusitala Edition) pp.24–5.
10 *Spectator* 3 January 1936 (*The Pleasure-Dome*, p.44).
11 Louis Macneice, 'An Eclogue for Christmas', *Collected Poems*, p.35.
12 Maurice Bardèche, *Stendhal romancier* (Paris, 1947) pp.215–16.

13 'Some Letters of George Orwell', *Encounter* (Jan. 1962) p.64.
14 G.S. Fraser, *The Modern Writer and His World* (1961) pp.88–9.

CHAPTER 3

(*pages 79–129*)
1   Cyril Connolly, 'Brighton' in *The Evening Colonnade* (1973) p.59.
2   The use of symbol and tableau in post-First World War expressionism is exemplified by the formalized structure and the use of choruses in
Ernst Toller's drama *Masses and Man* (translated by Edward Crankshaw
from *Masse-Mensch*, 1920).
3   Extract from *Cahiers du Quinzaine* translated in Marjorie Villiers,
Charles Péguy: A Study in Integrity (1965) p.278.
4   The idea of redemption through sexual love would be antipathetic to
Jansenism. Cf. a saying of the Jansenist Nicole: 'Il y a une galanterie
spirituelle aussi bien qu'une sensuelle, et si l'on n'y prend garde, le
commerce avec les femmes s'y termine d'ordinaire' (C.A. Sainte-Beuve,
Port-Royal (Paris, 1901) iv.515.
5   Oscar Kokoschka to Hans Tietze (1917), quoted in Wolf-Dieter
Dube, *Expressionism* (1972) p.187.
6   Richard Hoggart has written of working-class attitudes in his
generation similar to those of Ida: 'they do not think much about sin and
grace, good and evil, but they are sure there is a difference between right
and wrong' (*The Uses of Literacy*, 1957, p.98).
7   'I can't explain it all to you. I live without the sacraments. It's a risk.
But I have treasures of grace, superabundance of grace . . . My life is not
an ordinary one. My life is a stake.' Charles Péguy to Joseph Lotte, in
Alexander Dru, *Péguy* (1956) pp.68,69.
8   Jean-Paul Sartre, *Situations I* (1947–9).
9   K.W. Gransden, 'Graham Greene's Rhetoric', *Essays in Criticism*
(January 1981) pp.41–59.
10 *The Lawless Roads* (1939; ed.1950) p.139.
11 *The Lawless Roads* p.132.
12 Francis Wyndham, *Graham Greene* (Writers and their Work, 1955)
p.10.
13 Kenneth Allott and Miriam Ferris, *The Art of Graham Greene* (1951)
p.175.
14 Isaiah 53.1–12; cf.Matthew 16.24–5.
15 The paradox of God's absence from His world is the position
discussed by Pascal in the *Pensées*. ' . . . the fundamental clarity of the
tragic mind never allows it to forget that, in God, absence and presence
are indissolubly linked together. God's absence, and the paradoxical
nature of the world, exist only for a mind which cannot accept this state
of things, both because of the permanent demand for the unambiguous
and the unequivocal, and because of the constant awareness of being
under the eye of God which characterise it; on the other hand, this
presence is only a 'wager' and a 'permanent unproveable possibility'.
This is why the tragic mind is constantly haunted by both hope and fear,

and why it is always full both of fear and trembling and of hope, and why it is forced to live in uninterrupted tension, without either knowing or accepting an instant of repose.' Lucien Goldmann, *The Hidden God: A Study of Tragic Vision in the Pensées of Pascal and the Tragedies of Racine* translated by Philip Thody (1964) pp.67–8.

16 The subject of the priesthood as presented in Greene's novels has been thoughtfully considered by Leopoldo Durán, *El crisis del sacerdote en Graham Greene* (Madrid, 1974).

17 The same sentiment and almost the same sentence is to be found in Léon Bloy, *La femme pauvre* (1897; ed.1946) p.299: 'Il n'y a qu'une tristesse, lui a-t-elle dit, la dernière fois, c'est de N'ÊTRE PAS DES SAINTS'.

CHAPTER 4

(*pages 130–196*)

1 Greene's conception of peace, which ranges from release from care to the Christian assurance of salvation, is a leading motif from the last scene of Andrews in *The Man Within* onwards. There is a parallel with the use of the word — also both emotively and with a wide extension of meaning — by Ford Madox Ford, a writer admired by Greene: 'this strong impulse . . . it was a passionate desire to go where you could find exact intellect: rest. He thought he suddenly understood. For the Lincolnshire Sergeant-Major the word peace meant that a man could stand up on a hill. For him it meant someone to talk to.' *A Man Could Stand Up* in *The Bodley Head Ford Madox Ford* Vol.IV (1963) p.388.

2 For instance F.N. Lees in *Scrutiny* (October 1952) p.39.

3 J.P. Kulshrestha, *Graham Greene: the Novelist* (Madras, 1977) p.110.

4 Albert Camus, *La peste* (Paris, 1947) pp.234–41.

5 Significantly the writer in the Western philosophical tradition who is most severe about the defects of pity is the non-Christian Spinoza. 'Pity in a man who lives under the guidance of reason is in itself bad and useless . . . Now pity is sadness and therefore bad in itself.' *Ethics* (Everyman Edition) p.175. But the stiff-upper-lipped attitude is also found in the Stoics and in the many influenced by them.

6 Cf. 'Pity is not a substitute for love; when separated from it, it is ultimately destructive, a negative sharing of a failure, whereas love is creative.' Marie-Beatrice Mesnet, *Graham Greene and the Heart of the Matter* (1954) p.64.

7 George Orwell, *The New Yorker*, 17 July 1948, p.62.

8 Some early reflections of Bonhoeffer on Augustine's doctrine of pre-destination seem relevant here: 'These thoughts lead logically to the conception of the *massa perditionis*, the mass which endures a tragic destiny, seen as a natural happening.

'But in this pessimistic, almost Manichaean view there are also to be found the means for overcoming it. In the bodily consciousness of every man, which is given with sexuality, he is aware both that he possesses something quite personal, and that he is a natural being beyond his life as a person.' Dietrich Bonhoeffer, *Sanctorum Communio: A Dogmatic Inquiry into the Sociology of the Church* translated by R. Gregor Smith and others (1963) p.75.

9 'What we call a beautiful character has become beautiful at the cost of a struggle against itself, and this struggle should not stop until the bitter end. The evil which the beautiful character has to overcome in itself, and from which it has to sever itself, is a reality which the novelist must account for. If there is a reason for the existence of the novelist on earth it is this: to show the element which holds out against God in the highest and noblest characters — the innermost evils and dissimulations; and also to light up the secret source of sanctity in creatures who seem to us to have failed.' François Mauriac, *God and Mammon* (1929; English translation 1936), Chapter V quoted in Miriam Allott ed., *Novelists on the Novel* (1959) p.133.

10 The idea that human personality is only fully realized and completed by the test of action is lucidly expressed by the Catholic existentialist Gabriel Marcel, *Journal métaphysique* (Paris, 1927; ed. 1946) pp.228–9:

... une véritable dualité entre ce que je suis comme donné et ce que je suis comme réagissant (idéalement) ... La zone de l'épreuve est le champ même de la liberté. Dira-t-on maintenant que je ne ferai jamais que découvrir ce que je suis déjà? Encore faut-il distinguer deux sortes de réalité. Il est bien clair que l'épreuve me contraint à me mesurer avec moi-même. Serai-je ou non à ma propre hauteur? Là est tout le problème que seule l'action peut resoudre. (There exists a veritable duality between what I am as a given person and my nature in reacting to circumstances (in an ideal state) ... The test of experience is the very field of freedom. Must one say then that I can only discover that which I am already? Else it would be necessary to distinguish two levels of reality. It is quite clear that the test of experience compels me to come to terms with myself. Am I or am I not operating at my own appropriate level? That is the whole problem which only action can decide.)

11 *Lord Rochester's Monkey, being the Life of John Wilmot, Second Earl of Rochester* (1974) p.213.

12 Cf. Newman's view of the relation of coincidences to miracles: 'Providences, or what are called *grazie*, though they do not rise to the order of miracles, yet if they occur again and again in connexion with the same persons, institutions, or doctrines, may supply a cumulative evidence of the fact of a supernatural presence in the quarter in which they are found'. *Apologia pro Vita Sua, being a History of his Religious Opinions* (ed.1908) p.304.

13 David Lodge, *Graham Greene* (Columbia Studies in Modern Writers, New York, 1966) p.33.

14 Jules Michelet, *Bible de l'humanité* (Paris, 1864) p.403.

15 Cf. *In Search of a Character: Two African Journals* (1961) p.59: 'After living with a book for a year or two, he has come to terms with his unconscious — the end will be imposed'.

16 The ultimate alienation of these characters from their families and the world in general is another Quixotic feature: Scobie's failure to be understood by his wife is a case in point. 'The hero, the saint, the redeemer, is for no one so beside himself as for his own family, his parents and his brethren . . . The true relations of Don Quixote are those that are kindled by the flame of his noble knightliness, they are his spiritual relatives. The hero ends in having no friends; he is of necessity solitary.' Miguel de Unamuno, *The Life of Don Quixote and Sancho* (1905; translated by Homer P. Earle, 1927) p.102.

17 Blaise Pascal, *Pensées*, texte de Léon Brunschvicg (Editions Lutetia, Paris, 1946) p.169.

18 *Pensées*, ed. cit. p.291.

19 T.S. Eliot, *Essays Ancient and Modern* (1936) pp.150–1, 159.

20 *A Sort of Life*, p.51.

21 Frank Kermode, *Puzzles and Epiphanies* (1962) p.182.

22 'Convoy to West Africa' (*In Search of a Character*, p.123).

23 *In Search of a Character*, p.51.

24 It seems likely that Greene had been reading Teilhard de Chardin, *The Phenomenon of Man*.

25 Robert Browning, 'A Death in the Desert'.

CHAPTER 5

(*pages 197–237*)

1 BBC interview , January 1964.

2 Evelyn Waugh, *When the Going Was Good* (1946) p.199.

3 Roland Barthes, 'The Death of the Author', translated by Richard Howard, *Aspen Magazine* Nos.5–6 (1968).

4 *Why Do I Write?* (1948) pp.31–2.

5 Diana Trilling, 'America and *The Quiet American*', *Commentary* (1956) pp.66–71.

6 Review of *The Road Back* in *Night and Day*, 7 October 1937 (*The Pleasure Dome*, pp.171–2).

7 R.M. Nadal, Introduction to *Poems of Federico Garcia Lorca with English translation by Stephen Spender and J.L. Gili* (1942) p.xx.

8 *Collected Stories* (1972) p.107.

9 Geoffrey Thurley, *The American Moment: American Poetry at Mid-Century* (1977) p.234.

10 Alfred Kazin, *Contemporaries* (1962) p.159.

11 Kingsley Amis, 'Slow Boat to Haiti', *Observer* 30 January 1966.

12 Cf. Miguel de Unamuno, *The Life of Don Quixote and Sancho* translated by Homer P. Earle (1905) p.102: 'The insane are usually finished comedians; they take the comedy seriously, but they are not deceived; while they seriously play the part of God, of a king, or of an animal, they know well enough that they are not any of these things; they merely wish to be such, and that is sufficient'.

CHAPTER 6

(pages 238–259)
1 Geoffrey Jackson, *People's Prison* (1973).
2 'The South', in Jorge Luis Borges, *A Personal Anthology* edited by Anthony Kerrigan (1968) p.18.
3 Cf. 'As for the *mot juste*, you are quite wrong. Style is a very simple matter; it is all rhythm. Once you get that, you can't use the wrong words. But on the other hand here I am sitting after half the morning, crammed with ideas, and visions, and so on, and can't dislodge them, for lack of the right rhythm . . . A sight, an emotion, creates this wave in the mind, long before it makes words to fit it . . . and then, as it breaks and tumbles in the mind, it makes words to fit it.' *The Letters of Virginia Woolf* edited by Nigel Nicolson, Volume III 1923–1928 (1977) p.247.
4 Graham Greene, Preface to Kim Philby, *My Silent War* (1968) p.vii.
5 'It was now I began to develop a love for the landscape around Berkhamstead which never left me, so that Chesterton's rather inferior political ballade *'Of the First Rain'* moves me still like poetry with its key-line 'A storm is coming on the Chiltern Hills.' . . . the hidden spots of the Chilterns were all the dearer because they were on the very borders of Metroland. They had the excitement of a frontier.' *A Sort of Life*, p.107.

CHAPTER 7

(pages 260–281)
1 See David Lodge, *Modes of Modern Writing* (1977) for the attempt to apply the typology of metaphor and metonymy to twentieth-century English literature, modernist, post-modernist and anti-modernist.
2 The manner in which narrative fiction can be transformed into ritual celebration, especially in episodes of good fellowship, feasting and drinking, and therefore into a philosophic mode of comic approval or disapproval, has been magisterially described by Nicolas Bakhtin in his study of Rabelais (*The World of Rabelais*, Massachusetts Institute of Technology Press, 1968). *The Pickwick Papers* is an example nearer home and anti-celebration or ritual mockery can be found in the *Cena Trimalchionis* of Petronius' *Satyricon*.
3 The critic can only bring all he is and all he knows and then respond to the text. Cf. Iain McGilchrist, *Against Criticism* (1982), 'the only critical theory is that of no-theory, the only applicable abstraction the rejection of abstraction, the only general or central conception that which qualifies all general or central conceptions': pp.13–14.
4 The argument that in the nature of language every sign is a *signifier* whose *signified* is not some non-verbal original essence but another *signifier* is presented in Jacques Derrida, *De la Grammatologie* (1967); trans. Guyatri C. Spivak, *Of Grammatology* (Baltimore, 1976).
5 *Collected Essays* (1969), pp.23ff.: 'Henry James: the Private Universe'.
6 On James's desire for popularity and his critical distrust of his own talent see Maurice Blanchot's essay on *The Turn of the Screw* in *The Sirens' Song: Selected Essays* ed. Gabriel Josipovici (1982) pp.79–86.

BIBLIOGRAPHY

I. WORKS OF GRAHAM GREENE
Roman numerals refer to the numbers of the volumes in the Collected Edition.

(i) Fiction
The Man Within (Heinemann, 1929) XV
The Name of Action (Heinemann, 1930)
Rumour at Nightfall (Heinemann, 1931)
Stamboul Train (Heinemann, 1932) XII
It's a Battlefield (Heinemann, 1934) II
The Bear Fell Free (Grayson, 1935)
England Made Me (Heinemann, 1935) III
A Gun for Sale (Heinemann, 1936) IX
Brighton Rock (Heinemann, 1938) I
The Confidential Agent (Heinemann, 1939) VII
The Power and the Glory (Heinemann, 1940) V
The Ministry of Fear (Heinemann, 1943) X
The Heart of the Matter (Heinemann, 1948) VI
The Third Man and *The Fallen Idol* (Heinemann, 1950) XVI
The End of the Affair (Heinemann, 1951) XII
The Quiet American (Heinemann, 1955) XI
Loser Takes All (Heinemann, 1955) XVI
Our Man in Havana (Heinemann, 1958) IV
A Burnt-Out Case (Heinemann, 1961) XIV
The Comedians (The Bodley Head, 1966) XVII
Travels with My Aunt (The Bodley Head, 1969) XX
The Honorary Consul (The Bodley Head, 1973) XXI
The Human Factor (The Bodley Head, 1978) XXII
Dr Fischer of Geneva or the Bomb Party (The Bodley Head, 1980)
Monsignor Quixote (The Bodley Head, 1982)

Nineteen Stories (Heinemann, 1947)
Twenty-One Stories (Heinemann, 1954)
A Sense of Reality (The Bodley Head, 1963)
May We Borrow Your Husband? (The Bodley Head, 1967)
Collected Stories (The Bodley Head, 1972)

(ii) Plays
Three Plays (Heinemann, Mercury Books, 1961). The plays are *The Living Room* (1953), *The Potting Shed* (1958), and *The Complaisant Lover* (1959).
Carving a Statue (The Bodley Head, 1964)

(iii) Travel and Autobiography
Journey Without Maps (Heinemann, 1936)

The Lawless Roads (Heinemann, 1939)
In Search of a Character: Two African Journals (The Bodley Head, 1961)
A Sort of Life (The Bodley Head, 1971)
Ways of Escape (The Bodley Head, 1980)

(iv) Miscellaneous
Babbling April (Basil Blackwell, 1925). Poems.
British Dramatists (Collins, 1942)
Why Do I Write? (Percival Marshall, 1948)
The Lost Childhood (Eyre & Spottiswoode, 1951). The first collection of essays.
Collected Essays (The Bodley Head, 1969)
The Pleasure-Dome. Collected film criticism 1935–40. Edited by John Russell Taylor (Secker & Warburg, 1972)
Lord Rochester's Monkey (1974; Biography of Rochester written forty years before.)

II. WORKS ON GRAHAM GREENE

Allen, Walter. *Tradition and Dream: The English and American Novel from the Twenties to Our Time* (Phoenix House, 1964).
Allott, Kenneth, and Farris, Miriam. *The Art of Graham Greene* (Hamish Hamilton, 1951).
Atkins, John. *Graham Greene* (John Calder, 1957; rev. ed. 1966).
Auden, W.H. 'A Note on Graham Greene', in *The Wind and the Rain*, Summer 1949.
Burgess, Anthony. 'Politics in the Novels of Graham Greene', in *Journal of Contemporary History*, April 1967.
A.F. Cassis, *Graham Greene: An Annotated Bibliography of Criticism* (Metuchen, N.J., and London, 1981).
DeVitis, A.A. *Graham Greene* (Twayne Publishers, New York, 1964.)
Evans, R.O. (ed.). *Graham Greene: Some Critical Considerations* (University of Kentucky Press, Lexington, 1963).
Chapman, Raymond. 'The Vision of Graham Greene' in *Forms of Extremity in the Modern Novel* ed. Nathan A. Scott (John Knox Press, Richmond, Va., 1965).
Duran, Leopoldo. *La Crisis del Sacerdote en Graham Greene* (Biblioteca de Autores Christianos, Madrid, 1975).
Gregor, Ian, and Nicholas, Brian. 'Grace and Morality', in *The Moral and the Story* (Faber and Faber, 1962).
Gransden, K.W. 'Graham Greene's Rhetoric' (*Essays in Criticism*, January 1981).
Hynes, Samuel L. *Graham Greene: A Collection of Critical Essays* (Twentieth Century Views. Prentice-Hall, Englewood Cliffs, New Jersey, 1973).

Johnstone, Richard. *The Will to Believe: Novelists of the Nineteen Thirties* (Oxford University Press, 1982).

Kermode, Frank. 'Mr Greene's Eggs and Crosses', in *Puzzles and Epiphanies*: Essays and Reviews 1958–1961, (Routledge & Kegan Paul, 1961). Also in 'The House of Fiction: Interviews with Seven English Novelists', in *Partisan Review*, Spring 1963.

Kulshrestha, J.P. *Graham Greene: The Novelist* (Macmillan Company of India, Madras, 1977).

Kunkel, Francis L. *The Labyrinthine Ways of Graham Greene* (Sheed and Ward, New York, 1959).

Lewis, R.W.B. 'Graham Greene: The Religious Affair' in *The Picaresque Saint* (Gollancz, 1960).

Lodge, David. *Graham Greene* (Columbia Essays on Modern Writers, 17, New York, 1966).

Lynch, William F., *Christ and Apollo: the Dimensions of the Literary Imagination* (New York, 1960).

Maclaren-Ross, J. *Memoirs of the Forties* (Alan Ross, 1965).

Madaule, Jacques. *Graham Greene* (Editions du Temps présent, Paris, 1949).

Mesnet, Marie-Beatrice. *Graham Greene and the Heart of the Matter* (Cresset Press, 1954).

Nott, Kathleen. 'Augustinian Novelists', in *The Emperor's Clothes* (Heinemann, 1953).

O'Donnell, Donat (Conor Cruise O'Brien). 'Graham Greene: The Anatomy of Pity', in *Maria Cross: Imaginative Patterns in a Group of Catholic Writers* (Chatto & Windus, 1953).

O'Faolain, Sean. 'Graham Greene: I Suffer, Therefore I am', in *The Vanishing Hero: (Studies in Novelists of the Twenties* (Eyre and Spottiswoode, 1956).

Orwell, George. 'Some Letters', in *Encounter*, January 1962.

Pryce-Jones, David. *Graham Greene* (Writers and Critics, Oliver and Boyd, Edinburgh, 1963; rev. ed. 1973).

Stratford, Philip, *Faith and Fiction: Creative Process in Greene and Mauriac* (University of Notre Dame Press, 1964).

Wobbe, R.A. Graham Greene: *A Bibliography and Guide to Research* (Garland Publishing, Inc., New York and London, 1979).

Waugh, Evelyn, 'The Point of Departure', in *The Month*, September 1951.

Wolfe, Peter. *Graham Greene: The Entertainer* (Southern Illinois University Press, Carbondale, 1972).

Wyndham, Francis. *Graham Greene* (Writers and their Work, Longmans, 1955; rev. ed. 1968).

INDEX

Books of general Christian interest as well as books on theology, scripture, spirituality and mysticism are available from the publishers Burns and Oates and Search Press Limited. A catalogue will be sent free on request. Please apply to:

Burns and Oates/Search Press Limited,
Wellwood, North Farm Road,
Tunbridge Wells, Kent TN2 3DR
Tel. (0892) 44037/8.